Growing Food God's Way

How Paul Gautschi Takes Us
Back to Eden and Beyond

2nd Edition

David Devine

Book Publishers Network
2950 Newmarket St, Suite 101-358
Bellingham, WA 98228

ISBN: 978-0-9907552-0-3

Library of Congress Control Number: 2021904160

All Scripture references taken, or adapted, from the
King James Version (KJV) of the Holy Bible.

Websites and email addresses listed within were operable at the time of printing, but the author cannot guarantee the URL host will maintain the site(s) in perpetuity. They are a reader resource and not intended to be an endorsement either way.

This book makes no attempt to give readers medical advice, which should be sought from competent doctors, naturopaths, chiropractors, and other healing arts practitioners.

Cover design: Preston Devine
Indexer: Daniel Heila

For information, email David at: info@growingfoodgodsway.com.

Printed in the United States of America

To my parents, by birth and marriage:
Marvin and Vivian Devine (a wonderful dad and mom) plus
Chester and Virginia Gelnett (who raised my wife).

To Phyllis, a gifted and wonderful wife, and
our Devine family: Jonathan, with Malcolm; Jason and Hannah,
with Elijah, Lily, Rebekah, Annika and Kyle;
Preston and Casey, with Tobias;
Mallory, Matthew, Elsie, Jared, Seth, Sterling,
and Victoria for all their love.

To Lauri Devine (1949-2020), the best sister.

And especially . . .
to the Savior who loved us before we loved Him.

Paul and his trusty hard rake.

Contents

Paul making a row for seeds.

Foreword

A S AN INTEGRITY FOOD FARMER, I eventually wearied of audiences assuming that I was anti-God, anti-Israel, pro-abortion, pro-tax just because I embraced earth stewardship. To help cut through the stereotype, I began calling myself a "Christian libertarian environmentalist capitalist lunatic farmer."

During media interviews, journalists routinely appear shocked that someone who lugs a Bible around in his travel bags also promotes caressing our ecological womb. Those phrases are supposed to come from earth-worshipping, free-love hippies, not firebrand fundamentalist preacher-types.

Blaming the Bible specifically, and God generally, for all the environmental ills plaguing the world is a favorite theme from mainline environmentalists. Unfortunately, the perception is based in fact. From the crusaders to the conquistadors, carelessly invoking divine authority more often than not leads to societal and environmental catastrophes.

The Old Testament, which starts with **God** the Creator, establishes quite clearly His ownership over this planet we call Earth. Further, this Holy instruction manual places human-kind in a garden of abundance to be stewarded, loved, nurtured, and caressed. In the land of Canaan, the Israelites received a specific geographic region with clear earth-care and societal admonitions with the promise of ongoing abundance and health if they adhered to divine instructions . . . and devastating catastrophes if they did not.

Clearly, God has an interest in His handiwork and assumes that His people will steward this Divine real estate according to a sacred template. He is not a disinterested owner as the deists would have us believe. He is not a doting daddy devoid of discipline and plan as the free thinkers would have us believe. He is not a dispassionate bystander as the dominion evangelicals would have us believe, neither is He a marionette manipulator as the hyper-sovereignty-ists would have us believe.

God caringly seeks stewardship diplomats to be His hands and feet to extend redemption to a fallen landscape. Indeed, if earth stewardship means anything, it means re-establishing the physical world as an object lesson of spiritual truth. He wants our pilgrim footsteps to leave behind farm and foodscapes that illustrate forgiveness, beauty, abundance, order, healing, and righteousness. When visitors leave our farms and gardens, they should revel in having just seen a visceral representation of God's grace, abundance, and attractiveness.

My family operates Polyface Farm in Virginia's Shenandoah Valley. When European settlers in the early 1700s found this verdant silvo-pasture of alpha soils, they inverted the perennial biomass-covered landscape with the plow. Over the next century and a half, some three to eight feet of topsoil washed away into the Chesapeake Bay. Eventually this rich valley wore out. Grain production headed west. The Shenandoah Valley gradually became an orchard region and eventually a grass and livestock region. Pockets of rich soil still exist, and are still being plowed, but the rock outcroppings dotting most pastures throughout the region attest to the devastation of the plow. **Sir Albert Howard**, godfather of modern scientific aerobic composting, said:

> *It is the temptation of every civilization to take what nature took thousands of years to create and turn it into cash.*

What an atrocity that the story of civilization is also a story of environmental disaster. God weeps. The earth groans. Despair and pessimism rule our day as this historical record and its guilt, the full import of the damage is now apparent to all. Unfortunately, too often this guilt makes humans afraid to engage the environment, as if interacting with the ecology cannot be done with integrity. This leads to environmentalism by abandonment, locking up areas into parks and wilderness areas devoid of human presence.

But God never leaves us without provision. *Into this bleak landscape step stewards who follow a path of truth that begins with humility and culminates in following God's design.* Some of these great mentors do not acknowledge God. Some do. And those who do add a robustness to their findings and a freedom to express the spiritual implications to these visceral object lessons.

When our family put these principles into action on our wornout piece of earth, it responded like a lover. Water permeated the soil instead of running off. Soil grew. Earthworms proliferated. Vegetation now stays green much farther into a drought. We have far more diversity in both plants and animals. The farm supports many incomes instead of none and hosts countless visitors and customers. It's a place of abundance. Our motto: *Healing the land one bite at a time.*

That land healing is a remarkable demonstration of what God does in the human heart with the human soul. It is no less dramatic and no less real. As a steward and partner with God, the ultimate landscape architect, I have the distinct privilege and honor to be on the Father's team.

Paul Gautschi is another of those team members. Author **David Devine**, in an uncompromising and spiritually aggressive tone, captures the work of this landscape healer with clarity and optimism. While Paul and I are quite different—he comes from a plant-based scheme and I come from a livestock scheme—the basic principles of soil building and healing are identical and spot on. What a delight that Devine leads us down Gautschi's path in such outspoken credit to the Author of the design.

What I especially appreciate about this book is that it offers another example of earth stewardship from the Judeo-Christian heritage. It shows that we can love God and love the earth too.

While I could argue some points, and might even label some as extreme, all prophets are labeled extremists in their day. What's too much, lay aside for another day. It's okay to eat in small bites.

The mechanics of Paul's covering, the reasoning of his carbon-centric system, and the journey of his heart must be appreciated by everyone, and especially people in the faith community. The ramifications of Paul's findings are profound: soil building, no chemical fertilizers, integrated community abundance, human wellness (fewer doctors and pharmaceuticals), and landscape hydration rather than desertification.

These are not small outcomes.

Devine's writing style is akin to drinking out of a fire hose. Get ready. But above all, regardless of your current faith situation, appreciate the ecological principles and appreciate that Paul is a man with a child-like relationship with his Redeemer who dares to seek divine counsel for daily problems. That is a compelling way to live.

– Joel Salatin

Preface

THE FOLLOWING PAGES TRACK YOU THROUGH a man's life from a treadmill existence of working hard against nature, to revelation and marvelous results. In a sense, you are reading a biography of seventy-one year old Paul Gautschi, but he would rather we read this as a testimony to the Creator who lifted his soul from darkness into light . . . even the light of His Son Jesus. One of the outcomes of that light was how to grow a garden and an orchard without tilling, without chemicals, and nearly without watering.

In 1990, Paul's orchard was featured in a one-page *Sunset* magazine article.[1] Back then, that generation was not ready to embrace the message Paul shared. Seven years ago, his simple, yet overwhelmingly profound, message was introduced to the world via a free 103-minute online video called *Back to Eden*.[2]

It was viewed half a million times in only a few months and received over one million hits two years later from over 108 (now 155) countries. Paul tells me it has gone viral with the video being linked from untold numbers of faith, gardening, health, and self-sufficiency (prepper) blogs and websites.[3] To date (2020), it has been subtitled into Hungarian, German,

---

1 **Jim McCausland,** "No water or chemicals. . . lots of mulch, earthworms," January 1990 (Northern California) edition, page 118 [cover image used by permission].
2 www.backtoedenfilm.com/watchfreeorganicgardeningmovie.html.
3 Including www.growingfoodgodsway.com, the official website of this book.

Danish, Polish, Russian, Swahili, Japanese, Romanian, Hindi, Italian, Swedish, Norwegian, French, Slovenian, Polish, Portuguese, Hindi, and Chinese to benefit cultures, people, and villages that have been severely affected by inadequate water supply, the products of corporate agribusiness, and a government-dependent supply chain that is so deficient of true food value.

Paul near the herb garden.

Unless you've seen the video, you will be shocked that much of what we have been taught about gardening (and other things in life) has more or less been lies that lead to poor, and even contravening, gardening practices.

If you are on the drug grid, the debt grid, the depression grid, the supplement grid, the junk-science grid, an addiction grid, the junk-food grid, or even a religion grid, you can truly benefit from the minutes and hours you invest in reading this book cover to cover. It was written in order to give you more truth, more inspiration, more hope, and more ways to deal with the challenges you face today and the ones you'll face tomorrow.

Acknowledgments

MANY PEOPLE HAVE MADE THIS BOOK a reality and have been such a gift to me, yet I feel compelled to acknowledge YOU, the reader, because without you taking this to heart and applying the wisdom shared by Paul and others, his glorious message falls short of its purpose. This book, like all books, is a printed compilation of text that is bound with a cover, or as an eBook or audiobook, is simply a file on a device. They have no life in and of themselves, but your character, your personality, and your passion applied to the content to follow make this book alive, real, and dynamic.

God has shown me how precious you are to Him, so how can I do anything less than appreciate and acknowledge your part and your substance? Thank you for honoring all our efforts with the precious time you set aside to read and apply *Growing Food God's Way* 2nd edition.

I thank Paul Gautschi, my friend and mentor, for consistently being an example of living out God's grace in practical, yet faithful, ways. You inspire us not only to grow better food in our physical gardens but also to tend to the garden of our souls, whose "leaf shall not fade, neither shall the fruit thereof be consumed."

Thank you to **Joel Salatin** for sharing your writing talent and insights in the foreword, along with your helpful, free-spirited demeanor, love for people, and devotion to the Lord.

Thanks go to our Indiegogo crowdfunding supporters from all over the globe for faithfully investing in this book and its life-enriching messages. I am happy to give a special shout-out to our crowdfunding sponsor **Michelle Jensen**.

I thank friends—**John and Lauretta Smythe, Mike and Jonna Yant, Pastor John and Marilyn Thomas, Pastor Dennis and Ruth Brown, Earl and Heather Poole**, and **Ian Martinez** (all in Oregon), plus **Brad and Patti Worel**, along with **Rodger and Gwen Wehage** in Washington—for literally putting me up, as well as putting up with me, when I was without.

Thank you to manuscript reviewers **Melina Stephens, Dick Moss, Mel Cohen, T.G. Neason**, and **Marv Balwit** for your careful and observant skills.

Thanks to **Preston Devine** for your graphic design expertise.

I especially thank my best friend and wife, **Phyllis Devine**, for creatively designing the original book's interior and your love and desire to see this book (and your husband) succeed.

Introduction

Growing Food God's Way first began when David came to my garden for a tour in August of 2012. He went home and had an inclination that he needed to write a book about this. David has been back numerous times; plus we talked regularly, and I shared many of my personal letters with him.

Growing Food God's Way is a biographical work to show that this is doable, that it's not hard. You don't need a college education to do it because it's very simple. It's a book to try to help people with all kinds of testimonials and evidence to say, "This works!" So, I just think that it's a great handbook.

My desire for *Growing Food God's Way* is that people become set free and learn to know God. It's all about Him. Knowing God is so foundational to all of life. I love [the Holy Bible] in John 17, where it says: "And this is life eternal, that they might know Thee, the only true God, and Jesus Christ, whom Thou hast sent." Eternal life is knowing God; that's the bottom line.

To taste of my orchard and garden is to taste of God's loving favor and blessing, as I honor Him by restoring what He meant for living things. God arranges remarkable results to those who call upon Him in truth. We do not have to die to experience God's Kingdom. It came to life when I gave my life to Him!

– Paul Gautschi

CHAPTER 1

Paul Gautschi: The Messenger

GROWING FOOD GOD'S WAY BEGINS WITH the man who introduced
his garden to me and many thousands of others. His name is Paul
Gautschi.[4] If you're like most folks, you have never heard of this fellow
who lives, rather simply, on five acres in northwest Washington State.

Why would you, unless you heard his name referenced at a permaculture seminar, watched the *Back to Eden* video via the link sent
to you by a friend, ran across some YouTube video shot at his garden,
or heard him interviewed on a radio program? But Google his name,
and you'll have to scroll over twenty-five pages!

According to the 2020 US Census, there were 15,756 males living
in Jefferson County, Washington,[5] and Paul Gautschi was just one of
them, yet he is featured in this book. Why? Not because his example
is the best thing (in gardening) since sliced bread; not even because of
the sincere depth of his faith. Instead, it is the *object* of his faith that
desperately needs to be shared with the world, certainly the farm and
gardening world, but also the business world, the academic world, the
health and fitness world, the world of faith communities, and so on.
You will see that Paul lives on a tankful of blessings and that his garden and orchard provide undeniable results of an undeniable Creator.

---

4 Pronounced *gowt-chee*.
5 https://www.census.gov/quickfacts/jeffersoncountywashington

The manner in which Paul grows food has caught the attention and praise of the esteemed Rodale Institute.[6] Moreover, **Dr. Joseph Mercola**[7] has received revelation about Paul's methods and wrote a positive review of the documentary featuring Paul.[8] In it, he describes Paul's garden as "a simple organic gardening method that can not only transform your personal garden, but may even be part of the food solution needed on a global scale as well." He was so inspired he called his local tree cutting service and received three truck-loads of woodchips for free! In 2017, fanatic permaculture vlogger **Justin Rhodes** highlighted Paul's garden in "The Great American Farm Tour."[9] Justin told Paul that his was the most requested tour stop by thousands of viewers. Years prior to that, a progressive prepper, code-named **Thatnub,** filmed Paul's tours and special events like his pruning demonstration. People follow him on his L2Survive YouTube channel.[10]

Finally, in a 2012 edition of *Mother Earth News,*[11] an article entitled "Grow More Food In Less Space (With the Least Work)" noted two gardening methods that have been around for decades: square foot gardening and biointensive gardening. Contributor **Linda Gilkeson** notes that one method comes with a high up-front cost and the other comes with high up-front labor. (I note that both methods can benefit from the approach—soil covering—that *Growing Food God's Way* entails.) The article validates no-till and mulch covering: "Research has provided sound reasons why minimizing soil disturbance is a good idea: Reduced tillage systems result in higher populations of beneficial fungi that move nutrients and water through the soil column." She later affirms: "Creating minimal disturbance has led to a bountiful garden with less work on my part."

---

6 It is a premiere think tank of everything organic. See www.rodaleinstitutte.org.
7 www.mercola.com.
8 See http://articles.mercola.com/sites/articles/archive/2014/06/21/back-to-eden-organic-gardening.aspx?e_cid=20140621Z1_DNL_art_1&utm_source=dnl&utm_medium=email&utm_content=art1&utm_campaign=20140621Z1&et_cid=DM47723&et_rid=560676611. Be advised that Dr. Mercola promotes a product later in the article. It has *nothing* to do with Paul's tending of his garden.
9 https://www.youtube.com/watch?v=fM2DMv0Arlc&feature=youtu.be.
10 https://www.youtube.com/channel/UCBI97edYBxQr-KfWkmk86QQ.
11 Linda A. Gilkeson, "Grow More Food In Less Space (With the Least Work)" *Mother Earth News*, Feb/Mar 2014, 41-45, www.motherearthnews.com.

Why Read This Book?

Because Paul is Exhibit A that:

- you can grow good food in ground so hard and sterile that it defies the shovel;
- you can, in a few seasons, grow amazing pasture grass for your animals;
- you can grow and eat foods that are "off the chart" nutritionally;
- you can enjoy fresh, raw foods (nuts, fruits, and vegetables) in season and locally grown;
- you can grow healthy food all year long;
- you can overcome whatever level of dependence you have for institutionally processed foods;
- you can turn your sick and tired body into a healthy, active one;
- you can exchange a life pattern of unforgiveness to a consistent forgiving pattern and receive a multitude of health benefits for doing so;
- you can be a catalyst for change in those who observe your garden and your life;
- you can purposefully destress in your own peaceful sanctuary where there is life and growth and deep, intangible substance;
- you can transform your life with new-found gratefulness;
- *you can grow excellent food with much less work!*
- The only question is, Are you ready?

- If you desire to live life with one or more of the above characteristics as Paul Gautschi is experiencing, then fasten your seatbelt, put your seat in the upright position, and stow your tray table. It's time to land in your own Garden of Eden!

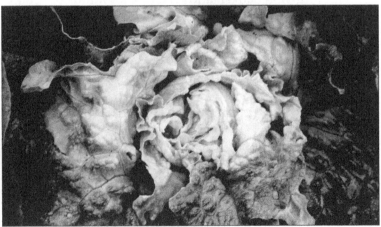

CHAPTER 2

The Dream and the Covenant

IN 1976, THE GAUTSCHI FAMILY OF FOUR purchased a nine-hundred-square-foot home on a standard subdivision lot in a Los Angeles, California suburb called Eagle Rock. Life was okay there, and the weather was idyllic, but as with many a Californian, they eventually concluded the LA environment was not conducive to safe and healthful living. At that time (1978), there were over seven million people living in Los Angeles County. That year, there were 173 days (47 percent of the year) that exceeded air health standard levels.[12]

Also, Paul had heard on the news that the odds of a female getting physically accosted in LA were 1 in 3.[13] Because he had a wife and two daughters, it seemed like just a matter of time before something horrific would happen. The last straw came in December of 1978 when, on Christmas Day, a drunk driver ran into two of the Gautschis' parked cars in front of their house. Of course, the driver had no insurance to fix the damages.

At the time they bought their house on Almaden Drive in the Eagle Rock neighborhood, they also purchased a rural lot in Sequim,[14]

---

12 An excess of 0.15 PM (particulate matter) over a one-hour average, almost six months of unhealthy city air to breathe.

13 In fairness to LA, I could not confirm this statistic, yet it is disturbing that the constant reporting of "crimes against the person" in the city would lend sufficient credence to terribly high incidences of violence to women.

14 Pronounced *skwim*.

Washington, for one thousand dollars down and one hundred dollars per month. Paul says: "In 1976, we bought the five acres in Washington. We had *no plans* to ever move up there." The Gautschis had a friend in Laguna Beach whose dad had bought a home up there. In doing some research, Paul read in *Sunset* magazine that pilots said they fly through clouds in all of Washington until they get to Sequim, which was cloudless. He continues: "Over the years, we observed folks in California making money in real estate, and we bought the lot as a kind of savings."

ON TO WASHINGTON

Now that Paul and **Carol Gautschi** had purposed to move, they needed to set priorities that would guide them to where they would move. The priorities were (1) fresh air, (2) clean water, and (3) live food. Such "did not exist in LA" in their opinion. In 1979 they joined the ranks of those leaving California, when 135,173 *more* people migrated *out* of California than migrated in![15]

The Gautschis had a small mortgage on their home. Keep in mind, in 1979, Federal Housing Administration (FHA) home loan

---

15 According to truck rental company U-Haul, Californians preferred to move to Nevada, Arizona, and Washington.

rates were upwards of 13 percent, not the historic lows Americans have seen since 2010. This bothered Paul, and he made a covenant with God, "If You will sell our house, I will commit to stay out of debt." I asked him why he made such a vow and Paul replied: "I had no right to be in debt. The Word of God says you cannot serve two masters.[16] You are a slave to whom you owe.[17] To be a slave to a bank when I was a slave to Jesus was not consistent." Once the family had agreed to a move, they put a For Sale By Owner sign in their front lawn on a Saturday. Upon arriving home from church the next day, a couple was standing at their porch and wanted to see the house. Once they did, they loved it and agreed to buy it for fifty-eight thousand dollars.

The sale went so swiftly that the Gautschis had to rent back for some weeks after selling just to get their stuff out. The sale made the Gautschis thirty thousand dollars in two years! With those funds, they paid for and built their house on the five-acre lot, put in a well and septic system, and paid for the move. Paul and Carol honored God and the covenant they made with Him to live debt free. That was how the Gautschis got off the debt grid.

The Gautschi family moved to Washington State in June of 1979. Though he didn't have a job waiting for him, Paul was motivated by three passages in the Bible:

> A skilled man will work for kings, he will not work for the common man.[18]
> A man's gift will make room for him.[19]
> A diligent man will succeed.[20]

Paul concludes: "Those three scriptures gave me the confidence that, no matter where I go, God is not limited to geography. Those

---

16 Matthew 6:24, "No man can serve two masters: for either he will hate the one, and love the other; or else he will hold to the one, and despise the other. You cannot serve God and mammon [money]."
17 Proverbs 22:7, "The rich ruleth over the poor, and the borrower is servant to the lender."
18 Proverbs 22:29, "mean" replaced with "common."
19 Proverbs 18:16, "A man's gift maketh room for him, and bringeth him before great men."
20 A paraphrase of Proverbs 12:27, "The slothful man roasteth not that which he took in hunting: but the substance of a diligent man is precious."

principles are eternal, and they work anywhere." Paul's part was to apply his gifts and do so diligently.

PLANNING HIS WORK AND WORKING HIS PLAN

To save money, the Gautschis purchased a fifteen-hundred-square-foot log-home kit from Real Log Homes out of Montana[21] for $12,500 in June of 1979.[22] Paul, Carol, and their three children (at that time)[23] began to occupy their new house in December (five and a half months after they started), though it was not completed till many years later. Paul admits: "I'd never built a doghouse before," so the prospect of constructing the family home was a huge challenge to a man who had been raised to do things right the first time. A neighbor was an expert in construction. He was their friendly and handy consultant as they ran into challenge after challenge. "I don't know what we would have done without him," Paul recalls.

They spent four thousand dollars for the well and two thousand dollars for the septic and permits. Additionally, they had to buy their own roofing, plumbing/electrical fixtures, paint, flooring, and heating system. As to the log home, Paul enjoys solid wood interior walls. They look homey and natural. Then he gleams: "If the kids mark it up, you can chisel it off." They chose a wood shake roof cover, which lasted thirty-four years, and then installed a lifetime metal roof.

But what did Paul do for a living in Washington? In LA, he was an independent arborist. Some of his jobs included trimming palm trees for the city at seventy dollars an hour. However, Sequim doesn't have such palm trees, so Paul got a winter job at Graysmarsh Farm [24]caning up raspberry vines all day. "It paid fifteen dollars a day, but I was glad to do it because it was all there was," says Paul. After a time, God brought him an "amazing job" at a nursery. His salary? One thousand dollars a month. It was a huge windfall for a family that was debt free. Their expenses were pretty much limited to gas, food, and electric.

---

21 www.realloghomes.com
22 This same model (with a gable vs. gambrel roof) is now around $67,000 delivered per the 2013 catalog.
23 Later, four more sons and daughters came along.
24 http://www.graysmarsh.com/.

Paul was pruning the nursery plants, and one day a customer took note of his skill with plants. From that encounter, Paul was hired to prune the man's trees in an upscale Sequim neighborhood of about one thousand homes, set amongst many natural fir trees. His tree work so dramatically improved the looks of the property that, by word of mouth, Paul received "all the work I wanted for thirty-four years." He has never had to advertise his business. Doing that first job exceedingly well set him up for life, as God honored His scriptural promises.

One customer in that community had Paul prune six of his trees. Over a decade later, the man died, and the new owner hired Paul to remove some of the trees. Here is a revelation Paul received about thinning trees in his own words: "It was twelve years in between (when I thinned them and took them out), and you could go back and see the growth rings. The first hundred years they were as tight as they could be, then all of the sudden, there's this huge width . . . and you could count the twelve years and see back to the time where I thinned them and how it just stimulated the growth. For me it was an amazing revelation, like 'Wow, look at the impact of pruning a tree.' God was just showing me stuff that you would never get out of a textbook."

WHEN LIFE GIVES YOU DANDELIONS, MAKE DANDELION TEA

As mentioned, the Gautschis paid four thousand dollars for the 213-foot well that was drilled in 1979. When it became time to do a flow test, the output of the well was discovered to be only one-half gallon per minute (½ GPM). That is about as close to zero GPM as you can get. Now the blessing of being debt-free was additionally ratified by the fact that, at the time, mortgage companies would not lend on a rural property with a well producing less than 3 GPM. They couldn't have gotten a loan, even if they had wanted one!

But the greater impact on Paul was: How do I get water to my new orchard when there is barely enough to take a shower or run a dishwasher? Recall that his goals were to have fresh air, clean water, and live food to feed his family.

The Gautschis were told, in 1976, that the land they were buying was extraordinarily affordable because the area was known for its water problems. Now the chickens had come home to roost, so to speak, and they were stuck with a sub-standard domestic water source. Understandably, a certain sense of panic would be justified at this point, but that doesn't solve anything. Paul needed answers, not more stress.

Looking back, he readily admits that if he had drilled an adequate well, he never would have learned the Lessons from the Forest . . .

CHAPTER 3

Lessons from the Forest:
The Covering

O VERWHELMED BY THE FACT THAT HE had no water for his orchard, Paul took this pressing need to his "Dad" (heavenly Father), not in the way of saying to Him, "Give me more water," but in a more surrendered posture that said, "God, how am I going to grow food without water?"

Dad directed him to the cedar and fir trees that surround his property. There, in August (after many rainless weeks), he saw green, healthy, thriving trees. Paul told the Lord: "If You can show me how You do these trees, then I can do an orchard." As he walked among the towering trees, his attention was suddenly drawn to the ground. On top was nothing out of the ordinary, just fir needles, small twigs, and other organic matter. As he dug deeper, he found something remarkable—rich, moist humus[25] beneath the ground

---

25 Humus: dark earth made of organic material such as decayed leaves and plants (Cambridge Dictionary).

cover. That raised a new question: "Where did the moisture come from?" Then he recognized that God used the organic cover (mulch) upon the soil to retain accumulated rain water, which kept the subsoil from drying out.

Paul planted the orchard using straw and sheep manure for the covering. Afterwards, he discovered *woodchips have far superior properties* and has used them ever since. In fact, his orchard soil lies under eight to ten inches of decomposed woodchips. After twelve years of leaving it all alone, he added about four inches of free woodchips to the orchard for better weed control in late 2013, and some in 2019.

WE WILL, WE WILL, ROCK YOU

Next, Paul tells of a property that he owns in the town of Sequim: "My place in Sequim[26] is riverbed, it is 85 percent rock. It would be impossible to till. You could never till . . . because it's all rock. I'm growing the most amazing, beautiful, stuff there—carrots, potatoes, fruit trees, tomatoes, peppers, figs, peaches, and apricots—just from the woodchips over the rocks. I put the woodchips over the rock, then went down to the level where the rocks started, planted potatoes, and they all grew well. All those rocks, down below, are still there, releasing minerals. Nothing's changed; we just covered it. That's the favor of God."

This prolific lot is kind of a community garden for Paul's friends in the area. Paul affirms: "The thing about God is He is not challenged by anything. Once something's there and creates a cover, it's not an issue. We have to adjust our minds and get humble and say: 'You know, God, I may not be able to wrap my mind around it and understand it, but I will, by faith, believe You are doing it. You're doing it; it's there in my face, so I can do what You're doing. I can plant stuff in rock.'"

WHAT ARE WOODCHIPS?

First, let's consider what woodchips are not; they are not bark dust or sawdust, and they are not only bark chips. Those are readily

---

26 The Gautschis have a rental property in town on a large lot where he (and others) grow food.

available at garden centers and lumberyards. Though they are organic (unless dyed to be a uniform color), they are deficient for your garden compared to the real thing. Woodchips are a form of mulch, composed of a mixture of chipped tree branches, bark, and the all-important leaves or needles.

There are three kinds of woodchips:

 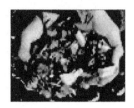 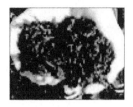

1. Fresh, or green, chips
2. Partially seasoned (composted) chips
3. Composted chips (left to sit and decompose for at least a year)

To use peanut butter terms: extra chunky, chunky, and creamy.

The key to the right material is that it contains twigs, branch particles, and green leaves, and needles. Just the other day, an arborist was working around the corner of my lot. Of course, I walked over there to observe what was being ground up. As it was the tail end of winter, there were not green leaves. Thus, I had to pass on the opportunity to have them dump at my place.

On the topic of discerning what not to take, you may tell the arborist that you do not want a load that contains invasive plant species like Scotch broom, holly, blackberries, vetch, or ivy. The more indigenous the woodchips are to your area or neighborhood, the better opportunity you will have to maximize the benefits of covering. Paul says: "You don't want them all the same size. God, in nature, makes things in multiple sizes. It is an amazing design. If they are all the same size, you have issues like floating." As well, same-size materials tend to compact. So, why is covering so relevant to plant growth?

GOD HAS US COVERED

Upon any clear-minded observation, we see that God designed everything in nature to have a covering: humans have skin, animals have fur, trees have bark, birds have feathers, and fish have scales. Even when you were in your mother's womb, God covered your life-long covering (skin) with vernix to protect it while you were growing in an all-liquid environment.

Likewise, soil is a living organism, and God designed it to be covered with something. When you take the cover off, the soil becomes vulnerable and suffers consequences. Covering keeps the topsoil in place by keeping erosion in check. Paul notes that man, in his fallen state, has taken the covering off by plowing and tilling. These practices deplete topsoil over time. Paul points out to visitors: "It takes one hundred years to build one inch of topsoil."[27]

One of the mind-blowing aspects of the covering is that the wood-chips are lighter than dirt, yet a storm of wind that blows topsoil away does not blow the woodchips away. The covering stays and continues to do its job. It is not uncommon for the Olympic Peninsula (the area that includes Sequim) to receive up to 60 mph[28] wind gusts during a storm. When such a storm occurs during autumn, all of Paul's fallen leaves blow away, but the woodchips and underlying topsoil remain.

Consider how the natural forest cover has an astounding ability to displace surface water. Paul tells of the Hoh Rainforest that is only seventy miles west of Sequim. There the forest floor has been documented to displace fourteen feet of rainwater a year![29] The obvious inference is unless you get over fourteen feet[30] of rain a year, the surface water that does come your way is no match for a good covering (of woodchips).

But what about water retention in dry climates? The LA Basin is essentially a desert. There were hot summer days when Paul, as a young boy, wanted to go fishing and needed worms for bait. Since worms were not a budget item in the Gautschi household, Paul would have to find his own. In other parts of the US West Coast, you can stick a shovel in the ground and dig up worms easily. Not in Los Angeles. Paul learned that the only place to get them was where the worms had moisture. That, in a desert, was under a large rock. So, a covering

27 According to Professor **David Pimentel** (Cornell University – Ecology and Agricultural Science), "It takes approximately 500 years to replace 25 millimeters (1 inch) of topsoil lost to erosion."
28 Equivalent to about 100 kph.
29 http://www.sevenwondersofwashingtonstate.com/the-hoh-rain-forest.html
30 Equal to 4.26 meters.

displaces volumes of water in a rainforest but also retains water in a desert. This is not a coincidence; it is by *design*. We can choose to go against the design, but we will always reap the consequences of doing so and forfeit all the benefits.

Hoh Rainforest.

Paul reminds us: "All plants can do is pick up nutrients through water.[31] When the cover is on the ground, the cover makes compost tea. Whatever is in the water is what the plant has to eat. This has been going on in nature for six thousand years of recorded human history. This is not something that can fail. This is not a new concept. That's what I love about it. *It's impossible to fail.* So, it is not like I'm trying to sell you on something *if* it works. This is a demonstrated thing, but because of the blindness and disconnect [to, or with, God], we do not get it."

Bioremediation

Paul tells of some friends in Battleground, Washington: "They built this beautiful home and did this septic system, designed by the county, which cost them about twelve thousand dollars. It failed to function as needed. The county told them to use a different grade of sand and to haul thirty yards of the old sand out and get rid of it; then

---

31 This is essentially true, but not exclusive at the microbial level.

bring in some new sand: do it all over again at their expense, when it was the county's mistake. You know what we did? We simply buried the [existing] mound in woodchips and planted Mediterranean pink heather on it.

"The whole thing is gorgeous today, and the septic is working properly. Free woodchips and a few one-gallon plants, resulted in no standing water. With the heather, the roots don't go deep, but they are pulling moisture out. It blooms all winter and is beautiful and working. *Woodchips are amazing; the problems they will solve for you.*" Applying a woodchip cover to most soils (even rocks) is akin to "biografting" the land.

David's Theory of Biografting Soil

Imported ground cover (woodchips) tend to, within one season, convert from the role of a foreign mass of ground cover to an integral and beneficial element of the soil via decomposition and assimilation by natural processes.

It is the testimony of a number of gardeners that initial application of woodchips, or soil and added compost, over native soil will cause a positive reaction in the soil, which often results in new or increased earthworm activity, and can be followed by a period of limited growth of plant material as the woodchips and the soil attempt to assimilate into a cohesive mass of living organisms (biomass).

The natural inertia that would be dedicated to seed germination and plant growth can be, of necessity, co-opted by the host soil's efforts to convert the woodchips from the role of cover (visitor team in baseball) to the role of becoming an extension of the host itself (the home team). This process can have the effect of delaying growth *temporarily*. It could be days or weeks, depending upon weather conditions and when you applied the cover.

Biografting versus Biomimicry

Biomimicry has been defined by biologist **Janine Benyus** as, "new science that studies nature's models and then imitates or takes inspiration from these designs and processes to solve human problems."[32] For instance, Velcro was inspired by the tiny hooks on the surface of burr-like seeds in nature. Look how common Velcro is in our lives. Another example would be using an electric or power leaf blower that mimics intense wind to allow us to blow our leaves to a desired location, or even hair blowers to dry hair quickly.

So, isn't that what Paul did to solve his problem? The short answer would be yes, but that is misleading because biomimicry takes cues from God's design (nature) to implement products and processes *in the lab*. Rather, Paul said to God: "I want to imitate

---

32 Janine Benyus, *Biomimicry: Innovation Inspired by Nature*, New York: HarperCollins, 1997.

You." He used natural things (woodchips) to restore the land to its God-given properties and producing capacities. He was (and is) imitating God's restorative nature and sharing that freely (as God freely revealed it to Paul).

It is better described as "Theomimicry," and it is something we all can do and share with others. Conversely, biomimicry, if successful, typically leads to legal patents and industrial process changes.

Paul does not call what he did "biografting"; that is simply how I relate to it as a clear step towards bioremediation. It is not a new term, just one not typically applied to the care of soils. Like tree grafting, you are starting out with one thing with a desire to end up with another thing—a better or different fruit, or in our case, better soil in your garden, orchard, or vineyard. It is remediating the surface of the terra firma to what God originally designed before man had taken off the cover and compacted it.

Read an insightful excerpt from Ms. Benyus's book (pg. 95):

> Despite what we would call "limits," nature manages to craft materials of a complexity and a functionality that we can only envy. The inner shell of a sea creature called an abalone is twice as tough as our high-tech ceramics. Spider silk, ounce for ounce, is five times stronger than steel. Mussel adhesive works under water and sticks to anything, even without a primer. Rhino horn manages to repair itself, though it contains no living cells. Bone, wood, skin, tusks, antlers and heart muscle—miracle materials all—are made to live out their useful life and then to fade back, to be absorbed by another kind of life through the grand cycle of death and renewal.

It is encouraging when a secular biologist acknowledges the miraculous. Imagine what she could discover directly from the Miracle Maker by honest inquiry as she seeks to take cues from His actors: ducks, rhinos, shells, forests, rivers, and so on.

What Makes Woodchips Effective?

In order to truly appreciate the benefits of using woodchips as a covering, let's examine a more common item, wool, and its amazing properties.

A single strand of wool is of no account, but aggregate wool fibers do amazing things. They:
- are hygroscopic (able to absorb ambient moisture from the air);
- have a "memory" to bounce back to their original shape;
- supply fantastic warmth;
- are flame resistant (and self-extinguishing if ignited);
- are resistant to dirt, mildew, and static electricity;
- insulate well; and
- provide for great acoustics.

In a similar vein, woodchips:
- are also hygroscopic (literally soak in moisture from the atmosphere);
- insulate soil from extreme cold;
- cool land surfaces in extreme heat;
- retain sub-surface moisture in droughts;
- release or redistribute excess moisture;
- are resilient to prevent compaction (even under extreme weight);
- can neutralize soil pH;
- add minerals and essential elements to the soil;
- at times, provide spores that enable quicker decomposition of beneficial plant material;
- protect the soil from airborne weed seeds and make weed removal easier;
- allow for cleaner harvests of produce, with little or no dirty residue;
- filter out harmful liquid soil inputs; and
- act, in conjunction with rain, to make natural compost tea that . . .
- stimulate increased earthworm, nematode, and microbiologic activity in soils.

So Why Would Anybody Not Use Woodchips?

Like any new approach, there is the fear of the unknown. For many, it is a matter of pride and prejudice: too proud to be taught something because they already consider themselves experts, and the prejudice of myopically sticking to the ways agricultural schools and extension agents have treated the land for generations, while discounting viably improved practices. Sort of like "once a land tiller, always a land tiller." It takes humility (which does not come easy to us) to admit that what we believed and practiced was counterproductive. Bear in mind, Paul learned it from the source, the Creator directly. He could have said: "That's not the way my professor did it," and resisted, but he would have missed the benefit of covering. It takes compelling evidence and, better yet, personal experience to rise above our complacency and habitually playing it safe by doing what we have always done in the past.

What Is the Secret of a Covering?

The prime benefit of a woodchip covering is the creation and maintenance of a soil environment that encourages vibrant root growth. Roots are wired to grow but can be thwarted by resistance. They are usually no match for stiff, clay-dominant soils or other systemically compacted soils (e.g., hardpan).

Not all roots are created equal, in that some plants put out hardier roots than others. A strong root capacity is why a weed grows where other plants do not. All plants need energy to survive, and roots are soil-nutrient receivers. The more prolific the root system is, the more energy (in both reproduction and growth energy) the plant will receive.

Paul's woodchip soil surface is porous (to let air and water in) and is loose enough to not only allow for unfettered root growth but also encourage it! These roots are empowered to travel more laterally, rather than straight down. Paul traced one of his dwarf apple tree's roots thirty feet from its trunk! A back-to-Eden gardener in Chelan, Washington, traced a tomato plant's roots out fourteen feet! No wonder he had a bumper crop of tomatoes; no wonder Paul has remarkable apple growth on his trees!

The tree shown here is only two years old and is laden with apples. Paul says that "boxes of apples" had already been taken off before I photographed it in October of 2013.

The following photo is even a younger tree. See the apples that have come on in its first year!

Woodchips Time Tested

French biologists in Quebec studied natural ramial chipped wood, or RCW (woodchips from small to medium-sized branches; "rami" means small). Below are their findings (my emphasis added in boldface):

Results of World-Wide Experiments[33]

Twenty years of experiments with RCW in both forestry and agriculture in Québec, Africa, Europe and the Caribbean conclude that RCWs provide:

- **Better soil conservation** due to the water retention capacity of humus content (up to 20 times its weight) and the capacity of water accumulation and management by soil organisms;
- **[Beneficial pH modification]** An increase in pH from 0.4 to 1.2 or, under tropical conditions, in alkaline soils, a decrease in the range of 2.0.;
- **A yield increase** up to 1000% for tomatoes in Sénégal, and 300% on strawberries in Québec;
- **A 400% increase in dry matter**[34] for corn in both Côte d'Ivoire [Africa] and the Dominican Republic [Caribbeans]
- **A noticeable increase in frost and drought resistance**;
- **More developed** and highly-mycorrhized[35] **root systems**;
- **Fewer and less diversified weeds**; elimination of pests (under tropical conditions, a complete control of root nematodes, the worst and most costly pest in vegetable garden growing);
- **Enhanced flavor** in fruit production;
- **Higher dry matter,** phosphorus, potassium and magnesium content in potato tubers;
- **A soil turning from pale to deep brown** in the same season.
- **A decrease or complete elimination of pests.**

A particular affinity for chipped twigs resulted from the study: "More than 75% of nutrients are stored in twigs. Twigs are the center of life, stemwood being the result of the whole crown activity. Twigs, once chipped and brought in close contact with the soil, momentarily replace the rootlets that are constantly transformed into short-lived aggregates by the soil microorganisms. These aggregates are the managers of soil nutrients and energy for the ecosystem's own sake. They

---

33 Céline Caron, Gilles Lemieux, and Lionel Lachance, *Regenerating Soils with Ramial Chipped Wood*. Publication N 83, Quebec, Canada: Laval University, 1992, page 3.
34 Dry matter in plants includes minerals, proteins, vitamins, and antioxidants.
35 Symbiotic relationship with a fungus. http://www.definitions.net/definition/mycorrhized.

enable biological actors to play their vital role, from virus to mammals, using available energy and nutrients."[36]

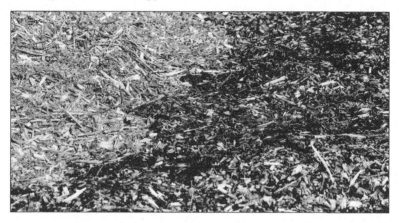

Woodchip Myths

Another reason so many people fail to use woodchips is that some public perceptions about woodchips rely less on soil science and more on superstition:

Myth #1: Woodchips will acidify the soil.
FACT: There is no evidence that supports this myth. It may be said that pH can fluctuate in the lower decomposing (biografting) layer of the chips, but this has not been shown to adversely affect the actual soil layer.

One day, Paul called to tell me about a gardener near Montreal, Canada. Three days later, and a half-hour three-way call with a French interpreter, I heard **Jurek**'s story first-hand. He and his neighbor, **Nicole**, were offered a free load of woodchips but were advised that the organic matter would be ten percent pine needles. Because of Myth #1, they were concerned about acidity with adding the chips and needles, so Jurek borrowed a Kelway[37] soil pH tester (probe). With it, he tested three areas of his wife's garden to see what the pH was prior to covering with woodchips. The results? Already acidic —5.5, 5.8, and 6.5! It didn't make sense to add pine needles to acidic soil, so Nicole called Paul,

---

36 Céline Caron et al., *Regenerating Soils*, page 7.
37 Distributed by Kel Instruments Company in Wyckoff, New Jersey, 201-847-8353.

and he was very reassuring that it would be fine to use those chips. Nonetheless, Jurek preferred hard evidence that this was not going to be the wrong thing to do, so he went to a forested area by his country plot and came to an area with pine needles on the forest floor. He inserted the Kelway probe, and it read a perfect 7.0 pH! I asked Jurek if he had any reservations about the load of chips, and he said: "None." When Paul was told about this, his response was: "I love it! This is the nature of the Father; total perfect order and balance." Then he pointed to Romans 1:20: "For the invisible things of Him from the creation of the world are clearly seen, being understood by the things that are made, even His eternal power and Godhead; so that they are without excuse."

Myth #2: Woodchips will rob soil of nitrogen.

FACT: More studies validate that woodchips enhance the soils they cover. At most, the chips may temporarily ameliorate surface nitrogen when they are first applied. (See biografting dynamics above.) The only known problem with woodchips and nitrogen is if you till them into your soil. So, properly applied, they are not a problem. To misuse the woodchips is a self-fulfilling prophesy.

Myth #3: Cedar chips (an insect-repelling wood) leach chemicals that can kill other plants or seedlings.

FACT: Woodchips of only a few species—including black walnut, sour orange, red maple, red cedar, eucalyptus, box elder, and mango—actually contain such (allelopathic) chemicals. Most cedar varieties don't have those natural chemicals. I use cedar chips around the house and barn foundations to ward off carpenter ants and termites. Note that Paul would take the varieties mentioned above and leave them in a pile to break down over time into organic mulch.

Myth #4: Woodchips are a fire hazard.

FACT: This myth stems from occasional reports of fire at commercial mulch facilities hosting huge piles of woodchips, where the heat generated by the biomass within the pile accelerated into actual fire. The pile of woodchips delivered by your local tree service, if left alone, will generate heat (you will see steam in colder areas) but lacks sufficient mass to gravitate to ignition. If you are uncomfortable with it, spread the chips as you get them or make multiple, smaller piles. For the latter, just know that you are undoing the very process you desire in your compost bin.

TAKING INVENTORY

Are you struggling with the thought of converting your precious garden to what has been described in this book?

Does the thought of covering ALL your growing areas with wood-chips seem loathsome to you?

Like my friends **Lance and Chris Riste** in central Washington, you could plant some seeds in tilled soil and the rest in covered soil, but they were sure sorry they didn't do the whole thing in woodchips.

Paul tells me of a pumpkin farmer in Washington that planted half his pumpkins in woodchips and half "the old way." At the end of the 2013 season, he called Paul and said: "I am never going back to the old way!" Turns out he had to constantly water the tilled area and didn't water the woodchip area at all. As the pumpkins came on, he noticed that the leaves in the tilled area were wilty, as if he hadn't watered, though he applied water all through the day.

He asked Paul about this, and Paul reminded him that his com-pacted soil was not allowing enough root development to take in the water, so that was why the leaves seemed starved of hydration. By the way, the covered pumpkins grew wonderfully, as they were fully hydrated naturally.

Finally, there was a soil-covering enthusiast in the Midwest that convinced her elderly dad to do a portion of his garden in woodchips last season. Paul later got a call from her, and she explained how they were not able to grow any mustard greens (which were planted in the original garden area). As it turned out, one seed must have made it across to the woodchip-covered area, and a plant grew there on its own. In fact, it grew so well and produced so much, the lady's mother was able to use those mustard greens for several meals!

> *Ninety-nine percent of the failures come from people who have the habit of making excuses.*
> – George Washington Carver

COVERING ROCKS!

Rocks are concentrated aggregates that slowly release beneficial minerals into the soil.

Paul continues:

> Every one of these rocks [above] was in my garden. You can imagine how much labor it was [to remove them]. It was this (seemingly) endless, difficult task. Every time I tilled, they just kept coming up. I'm looking at all this incredible mineral content I took out of my garden. There is still some in there. The rocks are still out there in my orchard. I got it with the orchard, but I was so stupid I just thought, "I can do this garden on my own, God," so I did it my own way without asking, and that was so dumb. I am thankful it [the altar/rock pile] is here because it reminds me of . . . the stupidity of not asking God . . . of leaning on your own understanding.
>
> God said not to put your tool on His handiwork or you will pollute it.[38] The nature of man is to try to make it fit. God said, "Don't you touch those rocks." I think that's a principle for everything. Anytime you

---

38 Exodus 20:25, "And if thou wilt make me an altar of stone, thou shalt not build it of hewn stone: for if thou lift up thy tool upon it, thou hast polluted it."

change an altar—the natural order—it has to be negative and degrading because God designed the place to
be good. He has the place of all wisdom, all knowledge,
so everything He did was *the max.* To change that is
only negative and degrading; you cannot improve
upon God. God made it perfect.

I love the Creation, the whole design. Every day
during Creation, He would go out and do the inspec-
tion because there was no one higher than Him, and
He would say, "It is good," and I think that is saying
a lot. That infinite, omnipotent, omniscient God who
can do it all says, "This is good."

Paul shares: "Lake Crescent's banks [in Washington's Olympic
Peninsula] have dark green trees. They grow in rock. . . . Think about
the trees . . . it's a slope . . . anything that hits, runs off . . . it's not like its
flat . . . going to hold it. Because of the genius [of God], the needles fall
in the cracks and are holding moisture, and those trees are thriving all
summer long. . . . Rocks are a benefit, an asset to your garden. Rocks
are a wonderful cover; things grow very well in them.

"The Japanese are very connected to nature; they're very intuitive
that way and prune the best of any culture on the planet. They are
very, very sensitive to the ground, where they are growing things. . . .
Do you know how they cover the ground there? They meticulously
lay rock in and around all their plants and trees, beautifully laid, so
it is attractive. And they are doing that to retain moisture and release
minerals to their plants. So, it [the covering] is a demonstrated thing
in all kinds of places."

If you have started your own rock altar out of a misplaced con-
cern about rocks in your garden, then consider joining Paul in removing our bias against rocks.

Reading about nature is fine, but if a person walks in the
woods and listens carefully, he can learn more than what
is in the books, for they speak with the voice of God.
– George Washington Carver

CHAPTER 4

Paul's Garden and the Genesis Curse

*Cursed is the ground for thy sake; in sorrow shalt thou
eat of it all the days of thy life; Thorns also and thistles
shall it bring forth to thee; and thou shalt eat the herb of
the field; In the sweat of thy face shalt thou eat bread, till
thou return unto the ground.*

— Genesis 3:17-19

IN THE VERSE ABOVE, GOD IS speaking to **Adam** after he and **Eve** disobeyed. As the first members of the human race, they lived on an earth we wouldn't recognize. As beautiful as our current world is with its majestic sunsets, rhythmic oceans, and verdant forests, we have to remember that our planet is in a *fallen state*.

Their world was not subject to temperature extremes; they did not receive rain from the sky, nor did they need to because the earth was one global greenhouse with a perfect mixture of super oxygen, ambient moisture, and consistent warmth. In finite terms, it was spring all year. There was a peace and rest about the Garden of Eden that, far from doing it justice, could best be described as personal and global harmony because everything and everyone was connected to the Creator.

What also may be beyond our ability to grasp is that Adam and Eve were given dominion over the entire worldly empire. They could do anything; they could go anywhere. They could whisper, or they could yell anywhere, anytime, and no one would hold it against them. No bird, animal, beast, reptile, or insect on the planet would harm them. They ate whatever plant they desired and drank from any pond, brook, or waterfall. They were truly FREE!

There was only one caveat—one tree (out of so many) that God said to leave alone. It was beautiful, possibly the most majestic of fruit-bearing trees. This was the tree of the knowledge of good and evil.[39] The fruit was lovely to behold. Perhaps it had an aromatic presence, like blooming lilacs. But no matter, it was off limits, and the penalty for intruding upon that particular tree was severe, and everyone in the world knew it![40]

This was the glorified life of Earth's first inhabitants. Not the Earth we know, but the Earth especially blessed by its Creator. Centuries of astronomers, the Hubble[41] telescope, and NASA's Kepler[42] roving space observatory confirm that no other observable heavenly body was given life forms as earth was.

THE FALL

Once the two humans offended God's law or broke His covenant, He had to fulfill His promise and carry out His sentence: Adam and Eve were demoted from a spiritual bent to a mortal one and were now under a sentence of certain physical death. They were banished from the garden and, in the process, the Earth went from a glorious and perfect planet towards what it is now, subject to earthquakes, floods, hurricanes, tornadoes, drought, insects, extreme heat, and extreme cold. Worse than all of that is that man was left separated from God and Satan became Liar in Chief and the prince of the earthly realm. So now, Adam went from God's benevolent ruler of the earth to both predator and prey in portions of the animal kingdom *and* indentured servant in the realm of growing food. Adam's breaking of the ground

---

39 Genesis 2:9.
40 Genesis 2:16-17 (all two of them!).
41 Named after Edwin Powell Hubble, 1889-1953, pioneer of modern astronomy.
42 Named after Johannes Kepler, 1571-1630, pioneer of geometric astronomy.

was symbolic of his breaking away from God. It was a departure, a desperate act of a desperate man that now had to grow his own food and was subject to harsh elements and threatening species.[43]

The Bible talks of generational sin,[44] which is a tendency of wrong thoughts and behaviors that can proceed from grandfather, to father, to son, and so on. Current gardening practices have essentially been handed down from previous generations.

The concept of breaking up soil and trying to manipulate it into something functional is merely Adam's post-Eden way (thousands of years ago) mixed with some modern chemicals and such. In so doing, we are still under the curse, and so was Paul, hook, line, and sinker.

Paul's orchard experience produced fantastic results, but he says that we are creatures of habit and our human nature is to do things as we were taught and *not* to inquire from God. He was grateful for God's plan to sustain an orchard with a covering, but it did not occur to him to apply this revelation to his garden.

Paul roto-tilled his garden, he imported organic material, he removed tons of rock from his garden, and he rotated where things were planted; he did all that he knew to be the right things as far as gardening was concerned. Yet his was a treadmill experience. He fought with weeds every year for seventeen years from the first tilling each April, all because he forgot God's lessons from the orchard.

---

43 Genesis 3:17-19, 23.
44 Also encompassed by the term "iniquities."

CHAPTER 5

Lessons from the Orchard

And God said, Behold, I have given you every herb bearing seed, which is upon the face of all the earth, and every tree, in the which is the fruit of a tree yielding seed; to you it shall be for meat [food].
— Genesis 1:29

MOST READERS OF THIS BOOK KNOW the traditional routine of home gardens: Till them in early spring (in the Pacific Northwest), let them dry out a bit, and till again. When the weeds come up, till again (and again if necessary).

Build your furrows, or mounds, and plant your seeds and/or your various starts; then water and continue weeding as the weeds come up. On the latter discipline, if you slack off a week, it might as well be a month, as weeds tend to multiply at an insatiable rate. So we hoe or till (yet again) at a shallow setting, or we hand pull; or worse, we spray the weeds.

HOE, HOE, HOE

Such was Paul's life for seventeen years after he had discovered the covering for his orchard. It was more and more demanding on his body, but even worse, it was taking too much joy from his gardening experience and giving him only average results. Then one day, as he describes it: "I'm on my knees in my orchard . . . pulling weeds, and for no reason, I just stuck my hands and started moving these woodchips . . . just to see how far I could go . . . and I'm down to my elbow in this beautiful, black, gorgeous compost, and I got up screaming angry . . . I was really upset. I said, 'There's something wrong with this picture!' I have been killing myself trying to get this in my garden. I don't have eight inches of anything that looks like this, and I did nothing here [in the orchard], and I hear inside (it was just so clear): 'Well it works in your garden the same way; *you didn't ask*.' Oh, I was so angry with myself. I threw that tiller away, and I started covering that garden with woodchips. It just hit me up-side the head, like *duh*, and again . . . I didn't ask! I'm doing this traditional stuff, frustrated every time—setting this stick down six inches, hitting this hardpan; seventeen years . . . nothing's breaking up, and I'm thinking, '*What's up with that?*'

"I tell people, 'I can't believe how hard I worked to fail.' I really worked hard, I was diligent; I wasn't lazy. I was so frustrated. Every spring you go out April 1, and it's all mud, and you try to till and there's all this mud, and as soon as you till . . . in three to five days . . . it's all covered with weeds! I'm telling you, it was labor intensive, and I was committed and dedicated to feed my family, and I worked really hard under severe challenges [he exhales deeply] going backwards."

Well, it wasn't that he "threw away" his tiller; it was more like banishing it from the garden to never return (that sounds kind of Biblical too). Here is the rest of the story as told by Paul: "When my wife saw me sell the tiller, she was really upset. She said, 'Paul, you sold your tiller? *Are you okay?* Do you realize what you did?' And I said, 'Don't you see the garden? Don't you see the orchard?'

"It was a 1974 Troy-Bilt tiller, the first four-speed, seven-horse-power model. As far as tillers go, it was the best ever made. I bought it in New York in 1974 for seven hundred dollars. I used it in LA until 1979, worked it really hard, brought it up here, worked it all those years, and I sold it for $825 because it was a quality item and I maintained it. The guy I sold it to was going to buy a brand-new one for $1,500,[45] but mine was in such good condition and he saw how well it worked.

"When people called me [on the ad for the tiller], they would ask, 'Why are you selling this?' I said, 'Nothing is wrong; the tiller is great. It's just not what we're supposed to do.' As this guy was loading his truck, I took his wife out to the orchard and told her, 'After he prepares your yard, you come back to cover the ground with woodchips, and he can sell it too because this [tilling] is not what he's supposed to do.' She couldn't believe it. She said, 'This is so beautiful.' But this guy was so excited."

Paul adds: "Remember *Pilgrim's Progress*?[46] Pilgrim is packing this load on his back for his whole trek till he comes to the mountain where he views the cross,[47] and that thing fell off his back. He was free. I felt that same sensation as I watched that tiller going out my driveway; I sensed this load coming off my back. I'm telling you it was dramatic; it was like a spiritual encounter, like '*WHOA,*' *I just got set free.*' It was heavy-duty amazing."

45 A 2020 Horse 20-inch 305cc (9 HP) Troy-Bilt tiller lists for $2,700 at tillersdirect.com.
46 *Pilgrim's Progress* by John Bunyan (1628-1688) is an allegory of a man (Pilgrim) and his journey to the Celestial City (Heaven).
47 Representing the cross of Jesus's crucifixion.

THE TREADMILL LIFE

Before placing the covering, every April Paul would lay out where his plantings would go. This was done with stakes and string. When he put the stakes in the ground, he could only get them down six inches before they would hit hardpan. Here is his account: "I was whining at God about my hardpan, and He didn't answer me. He didn't answer me. I mean . . . it was nothing, no spontaneous thoughts. I had a sense like 'that was different.'" He continues: "I am pushing my stick down at the end of my rows after seventeen years of bringing in truckloads of beautiful chicken manure . . . all kinds of manure, tilling in grass and stuff. I'm talking truckloads every year and tilling it in. And I'm still pushing this stick down, and I hit this (like) cement, and I'm whining to God about this hardpan all this time, and I got nothing. Dead silence. So then, I repented and started putting the cover, the woodchips, down.

"Three years into it (I'll never forget this as long as I live), I'm out there in the morning and pushing that stick down, and I heard this spontaneous thought: *'Give it a push.'* And I gave it a push and it broke loose and I thought, 'Wow, that hardpan is breaking up!' Simultaneously over in my garden is this robin pulling these worms out, and I hear inside: *'I sent those worms to break up your hardpan, but you kept killing them with the tiller. Now that you aren't killing them, they are breaking up your hardpan.'*

"I started to cry. I was so moved I began to cry, realizing that in my ignorance, my honest ignorance, I am doing all this damage to my garden, having no clue. Here I'm killing those worms every year, consistently killing with this tiller, thinking I'm doing all the right things bringing in this tiller, and I'm killing this environment God created. Now that I'm not touching it, all these amazing developments are happening. And again, you see, the natural mind just doesn't go there."

DEFIANCE VERSUS DEPENDENCE

Paul's circumstances didn't change, but his attitude did. He didn't surrender to the circumstance, sell the property at a loss, and look for land with a better well; he surrendered to the Lord he believed led him to that five-acre lot and was blessed to stay and flourish there. As the saying goes, he *bloomed where he was planted*. Do not miss the fact that the blooming came from dependence, not defiance. The often-quoted phrase *God helps those who help themselves*[48] is not in the Bible and is false justification for our self-efforts that are apart from God. The key to true sufficiency is not pulling ourselves up by our bootstraps but is in total dependence on God. He knows us better than we know ourselves.

In 2 Corinthians 3:5, we read, "Not that we are sufficient of ourselves to think anything as of ourselves; but our sufficiency is of God."

English-born minister **Leonard Ravenhill** (1903-1994) made the observation: "The self-sufficient do not pray, the self-satisfied will not pray, and the self-righteous cannot pray."

WHY DEFY LOVE?

God's love for us is too vast to even comprehend. The 1917 composer[49] of the hymn "The Love of God" makes a valiant attempt to capture the depth of God's love for us with the following prose:

> *Could we with ink the ocean fill,*
> *And were the skies of parchment made,*
> *Were every stalk on earth a quill,*
> *And every man a scribe by trade;*
> *To write the love of God above*
> *Would drain the oceans dry;*
> *Nor could the scroll contain the whole,*
> *Though stretched from sky to sky.*

Also, the **Apostle Paul** wrote these words to believers in Romans 8:35-39:

> Who shall separate us from the love of Christ? Shall tribulation, or distress, or persecution, or famine, or

---

48 Attributed to Benjamin Franklin.
49 Composer Frederick M. Lehman; who wrote it (on break) in a citrus packing plant he was working at in California.

nakedness, or peril, or sword? As it is written, for thy sake we are killed all the day long; we are accounted as sheep for the slaughter. [No],[50] in all these things we are more than conquerors through Him that loved us. For I am persuaded, that neither death, nor life, nor angels, nor principalities, nor powers, nor things present, nor things to come, nor height, nor depth, nor any other creature, shall be able to separate us from the love of God, which is in Christ Jesus our Lord.

MORE REVELATION

Long after the *Back to Eden* video was filmed, Paul gained further insight about the awesome properties of the covering. He tells us: "For years I knew it was an insulator of the ground and a means of moisture control, but it also acts as a filter. . . . Folks are concerned with chemtrails.[51] The cover filters out metals in the air." The confirmation for Paul was a call from a woman in Louisiana; her garden was twice ruined by saltwater from hurricane storms. Paul recalls: "I asked her if there were any woods in the area. 'Yes,' she replied. Then it dawned on her that they were not affected by the saltwater."

As the forest cover protected the trees, the garden cover will protect her garden. True enough, saltwater is a natural element, and manmade chemicals are not, but the concept and applications are similar.

I discussed with Paul the various types of soil, from extreme clay (no percolation properties) to extreme sand (grainy with hyper-percolation properties). He is firmly convinced that the covering can (and will) compensate *any* soil type, even rocks! He says, "God demonstrates that He is not challenged by soil types . . . so WAKE UP, wake up human race! The covering perfectly balances it out. I love God! He makes everything perfect."

---

50 Replacing the Elizabethan term "nay."

51 Aluminum oxide and barium salt displaced into our air via jet turbine dispersion, by certain aircraft, at high altitudes.

Ours for the Asking

Paul showed me a letter and said, "I got this letter from this lady who flew all the way from Florida to come out here, and she wrote this letter of thanks and says, 'And all I have to do is ASK.' She got it," he says with a smile.

Paul adds, "The Word says: 'You have not because you ask not.'[52] It's amazing how our minds are so clouded. I think the Enemy[53] is blinding our eyes so we cannot see the light of the glorious gospel of Jesus. Everything about God is Good News, it's all Good News. And he [Satan] has really made an effort to blind our eyes so we don't get it, and we don't ask. [Jesus says,] 'Ask and you shall receive'[54] God says, 'Call unto Me and I will answer you, to [show you] great things.'[55] It's all over the place; it's not like it is hidden or subtle [in the Bible], but we don't do it. And then when we do it, I don't think we have the faith to believe what we're hearing.

"So many times, it is the opposite of what we think, so we chuck it and say, 'That couldn't have been God,' and we don't get it. I would not have a garden today if I hadn't had that encounter with God because I couldn't keep it up with my legs. I'd have quit from frustration, but

52 James 4:2.
53 Satan.
54 John 16:24.
55 Jeremiah 33:3.

it changed my whole life around, that lousy well. You come to that place, encountering God. In the natural, it was a negative thing, but God used it to get my attention."

There's a new term for growers of things who pay attention to God, so read on about relational permaculture and you.

CHAPTER 6

Relational Permaculture and You

He that dwelleth in the secret place of the Most High
shall abide under the shadow of the Almighty.
— Psalms 91:1

IF YOU PARTICIPATED IN A WORD scavenger hunt and were given the terms "permaculture" and "relational," this is a taste of what you could find:

Permaculture: An agricultural system or method that integrates human activity with natural surroundings so as to create highly efficient, self-sustaining ecosystems.[56]

Relational: pertaining to relations; a significant connection or association between and among things.[57]

Paul is always challenging audiences at various venues and visitors to his garden to "get connected" and to "track with me on this" so that we will finally tap in to the same source of truth and wisdom that he has found.

There is an element of mystery in relational permaculture that requires extra-spiritual perception, or ESP. Paul's mysteries were: *How can I grow good food without watering? Can I be successful without*

---

56 Adapted from Merriam-Webster, com/dictionary/permaculture.
57 Adapted from *Webster's New Universal Unabridged Dictionary*, New York: Gramercy Books, 1989.

herbicides and pesticides? Is there an easier, better way than tilling? Those answers came when his extra-spiritual perception kicked in. He is not a gardening savant, just a regular guy who simply went from asking himself these questions to asking God or, as he puts it, his Dad.

We know his kinship with the Lord is personal, heartfelt, and real when he refers to the Most High as his Dad. Note that with mysteries in life, if we ask ourselves, then we are responsible for the answers. But if we ask God (in faith), then the responsibility of answering falls on Him, and He is more than able to respond. Indeed, God delights in revealing Himself in life's challenges.[58]

THERE IS A CONDUCTOR

Thousands of interrelations occur to make good food grow, from nematode[59] activity in the subsoil of terra firma to pollination of flowers from bees in the air. Add to that sunlight, wind and rain, sounds, and more. If viewed as a symphony, we can liken these relationships to various instrument sections: percussions provide tempo, strings for melody, woodwinds and brass for harmony. The important element of this analogy is that *there is a single conductor* that guides all the instruments to produce a beautiful result.

In creation, that single conductor is the Creator. It is a self-evident truth, similar to concluding, that every painting has a painter.[60] In this case, the museum is your garden. It would be foolish to worship the painting when it is simply a product of the Painter. To believe in, and be in awe of, the Creator is a key step of getting to know the God of the universe.[61]

IS GOD REAL?

What makes it a more difficult step for many is their level of indoctrination and adherence to the philosophy of evolutionism.

---

58 "But let him that glorieth glory in this, that he understandeth and knoweth Me, that I am the LORD which exercise lovingkindness, judgment, and righteousness, in the earth: for in these things I delight, saith the LORD." Jeremiah 9:24

59 Nematodes are minute, worm-like organisms.

60 Adapted from *God Does Not Believe in Atheists* by Ray Comfort.

61 "But without faith it is impossible to please Him: for he that cometh to God must believe that He is, and that He is a rewarder of them that diligently seek Him." Hebrews 11:6.

We were spoon-fed it in grade school, middle school, high school, and college. Even the best university agricultural programs pay homage to this religiously popular, yet scientifically unsubstantiated theory, so we need some serious injections of truth to overcome these anti-Creator antibodies that have resulted in personal and national spiritual lethargy.

Suffice it to say that you may have some real doubts as to a Creator whose face you cannot see. Thousands of believers have been there too, so your feelings are validated by many common human experiences. Yet you cannot see television signals in the air, but you watch TV. You can't see cell or Wi-Fi signals, yet you believe your cell phone will work and use it in faith (without question).

Famed aerospace engineer and the father of rocket science, **Wernher von Braun** said: "One cannot be exposed to the law and order of the universe without concluding that there must be design and purpose behind it all. Through a closer look at creation we ought to gain a better knowledge of the Creator."

Also, from US **President John F. Kennedy**'s 1961 inaugural address: "Let us go forth to lead the land we love, asking His blessing and His help, but knowing that here on earth God's work must truly be our own."[62]

So as not to offend, let's start out with a creation perspective of the garden. We see, smell, and taste of our gardens; they are real to us, so it's a good platform for everyone. The Holy Bible says in Genesis 1:11-12, "And God said, Let the earth bring forth grass, the herb yielding seed, and the fruit tree yielding fruit after his kind, whose seed is in itself, upon the earth: and it was so. And the earth brought forth grass, and herb yielding seed after his kind, and the tree yielding fruit, whose seed was in itself, after his kind: and God saw that it was good."

What has been your gardening experience? When you planted radish seeds, did cucumbers come up? Did your perennial rhubarb morph into zucchini one year? Of course not. Herbs, plants, and trees bear after their own kind. We rely on that when we plant; as did my European ancestors, as did Native Americans centuries ago and do to this day.

---

62 Records of the White House Signal Agency, WO#30806, RG274: John F. Kennedy Presidential Library and Museum, Boston, Massachusetts.

Jesus said: "Truly, truly, I say to you, unless a grain of wheat falls into the ground and dies, it abides alone; but if it dies, it brings forth much fruit."[63] He was foreshadowing His own death and the "much fruit" that came about after He was resurrected. More about that historical event later.

On the following page is a photo of a geologic formation found in the western United States. My question to you is: *How did it come to be?* Before you look at it and try to discern its origin, you must resolve in advance that Intelligent Design is NOT going to be the answer. Ready? Turn the page.

---

63 John 12:24.

Feels silly, doesn't it . . . believing that chance and millions of years formed the images of Presidents **Washington, Jefferson, Theodore Roosevelt,** and **Lincoln?**[64] It's as plain as your face (or in this case, their faces) that when you take the obvious explanation of design origin off the table, you have to spin an elaborate, yet very delicate, web of obfuscations and science fiction to convince rational people to think irrationally and then claim that such imaginative explanations are the only rational ones!

Modern science has *de-volved* into the confluence of irrationality and a religious adherence to the dogmas of humanism and naturalism. Pre-adulterated science, as practiced by the masters,[65] was classically defined as "the systematic study of the created universe." Webster's 1828 dictionary's first entry for "science" provides a similar definition, and later, the fourth entry includes a notable proverb (my boldface emphasis):

---

64 Adapted from **Dr. Donald Chittick,** author of *Solving the Puzzle of Ancient Man.*
65 Including **Newton, Copernicus, Einstein, Lister, Pasteur, Faraday, Maxwell, Kepler, Napier, Pascal, Faraday, Boyle, Hales, Hitchcock, Mendel, Planck,** and **Milne.**

SCI'ENCE, *noun* [Latin scientia, from scio, to know.]
1. In a general sense, knowledge, or certain knowledge; the comprehension or understanding of truth or facts by the mind. The science of God must be perfect.[66]

No science doth make known the first principles on which it buildeth.
                                    – Daniel Webster (1782-1852)
Creation, as a self-evident reality, was implicit in the classic definition of science. End of story.

Consummate Scientist

When you hear the word "scientist," whom do you think of? Many people say "Albert Einstein" because he advanced the theory of relativity and received the Nobel Prize in 1921 for physics. Listen to what he said as a scientist and caring human being (my emphases):

I want to know God's thought—the rest are mere details.
If the solution is simple, God is answering.
Look deep, deep into nature, and then you will understand everything better.
The intuitive mind is a sacred gift and the rational mind is a faithful servant. We have created a society that honors the servant and has forgotten the gift.
God did not create evil. Just as darkness is the absence of light, evil is the absence of God.
What really interests me is whether God had any choice in the creation of the world.
We should take care not to make the intellect our god; it has, of course, powerful muscles, but no personality.

---

66 http://webstersdictionary1828.com/Dictionary/science.

It is obvious that Einstein embraced both God and His creation in the matter of life's origins. Do you claim to have a more rational mind than Einstein? You don't have to be a rocket scientist to honestly assent to the evidences of creation, nor does being a rocket scientist automatically preclude you from such an assent, as we read from Dr. von Braun.

APPLIED LOGIC

As with many questions in life, the answer often lies within the question. When asked about the formation of anything, the solid implication is that there is a form-er, or one-who-formed. The foundations of the houses, dorms, and apartments we live in are likely poured concrete. The walls are straight, and the floors are level because the accumulation of the concrete was not left up to chance and vast amounts of time.[67] The concrete was poured into forms. The forms were made by the contractor to the architect's design and specifications.

Paintings transform a blank canvas by the design of the painter, dances are performed by the design and direction of a choreographer, and so on. Any rock formation has *One who formed it*.[68] Accordingly, any celestial formation has *One who formed it*. God, in His Word, does not try to hide the fact that He formed all things:

> And the LORD God formed man of the dust of the ground and breathed into his nostrils the breath of life; and man became a living soul. Genesis 2:7.

> But ask now the beasts, and they shall teach thee; and the fowls of the air, and they shall tell thee: Or speak to the earth, and it shall teach thee: and the fishes of the sea shall declare unto thee. Who knoweth not, in all these, that the hand of the LORD hath wrought this? In whose hand is the soul of every living thing, and the breath of all mankind. Job 12:7-10.

---

67 It has been said that chance and vast amounts of time are the rug that the myriads of evolutionism's incongruities are swept under.
68 Often with the aid of water, weather, and even volcanoes.

Before the mountains were brought forth, or ever Thou hadst formed the earth and the world, even from everlasting to everlasting, Thou art God. Psalms 90:2.

I have made the earth, and created man upon it: I, even My hands, have stretched out the heavens, and all their host have I commanded. Isaiah 45:12.

For thus saith the LORD that created the heavens; God Himself that formed the earth and made it; He hath established it, He created it not in vain, He formed it to be inhabited: I am the LORD; and there is none else. Isaiah 45:18.

By the word of the LORD were the heavens made; and all the host of them by the breath of His mouth. He gathereth the waters of the sea together as an [sic] heap: He layeth up the depth in storehouses. Let all the earth fear the LORD: let all the inhabitants of the world stand in awe of Him. For He spake, and it was done; He commanded, and it stood fast. Psalms 33:6-9.

[No] but, O man, who art thou that repliest against God? Shall the thing formed say to Him that formed it, Why hast Thou made me thus? Romans 9:20.

Still skeptical? Consider the following:

How many millennia would it take a sixteen-legged, crawling, leaf-eating bug to evolve into a six-legged flying winged species? How many transitional species from crawler to flyer would the fossil record reveal to us? What are the odds that such a feat could be replicated again, let alone become common?

Biologists have studied this phenomenon and observe that it takes only ten to fourteen days for a specific caterpillar (the crawler) to be transformed into a Monarch butterfly (the flyer).

God has made the metamorphosis of all butterflies to be an ongoing repudiation of evolutionism, just in case mankind was foolish enough to believe deceiving web-spinners like **Darwin**[69] and **Lyell**.[70] He also uses its beautiful transformation to remind us that He can (spiritually) transform our hearts from a heart of stone to a heart of flesh.[71]

Other proofs of God's infinite design are fingerprints and snowflakes.

Let Your Fingers Do the *Talking*

At this 2020 writing, the world's population stands at about 7.76 billion people,[72]and no two of them (even identical twins) have the exact same fingerprints. Now multiply by ten fingers per person!

Let It Snow

Modern science has revealed the individual uniqueness of snowflakes. It is estimated that one cubic foot of snow has a billion distinct snowflakes. From the Andes Mountains to the South Pole to the North Pole, the number of snowflakes that fall to the earth, each year, is estimated at one followed by fifteen zeros, which is a million billion![73] It defies the odds (since modern science seems to prefer a game of chance) that there would not be vast replications of exact, fully formed ice crystals, but there aren't, so far as can be known.

How Is Your Week Going?

Your week (and my week) is seven days long. That is true for every major culture out there. Did you ever wonder why a week isn't five days, or even ten days? It is seven days because God created the universe in six days and rested on the seventh.[74] He set up the seven-day week, and we all are living that out whether we know Him and love Him or not.

---

69 Charles Darwin, famous author of *The Origin of the Species; The Preservation of Favoured Races in the Struggle for Life*. Note that Darwin believed in favored races, but favored by whom?

70 Sir Charles Lyell, "high priest" of uniformitarianism.

71 "*A new heart also will I give you, and a new spirit will I put within you: and I will take away the stony heart out of your flesh, and I will give you [a] heart of flesh.*" Ezekiel 36:26

72 https://www.worldometers.info/world-population/.

73 https://www.livescience.com/1239-scientist-snowflakes-alike.html.

74 Genesis 1-2:3.

The Eyes Have It!

Like the 7.76 billion sets of fingerprints, no two humans have the exact same iris. Thus, high-tech identification systems use iris recognition to ensure secure entry to buildings and computer systems. Proverbs 20:12 reads: "The hearing ear, and the seeing eye; the LORD hath made even both of them."

Bombs Away!

The bombardier beetle is a member of the *Carabidae* family. Specifically, the genus *Brachinus*. Its natural predators include frogs. They would be easy prey for the lightning-fast frog tongue to capture it but for a 100 percent effective defense mechanism that the Creator blessed the bombardier beetle with. Perhaps no other species has rendered the philosophy of evolutionism so silly as this insect has.

Why? Because the bodies of these special insects produce two specific gases for defense and a catalyst agent to activate these gasses. From the rear of their thorax, they spew out 212°F gas at five hundred times per minute with accuracy. The result? Beetle – 1, Frog – 0. There is no way these gasses could be formed in the beetles over eons. The one chamber of gas without the other would be considered vestigial (unnecessary). Therefore, progressive evolutionism would have eliminated it as being useless for survival (vestigial). Even if both chambers were formed absent the catalyst agent, this amazing creature would not be able to blast its opponents at all.

Not only frogs are blown away by the bombardier beetle, but so are many (honest) biology teachers at high schools and universities in North America and beyond. They cannot reconcile the amazing properties of this insect as *not* being designed that way from the very beginning.

Frozen

The North American wood frog (*Rana sylvatica*) is one of a few species whose bodies can survive being completely frozen over the winter. Some biologists jokingly call them "frogcicles," but how these ectotropic (cold-blooded) frogs can endure extreme cold is no laughing matter.

During freezing winters, they were designed to go from what we might call a catatonic stage to a complete shutdown of lungs, heart, and brain. In the spring, they thaw out and return to active life again. To achieve such a restart requires such extremely complex genetic programming that eliminates chance and random mutations as implausible explanations.

Scientists do not understand what triggers the heart to begin beating again. The existence of these frozen frogs has had a chilling effect on evolutionism believers, causing some to *let it go*.

Genetic Smoking Gun

Truth has nothing to fear from the results of honest, investigative science. That is why the discovery of deoxyribonucleic acid (DNA) is an unsurpassed revelation of the reality of Creation and, by extension, a glimpse into the intricacies of the Creator. Through DNA, modern geneticists have determined that all men and women have a common female (source) ancestor.[75] You may already know her name was Eve, which means the mother of all living.[76]

Around 980 BC, the psalmist David (arguably) wrote about God and DNA:

> For Thou hast possessed my reins:[77] Thou hast covered me in my mother's womb. I will praise thee; for I am fearfully and wonderfully made: marvelous are Thy works; and that my soul knoweth right well. My substance was not hid from Thee, when I was made in secret, and curiously wrought in the lowest parts of the earth. Thine eyes did see my substance, yet being unperfect; and in Thy book all my members were written, which in continuance were fashioned, when as yet there was none of them. Psalms 139:13-16.

---

75 1987 article in the journal *Nature*. In a desperate attempt to cling to the unraveling *Shroud of Darwin*, the article alternatively plays down the significance of this finding. Comparing the mtDNA of 147 Africans, Asians, Europeans, Australians, and New Guineans, the study revealed "that every person on Earth right now can trace his or her lineage back to a single common female ancestor."
76 Genesis 3:20.
77 Essential organs, or "inward parts."

Evolutionism Is against the Law

The philosophy of evolutionism rests upon the notion that things improve as they evolve over time, even ridiculously vast eons of time. The second law of thermodynamics resulted from demonstrable, scientific proof that things deteriorate over time via a process called entropy.[78]

Thus, evolutionism clearly violates the second law, as they are diametrically opposed. Either the philosophy is right and the law is wrong, or the law is right and the philosophy is flawed. Modern scientists cannot have it both ways, yet that is what academia has been selling impressionable minds in colleges and universities all over the world for generations.

Amazingly, on June 26, 2000, then-US President **Bill Clinton** addressed the researchers of the just-completed Human Genome Project and said:

> *Today's announcement represents more than just an epic-making triumph of science and reason. After all, when* **Galileo** *discovered he could use the tools of mathematics and mechanics to understand the motion of celestial bodies, he felt, in the words of one eminent researcher, "that he had learned the language in which God created the universe." Today we are learning the language in which God created life. We are gaining ever more awe for the complexity, the beauty, the wonder of God's most divine and sacred gift.*[79] (Emphasis added.)

Moreover, then-director of the Human Genome Project, **Dr. Francis Collins** later replied: "It is humbling for me and awe inspiring to realize that we have caught the first glimpse of our own instruction book, previously known only to God."[80]

---

78 "The entropy of an isolated system not in equilibrium will tend to increase over time, approaching a maximum value at equilibrium." http://www.physicsforidiots.com/thermodynamics.html

79 Text of Remarks on the Completion of the First Survey of the Entire Human Genome Project. See https://clintonwhitehouse5.archives.gov/textonly/WH/New/html/genome-20000626.html.

80 Ibid.

What Dr. Collins calls an "instruction book," Paul Gautschi calls the "Owner's Manual."

World-renowned brain surgeon and secretary of housing and urban development, **Dr. Ben Carson** was sharing how people always ask him: "How can you be a man of science and a man of faith?" His response: "I don't think the two are incompatible at all, . . . I choose to believe in God by faith."[81]

Beethoven's Fifth

Imagine you attend a symphony concert and have an excellent seat. The pre-concert tuning is complete; the conductor walks in to applause, faces the musicians, and takes the podium. As he raises his baton, you quickly slip on the earplugs of your smartphone or tablet and listen to Super Bowl commercials from 1975 to the present, missing the entire concert. Can you imagine a more wasted evening? The fact is your evening was wasted because you tuned out the symphony and the conductor!

Paul will tell you that when you conceptualize, plan, prepare, plant, and tend a garden without being tuned in to the Creator, you are "tuning out the Conductor" and missing His cues. You may get acceptable results, but not the blessing that was intended for you or your family. Such was true of his own experience. So how do we go about tuning in to the Creator?

It's ALL about relationship! That's why it's called "relational" permaculture.

If you do not have this relationship, *please* go directly to chapter 9 ("Mystery Revealed") and be open to your awaiting transformation. Commit to not finish this chapter until "Mystery Revealed" becomes your personal message from the Lord to believe, repent, receive His forgiveness, and begin to connect with His love and eternal provisions. You cannot get such a relationship just by reading books or by hanging around any true believer you know or are related to, not even Paul Gautschi. As my Texas friend **Dr. Mike Davis** says: "True relationship with God does not come by *gracemosis*." This relationship is intimate, it is personal, and it is real—involving your spirit, soul, and body. Your soul embodies your mind, your will, your emotions and conscience. In

---

81 Dr. Carson speech at a Liberty University Convocation on March 28, 2012. See http://www.youtube.com/watch?v=i-Foz-EjZ3g.

short, nothing of ourselves is left on the table. We truly get to God by freely and willingly placing ourselves on His altar. We go to Him on His terms, not ours. God (Yahweh) does not have to play God. *He is God!*

Desire to Be First

The orchestral first chair violinist has a close relationship with the conductor that is musically beneficial. If that relationship was not sure, it would spell disaster.

Thus, how can we pattern ourselves to be like the first chair violinist? Consider that:

a) the first chair should honor and respect the Conductor (that is, adoration);

b) the first chair, while reading the music, maintains an eye upon the Conductor to see his or her cues (that is, communication);

c) the first chair has to trust the Conductor with his or her devotion (that is, consecration); and

d) the first chair leads others as she or he is led by the Conductor (that is, liberation).

A relationship with the Creator is one where we adore Him, communicate (by prayer) with Him, consecrate (set apart) our lives to Him, and share His glorious liberation with others because that is His heart, to seek and to save everyone![82]

As mentioned earlier, the first step towards relational permaculture is to honor and revere the Creator. Emanating from that is a huge sense of gratefulness to God.[83]

The second step is, while living your everyday life, to keep your eyes on the Lord. Don't look away and get distracted by problems, failures, and circumstances[84] or by the advice of co-workers, or even well-meaning friends and family. What is *He* telling you in His word? **STOP . . . PRAY (ask) . . . LISTEN.**

---

82 Luke 19:10.
83 Psalms 92:1, 4, 5; 1 Thessalonians 5:18.
84 Hebrews 12:2; Isaiah 40:26.

Third, trust God. US coinage says: "In God We Trust," but our actions as a nation (and as individuals) reveal that we tend to look to ourselves and so-called experts to meet our needs when all we ever need to do is simply trust Him.

KEEP THE FAITH

One year, God told Paul to plant some kale under Paul's cherry tree, and he initially chafed at the idea because "you just don't plant things under trees." In a display of trust in God, Paul yielded to what seemed to be a bizarre directive. That winter (2009) an arctic cold front blanketed Washington's Olympic Peninsula, and everything was covered in snow and ice. Because the faith-planted Russian kale had the covering of the cherry tree, those plants did not freeze and survived the cold to bear healthy and delicious kale.

Some people call that "blind faith" (as though it was a bad thing). What is the alternative? An "if it feels good I'll do it" faith? That is no faith at all. The fact is we exhibit blind faith all the time. When we fly on a commercial airplane, we do not know the pilots, where they received their flight training, how many hours they've flown, if they've ever been reprimanded or commended by the airline, if the Federal Aviation Administration (FAA) has its eye on them, what their temperament is, their medical history, how they handle stress, how much rest they've had, or even whether they are having a bad day.

What about the aircraft? Have we seen the maintenance records? Has the manufacturer issued any service orders? When was its last C-check?[85] What kind of cargo is stored below? How much fuel is it carrying? Yet, with no knowledge of any of these critical and rational things, we board the plane (in blind faith) and expect the pilot, flight crew, ground crew, aircraft, and air traffic controllers to get us to our destination safely and perhaps even on time. If we can exhibit blind faith in mere men, women, and machines, we should certainly commit all faith (blind or otherwise) to our Creator, who loves us.

The Bible has an excellent definition of faith: "the substance of things hoped for, the evidence of things not seen." (Hebrews 11:1)

---

85 Complete overhaul of engines. By FAA rules, commercial airlines must do this every fifteen to twenty-one months.

Faith is *not* the power of positive thinking that says "I can." Rather, it is appealing to and trusting the Creator knowing He can.

Additionally, Hebrews 11:3 goes on to say: "Through faith we understand that the worlds were framed by the word of God, so that things which are seen were not made of things which do appear." In other words, things our eyes can see are made of things we don't see, like cells, atoms, molecules, DNA strings, and such, on the microscopic side. Conversely on the astronomic side, the appearance of a distant star, which seems so small to us but is really an entire remote galaxy, is much larger than our own. God is telling us we cannot put full trust in our perceptions, as they are limited. Because of our physical limitations, faith is imperative.

The fourth step is to share your gift to others as you have been led by the Lord. Paul has faithfully followed this key step and testifies as to its benefits. The *Back to Eden* video was one opportunity for Paul to share his faith, Whom he has faith in, and the results of that faith.

AMAZING GOD, AMAZING RESULTS

Consider scientist, professor, inventor, and faith farmer George Washington Carver. While traveling to Tuskegee, Alabama, in 1896, he looked out the train window to observe the cotton fields of that state. Carver had been farming the fertile fields of Iowa. To see the horribly depleted soil the laborers were trying to work brought shock and disgust to him. As one of his biographers records:

> Cotton had ruled the South for 100 years, and year by year it drained the good from the soil, producing an ever-smaller yield from the same enfeebled piece of ground, so that more fields had to be planted, and great forests felled to make room for still more fields. Without the trees' protective cover and binding roots, the topsoil was washed away by the decades' rains and blown away by its winds, uncounted millions of tons of invaluable, irreplaceable, plant nutrients eroded away to the sea and were gone forever.

Here is a poignant account: "An old farmer would spurn George Carver's counsel to try a different crop with the heartbreaking words: 'Son, I know all there is about farming. I've worn out three farms in my lifetime.'"[86]

Yet, Mr. Carver was determined to find a viable alternative to cotton. That led him to the peanut, which was a novelty and not regarded as anything of marketable consequence at that time. But he took the matter to the Lord, his God. He asked and asked what good could come out of a peanut. As a result of his asking "Mister Creator, why did You make the peanut?" God revealed to him 325 uses for the peanut!

Can one grasp so many uses without sensing that God can answer the sincere prayer of His believers? He promises to do so "exceedingly, abundantly, beyond what we ask or think." (Ephesians 3:20)

As George Washington Carver said, "I love to think of nature as an unlimited broadcasting station, through which God speaks to us every hour, if we will only tune in."

PAUL'S PERSONAL REFLECTION ON HEARING FROM GOD

"My whole life, as a Christian, it was so difficult for me, hearing His voice. My wife is very intuitive; she gets words of knowledge.[87] I was just brain dead at that spirit level. But this experience just opened me up to realize that He's there, and for years, I was so doubting. Then we got this audio series from a guy teaching in Toronto named **Mark Virkler**[88] on *How to Hear the Voice of God*. It was so amazing. His testimony was just like mine: he loved God's word, he memorized it, he was so into God, and he hears about all these people hearing from God (you know—His still small voice), and he just can't get it! And then one day, the Holy Spirit revealed to him (and this one statement changed my whole life) *'His voice is a spontaneous thought.'* It completely opened the door and set me free to hear God! That one statement completely broke all the blindness. You're not looking for it. You may have asked the question. [Then] all of a sudden, you're walking

---

86 **Lawrence Elliott**, *George Washington Carver: The Man Who Overcame*, NJ: Prentice-Hall, 1966, 107.
87 God-given insights/revelations of people and things.
88 www.cwgministries.org/store/results.

around, and the thought comes in your mind, and if you connect, the Holy Spirit says: 'Remember that question you asked? There it is!'

"I so love God;, He is so amazing! He says, 'Out of the mouth of two or three witnesses, truth is validated.'[89] When I get a spontaneous thought, and it is God, the Holy Spirit will immediately take me to scripture to validate it, to confirm it. It says the same thing, and then I know I heard. Now it's becoming so normal . . . every day, all day long. It's just like a way of life.

"I think of how many decades I lived in this place of doubt, not knowing, and He was always there, but I didn't know it was a spontaneous thought. I'm thinking it must be a still small voice; I'm looking for sounds, for words, and these thoughts just come. So often, I'll ask the question: 'God, how would You approach this?' and many times it's not immediate. Maybe a day later, I'm outside, and all of the sudden, this thought just comes, or I'm in a place and He says, 'You see that?' And then I'll get it . . . that was that question I asked! This is the answer, and then the Holy Spirit will bring the Word to confirm it. When you get that, you have such confidence. You know you've heard from God and nothing moves you, where in the past, you don't know, and you wonder if . . . (kind of a double-minded[90] thing). The Word so connects and brings validity and understanding to life if you get it because it's an Owner's Manual and it just shows you. That teaching from Mark Virkler was such an incredible blessing to my life. For me, it set me free."

Prior to that, people of faith were telling him hearing from God is so normal. Paul declares: "In the Word, it is normal: 'My sheep hear My voice'[91] and 'Today if ye will hear His voice.'[92] So, I was seeing everything, but not having my own experience; this should be happening, but I'm not getting it. I lived in amazing frustration. 'God, what's wrong with me? Why can't I hear? Cause everybody else is.' And I'm really crying out and praying, doing my best to hear, but I'm not. That was such an amazing [phrase] to me, 'spontaneous thought,' and I see it really connects because many times when I'm hearing from God, I'm not even asking. I'm just out doing stuff, or I'm in other places doing this routine thing. Then this thought just comes (whoa!),

---

89 Deuteronomy 19:15.
90 Wishy-washy at best, schizophrenic at worst.
91 John 10:27.
92 Hebrews 3:7,15.

and then when it does, I'll realize, Wow! That was the question I was asking! That relates to that question I was asking."

Paul continues: "A lot of times it is beyond what I was asking, like: 'What? What an idea! I never would have thought of that!' That's what I love about the Holy Spirit—He is so faithful. I love that term, that He is a Helper.[93] He's a Helper, and this is why I love [King] David's testimony. He asks the question in Psalms 119: 'How shall a young man cleanse his way?' And then He responds by answering it: 'By taking heed according to Your Word.' Then he gives testimony: 'Thy Word have I hid in my heart; that I might not sin against Thee.'[94] Sin is missing the mark; just not getting it. This is what I'm so getting: When you hide His word in your heart, He is so faithful to confirm, to bring answers, to align you with His word . . . telling you, so you are on track.

"I love that word in Isaiah, where it says you come to the end of the road where you don't know which way to go and you are in doubt. You hear a voice behind you, which says: 'This is the way, walk in it.'[95] I just love that! It is so God. He is a good Dad and doesn't want us to be in doubt and wonder 'What do I do now?' He is so there for us. But in my life, I have been in such doubt . . . can't trust . . . so lacking in faith . . . not believing; it has to be just [a] perfect kind of thing, and I have to have all the pieces together to go on.

"God says, 'No—just believe, just trust; I'm there for you.' And again, that whole thing of trusting Him and not myself to make sure all the things are lined up. It was such a huge thing. I want to make sure everything is just right before I have said, 'This is of God.' God says, 'Little children, just hear and obey. (They don't get hung up.) Just trust Me.' You see, it all comes back to faith and without faith, He says, 'It is impossible to please God.'[96] I'm just seeing that faith is so bottom line, so foundational to all of life and God just won't operate apart from it."

Most Christians don't hear the voice of God because we've already decided we aren't going to do what He says.
— A. W. Tozer

---

93 John 14:16, 26. Also translated "Comforter."
94 Psalms 119:9, 11.
95 Isaiah 30:21.
96 Hebrews 11:6.

Carl's Recounting

In the early 1970s, a group of Christian Vietnam veterans rented a fifteen-acre piece of land with only a barn near Dayton, Oregon. Decades later, my own family moved to Dayton and lived across Highway 221 from that barn.[97] Our (then) eighty-year-old Swiss-German farmer friend, **Carl Rutschman**, who lived further south on that highway, thought he would tell me what went on across the street from us years ago:

"You see, these young Vietnam vets rented the place after we all got our beans in. They decided to plant beans as well, so they did. But it was weeks too late to get them in, and we all expected their first crop to be a disaster. One day **Wil Wilson,** lifelong farmer and neighbor to the commune (as the locals called it) told me he had seen the group of guys on their knees in a circle out in the middle of their field when he drove by. 'What do you suppose they were up to, Carl?' asked Wil. I smiled my trademark way and said, '"Looks to me like they were praying."' Well that summer, it came time to harvest beans, and to Carl's (and Wil's) surprise, "Those young prayer warriors not only had a crop, but they got a higher yield per acre than we did!"

That, dear thoughtful reader, is the power of relational permaculture: God's favor (when we depend on Him).

Paul quoted to me a portion of Proverbs 3:5: "'Trust in the Lord with all your heart.' Spirit—that's where the connection is, not in the flesh or the mind."

Three in One

Earlier, reference was made to symphony music playing melody, harmony, and rhythm. They support the whole, like a three-legged stool. God exists as our Conductor and has revealed Himself as the Father, the Son, and the Holy Spirit. He made humans in three parts too—spirit, soul, and body—to support the whole of our being. The universe is made up of time, matter, and space. To further break these down, time is past, present, and future; water is solid, liquid, or gas;

---

97 In what was known as the Grabenhorst place.

space is composed of width, depth, and height. Even down to the atom, it is predominantly made of protons, neutrons, and electrons.[98]

We don't have to be a genius to see a definite three-in-one pattern here. Does scripture validate spirit, soul, and body? Look to 1 Thessalonians 5:23-24: "And the very God of peace sanctify you wholly; and I pray God your whole spirit and soul and body be preserved blameless unto the coming of our Lord Jesus Christ. Faithful is He that calleth you, who also will do it."

Plants need air, water, and sunlight (warmth). For optimum growth, the proper combination of those elements needs to be present in various conditions in nature. The covering element of relational permaculture best provides this sustainability—as the woodchips act to draw and retain moisture where it is lacking—yet releases excess moisture when it would be detrimental to a plant or tree. As Paul testifies, in times of drought,[99] and in times of unrelenting rain, the covering equalizes and regulates moisture activity, as well as the pH, in our gardens and orchards.

The same phenomenon applies to temperature. When it is hot outside, the woodchips retain coolness in the soil, but when it is cold outside, the covering acts as an insulator to keep the soil warm. Woodchips are a key source of needed minerals and even a filter to protect soil from bad elements in the air carried by rain.

The key to good ground is a proper covering. Let's view it as formulas:

Good Ground – Covering = Lesser Ground
Bad Ground – Covering = Eroded Ground
Bad Ground + Covering = Good Ground
Good Ground + Covering = Great Ground.

98 Jobe Martin, lecture notes from a 2013 presentation in Redmond, Washington. Jobe, DDS, is a biology major who authored: *Evolution of a Creationist*.
99 For a video account of how a covered garden survived the severe 2012 drought in Missouri, see https://www.youtube.com/watch?v=h1olVuYMoQg&noredirect=1.

DEPLETED SOIL AND SOIL ENEMIES

Paul is adamant that Public Enemy #1 of our gardens is taking the cover off and exposing the soil. That especially includes the time-honored practice of tilling. In his book, *Restoration Agriculture*,[100] Wisconsin farmer **Mark Shepard** states:

"Tilling the soil exposes it to the elements. Exposed soil blows away in the wind. Its organic matter and minerals are oxidized by the sun rendering them useless for plant fertility needs. Tilled soil exposes it to the rain and, when uncovered, washes away in muddy streams with every storm. Little by little, precious soil vanishes until all that remains is the bleached skeleton of the planet."

Next would be chemicals. A fellow from Chile described his family to Paul as "a large table-grape producer" in that region during an August 2012 international phone call. He told Paul he felt concerned that they were part of a food supply chain that may be compromising "thousands of people around the world" because of the intense chemical protocol and government-required fumigation before export. Both the US and Chilean authorities impose mandatory fumigation. I liken it to the dairy farmer that delivers fresh, natural, nutritious, raw milk to a facility that degrades substantial food value under the rubric of "safety." The Chilean businessman met Paul in October of 2012 to look at his garden and grapes with a goal to see if he can radically change their growing techniques.

It is exciting news that an international farmer wanted to get off the corporate agricultural chemical grid! I was there when he arrived at the Gautschis' and spent five hours with Paul. He also brought along a PhD chemistry researcher from the States. As he was leaving, I asked the businessman, "So, do you think this will work for you back home?" He said, "I will try it out. It should be safer, less intensive, and produce a better product." Though it wouldn't resolve the fumigation protocol, he ended with: "I owe it to my family to try." I think we all owe it to our family to try, don't you?

100 2013 published by Acres USA ISBN-10: 1601730357

THE GAUTSCHI GARDEN

Arriving at Paul's garden, you are immediately impressed with the openness. No deer fencing along the garden perimeter, no bird netting over the berry plants. You freely walk through the orchard and all three garden plots (there is a small garden area under and between the trees left of the parking area). Paul's a giver—to visitors, to neighbors, even to his dog. He says that in the end "there is plenty to go around."

As to insects, there were none observed in the four-plus hours I was there for the first time in August of 2012. No slugs or slug trails. No aphids or other unwanted insects. Members of our visiting group asked Paul, "How is it that your kale doesn't have aphids?" He responded by asking us to break a leaf from one of his vegetables. We did, and it immediately began oozing liquid.

He said that his vegetables have so much moisture that when bugs bite it, they are either repulsed by the natural sweetness of the item or overwhelmed by the amount of liquid they encounter (like a human trying to take a drink from a fire hose). Either way, they move on. He does admit that if a plant has been damaged by the dog or a visitor or age (past ripeness), the compromised leaves can, and do, attract bugs because its innate resilience has been altered by some form of damage. Yes, entropy happens, even in our gardens.

Don't Be Bugged by Bugs

How does a God of love create pests? Paul tells us: "Bugs are a police force sent by the Creator to take out stressed, dilapidated, unhealthy plants. God brings insects into the world to maintain healthy plants, so they are the ones that go to seed and produce more healthy plants. The following is his account:

"One time, I looked at a row of celery in my garden and decided to thin it. As I pulled out these gorgeous plants, I thought it would be a shame to throw them out [to the chickens]. So I transplanted (bare rooted) the celery in the herb garden."

"Since its inception, I have never seen a slug in the herb garden . . . ever, though they are prevalent in the Pacific Northwest. The next day as I was going to the chicken pen, I saw the celery covered with slugs, all over it. I said, 'What's happening, God?' He told me what He always says: 'Just watch.' So, I did nothing about the slugs."

"The following day, there were no leaves on the celery, just stumps. I said to God, 'Are You going to tell me to just watch again?'" He replied, 'Keep watching.' The third day, there were no slugs, and God said to me, 'You don't get slugs in the garden because the plants are not stressed, but when you moved the celery, it put out a signal to the bugs: *I am stressed, I'm dying, take me out.*' The slugs sensed the signal and cooperated. The third day, the celery overcame the transplant shock and grew to be good plants."

It may be a unique phenomenon, but the bugs will not attack the good leaves and stems. Paul reminds us: "Insects do not have a pancreas; they cannot process sugars. Healthy, mineral-rich, sweet produce does not attract insects." Conversely, poor-quality or once-healthy-but-compromised fruit and vegetables do attract opportunistic insects. The presence and volume of, say, aphids is God's way of telling the grower/tender of the plant that all is not well. We need to look at all the cues we are being given to have a right response to the challenges that face us.

Wilted leaves can suggest underwatering. Bug intrusion may suggest a lack of natural fructose, moisture, and/or minerals within the plant. Nevertheless, Paul heard that produce with some evidence of bug activity sells for more in Japanese markets than the perfect-looking produce because Japanese consumers reason that if a bug was on the plant it was due to a lack of chemical pesticides! Perhaps the new ad motto there should be "Bug tested; mother approved."

FOOD VALUE ENEMIES

Premature Harvesting

Each plant or fruit in your garden, orchard, or vineyard is a reservoir of natural (God-ordained) elements: vitamins, moisture, proteins, fiber, acids, oils, and enzymes. It is the enzymes that help our bodies properly assimilate the vitamins, minerals, proteins, and fiber of the foods we ingest. Experts call them phytonutrients. "Phyto" means plant-derived, and you know what nutrients are.

In short, natural enzymes make the "food value" deposits to our bodies. If the deposits are not made, there is little, or nothing, put into our body's healthy food account. A number of the critical enzymes needed to make those deposits are not manifested in the food until just before ripening.

Thus, when the organic apple grower picks an apple before eight days of being fully ripe (with the latter enzymes not yet in place), she or he has robbed the bank of the complete essential goodness of the apple for the human body. That is, you can do everything right by covering and avoiding chemicals, but if you pick too early, you cheat yourself of the fruits of your labor. How many times in school assignments, in cooking, in medicine, in using the computer, in mechanical work, and so on has a lack of patience been the enemy of all effort? We do something impulsively in an effort to save time or expense, and to our horror, we have to do it all over again. So it is with the garden. In the Old Testament Ecclesiastes 3:1-2, we read: "To everything there is a season, and a time to every purpose under the Heaven: A time to be born, and a time to die; a time to plant, and a time to pluck up that which is planted." How many nut growers do you know that pick green walnuts right off their trees? Pecans? Filberts? Chestnuts? Almonds? Absolutely none, right? They don't pick before the nuts fall because they will be too green, yet corporate agribusiness and even family orchards pick many fruit crops early/green to extend the shelf life of the produce for market. By doing so, they sell us enzyme-deficient food that we think is good for us. It is a vast deception.

An Apple a Day . . .

Paul grows King, Gravenstein, Melrose, Spartan, Liberty, Fuji, King David, Sweet 16, Akane, Jonafree, Mutzu, Gala, Spartan, Jonagold, Freedom, Tsugaru, Cosmic Crisp and Honeycrisp apples on dwarf trees. The apples are fairly low to the ground, and the ground is soft because it is covered with about ten inches of wood-chips. He knows that the tree can figure out when the apples are ripe and lets them fall when ready. Essentially, the tree says to the apple: "You are ripe; there is no more I can give to you from this point on." So the apple leaves the mothership and falls to the ground, as if to say, "Beam me down, Scotty!" The key for our consumption is to not leave them on the ground. Once on the ground, they are susceptible to bugs and other entropic occurrences.

For new tree planting, he buys bare root apple tree stock from Burnt Ridge Nursery and Orchard[101] in Onalaska, Washington. Each year's inventory comes in February, and Paul goes early to pick out the ones that have good shape and the most fine-hair roots (that take up nutrients) among the woody roots (that stabilize the tree). Once you get your trees in the ground, he says to start planting your garden among them. Why? He says, "Because plant growth and tree growth are symbiotic. I learned that by reading the book of Acts. It was validated by my experience with planting strawberries, then potatoes, among the trees. My strawberries grew better in the tree shade than in full sun! God shows us in nature that plants and people thrive in community versus isolation."

Paul gets the most out of his garden because he is listening and observing faithfully. He shares: "I say [to God], 'Talk to me . . . show me what You're doing because I want to copy it.' And He does it the best. Anything that comes in contact with God gets changed."

On Pruning

In John 15:2-3, Jesus is saying, "I am the True Vine, and My Father is the Vinedresser. Every branch in Me that does not bear fruit,

---

101 https://www.burntridgenursery.com/.

He takes away. And every one that bears fruit, He prunes it so that it may bring forth more fruit."

Paul says, "It is a beautiful illustration of God; giving and receiving." As the tree gives of itself (branches, leaves, and stems), it is stimulated to grow and bear more fruit. He adds, "If you want a tree to grow, the most stimulating thing you can do to it is cut it. Nothing compares to the effect of pruning. Never do a drastic pruning. Never do more than one-third a year. Initially start with the deadwood and crossovers. If you do it all at once (heavy), you get suckers and no fruit. You do it slowly. Start with the front and get crossovers so you get structure. Put covering [down] and you're good."

Paul's only three pruning tools are a three-legged ladder, a Swiss hand pruner, and a curved Japanese pruning saw. He suggests not using lopping shears because they tend to crush, and they cannot get in as close to the limb or trunk as a saw blade can. He highly recommends the Felco #8 (bypass) hand pruner[102] and the Samurai Ichiban (triple-edge teeth) handsaws.[103] The Felco #9 is the left-handed version of the #8. His favorite ladder is built in Oregon by Tallman.[104] He buys his saws and pruners from the Bishop Company[105] in California, but there are many sources. I asked about his wheelbarrow. It is a Jackson M-11,[106] a heavier wheelbarrow than what many consumers are used to, which

---

102 http://https://www.felco.com/us_en/our-products/pruners.html ($59.50 in early 2021).
103 https://www.treestuff.com/samurai-ichiban-13-pruning-saw/ ($39.99 in early 2021).
104 http://www.tallmanladders.com.
105 https://bishco.com/pruning/pruning-saws/.
106 https://www.jacksonprofessional.com/tools/wheelbarrows/steel-wheelbarrows/.

has been a detriment to sales. Paul says that a weighty wheelbarrow is better for control and that the newer M-11s are actually lighter than the older one he has. Both models have a metal tub, versus plastic. Finally, Paul says, "My favorite tool [in the garden] is an asparagus knife. I use it for everything because it's so easy to get in and underneath for weeding and for moving plants. I guarantee you; you're going to love it!"

FREE INDEED

Paul loves to quote the Bible: "It was for liberty that Christ came to set us free."[107] Everything about God is free and sets free, and I love that in His character. It is so beautifully exemplified and shown in nature. I love that scripture where He says, "Come unto Me all you who labor and I will give you rest."[108] You have to ask the question, Why do we labor and why are we heavy laden? It's because of the fall of man. Jesus said, "Take my yoke upon you."[109] And what do we use a yoke for? We attach it to the oxen or the animals, then to some device to plow the ground! Jesus says [in effect], "I don't do things like you. Follow Me (and learn from Me); My yoke is easy, and My burden is light."[110] In this incredible environment, that which God Himself created, He shows His magnanimous, awesome, giving, generous nature, and it is so beautiful in comparison to the man-approach of tilling and putting back and constantly being on a treadmill running, never getting on top of it."

Pointing to his garden, Paul says to me, "All these woodchips just sit here. They don't do a thing. Anytime I choose to plant, [I] put a seed in, and it thrives. If I don't use it, it just waits for me and develops richer qualities. In the meantime, it doesn't blow away, it doesn't turn to weeds; it just stays! Where, conversely, anything I do, if I don't stay right on it, if I don't maintain it, I lose it and I become a slave to it. Again, it is this quality of God; setting us free."

Paul continues: "This is what blows me away: woodchips are inanimate objects. They don't have a brain. Are you getting it? This is an amazing God! When I read that scripture—'all of nature groans and travails'[111]—I'm getting it! This is more alive than we think it is. Maybe

107 Galatians 5:1.
108 Matthew 11:28.
109 Matthew 11:29.
110 Matthew 11:29-30 with some rewording by Paul.
111 Romans 8:22.

there is more going on in nature than what we attribute to what's there. It's very connected, and it is groaning and travailing, and you have to understand why: because everything we are doing is wrong."

"We are doing all this counterproductive stuff and pulling out all these weeds and trying to hold the ground in place. This is not ideal, but this is what we have got to do to protect because these people keep ripping the cover off. So, you can just sense the earth's grief and pain over unnecessary intervention. You see, people are just unwilling to accept that the Creator made this perfect."

FERTILE IS AS FERTILE DOES

Then there is the aspect that relational permaculture does not require the gardener to constantly fertilize. Paul relates an account of multiple plantings in the same row: "I planted a row of spinach in the spring, and it came up real nice and we enjoyed it. I pulled it out and planted another one, and it came up nicer than the one before. Next, I planted black Spanish radish. When that came up, my friend couldn't believe the size and how beautiful it was, and I said, 'Now, God, talk to me. Every time I planted in this row this year, each one was bigger and nicer than the one before, and I didn't fertilize.'

"This was so opposite of what my experience was in gardening. Every time something was taken out, I had to put something back, and here I'm putting nothing back . . . and I hear Him say, in Romans 1:20: 'For the invisible things of Him from the creation of the world are clearly seen, being understood by the things that are made, even His eternal power and Godhead; so that they are without excuse.'[112] I asked, 'So what attribute are You showing me here?' He took me to Philippians [4:19] where it says: 'My God shall supply all your needs according to His riches in glory by Christ Jesus.' What that means is when He gives something, He makes no deduction, no withdrawal. He is the same. God says, 'This compost illustrates My character: It gives, and it gives, and it gives, and there's no withdrawal; there's no negative. It just continually, continually gives, and that's who I AM.'"

---

112 The next two verses go on to say: "Because that, when they knew God, they glorified him not as God, neither were thankful; but became vain in their imaginations, and their foolish heart was darkened. Professing themselves to be wise, they became fools."

Have you heard a message from God ever in your life? Though you may have never read the Holy Bible, if you have personally seen a rainbow, you have received a message from God (Yahweh) in the sky. Not only was it a message, but it was also a promise from Him to never flood the entire Earth again, as He did in judgment thousands of years ago.[113]

---

113 Genesis 9:12-15: "And God said, This is the token of the covenant which I make between Me and you and every living creature with you, for everlasting generations: I set my rainbow in the cloud. And it shall be a token of a covenant between Me and the earth. And it shall be, when I bring a cloud over the earth, that the rainbow shall be seen in the cloud. And I will remember My covenant which is between Me and you and every living creature of all flesh; and the waters shall no more become a flood to destroy all flesh."

CHAPTER 7

Paul: Sinner in the Hands of a Loving God

"A new commandment I give unto you, That ye love one another; as I have loved you, that ye also love one another."

– John 13:34

LOVING FATHER OR DEMANDING JUDGE?

JONATHAN EDWARDS WAS A CELEBRATED COLONIAL American preacher in the 1700s. He turned out to be the grandfather of the third U.S. president, **Aaron Burr**. Edwards' 1741 signature sermon was called "Sinners in the Hands of an Angry God." As the title implies, the text serves notice to "the wicked" that they are on a downward path to Hell. It was an effective clarion call of the Great Awakening—to acquaint the country (and the western world) to the Lord as the ultimate Judge.

It is notable to look back on Paul's "God moment" where he gets seriously committed to God. Was it out of fear or the threat of eternal damnation? No. After feeling lied to and morally abandoned by his country, Paul was searching for lasting truth, a solid anchor.

Ultimately, he re-encountered the Way, the Truth, and the Life[114] in the person of Jesus Christ.

As he grew in his faith, he found God to be a loving Father, a loving Dad. Towards the end of the Sermon on the Mount (Matthew 5-7), Jesus tells the listeners, "'What man is there of you, whom if his son ask [for] bread, will he give him a stone? Or if he ask [for] a fish, will he give him a serpent? If ye then, being evil, know how to give good gifts unto your children, how much more shall your Father, which is in heaven, give good things to them that ask Him?'"[115]

Paul has been confronted with the goodness of God: His caring, His loving, His giving. He consistently shares that with all who come to his garden tour. Yes, there will come a judgement,[116] but our Father in Heaven loves us all the way to our death, desiring to receive us into His loving arms. If only we would stop running *from* Him, turn around, and start running *to* Him. We are the ones running away, but He always leaves the porchlight on for us. We leave Him, but He doesn't leave us. Jesus promises His disciples: "'I will never leave you or forsake you.'"[117]

That was so beautifully illustrated in the parable of the prodigal son in Luke 15. Even after the young man spurned his father, demanded an advance of his inheritance, and left home (and all his responsibilities) to eat, drink, and be merry—thus squandering half of his dad's life savings—the father was still looking for his son to return. When he finally did, the father ran out to greet his son before he even reached home. He lovingly embraced him and gave a feast in his honor!

As I began writing this second edition, evangelist **Billy Graham** passed away. My family watched his memorial service held in North Carolina. One of Billy's daughters shared about a time she was struggling in life. After years of marriage and raising a family, her marriage ended in divorce. She was lonely and met a man she did not know that well. He took an interest in her and they purposed to marry. Her parents counseled her against it and to wait so they could get to know

---

114 John 14:6.
115 Matthew 7:9-11.
116 "And as it is appointed unto men once to die, but after this the judgment: So, Christ was once offered to bear the sins of many; and unto them that look for Him shall He appear the second time without sin unto salvation." Hebrews 9:27-28.
117 Hebrews 13:5.

the man better. Her grown kids had a similar reaction, but she was focused on herself and didn't listen to any of them. She had a hasty wedding. In her words, "Within twenty-four hours, I knew I had made a mistake." This guy was Mr. Wrong, not Mr. Right.

She describes her divorce, five weeks later, as "escaping from the relationship." With two divorces to her account in life, she felt like the proverbial black sheep of the Graham family. Driving back to her parents' place, up the winding mountain road, she was crying and wondering what she could possibly say to her parents after the second divorce. At last, she approached the entrance to the long driveway to the Graham home, and there was her father standing alone, waiting for her. She stopped the car and got out. He embraced her, and the first words out of his mouth were "I love you." She said there was "no shame, no judgment, just unconditional love."

Jesus is the Good Shepherd that leaves the flock of ninety-nine to find the one sheep that has gone astray. "For the Son of man is come to save that which was lost."[118] If you are a lost one right now, He wants you to come back to Him forever. Repent of doing your own thing, your own way, with only you in mind, and let Him lead you to green pastures, and experience His peace by the still waters. Let Him prepare a table for you in the presence of your enemies.[119]

So is it the wrath of God that draws people unto Himself? Romans 2:5-9 reminds us that:

- He will render to each of us according to our deeds;
- the proud, impenitent heart stores up "wrath for the day of wrath";
- indignation and wrath are reserved for all contentious liars that wallow in unrighteousness; and last,
- tribulation and anguish will await every soul that does evil.

God is omnipresent, everywhere. That means He is in the church meeting, and He is in the burlesque bar and tavern. He is on the school campus, and He is in the operating room. The presence of God is a settled thing. The issue is: What is His role in these environments? Maybe He has your credit card limit-out so you can't run up a higher

118 Luke 19:10.
119 Psalms 23.

bar tab and drive dangerously. Maybe you missed the expressway exit you wanted, and He saved you from a bad accident you would have encountered. His role is vast, and His love is even greater.

Fatherhood-Winked

Sadly, our earthly fathers, who are to be our personal glimpse to the fatherhood of God, cannot begin to adequately represent Him. Consequently, many children grow up having a jaded view of God as their Father. Does He drink too much? Does He have annoying habits? Is He so prone to anger? Does He listen any better? When our earthly dads fail to show us God's grace, His wisdom, His unconditional love, then we tend either to turn inward or to seek what was unprovided from other sources.

As was mentioned in chapter 10, Paul's closest parental relationship was not with his father. Like so many, he had to work at getting his mind wrapped around the fatherhood of God. Once he did, he was free to embrace that reality and live in the light of his heavenly Father's love and favor.[120]

Paul reminds us that Romans 2:4 asks whether we despise the riches of God's goodness and forbearance and longsuffering, not knowing that "the goodness of God leads us to repentance." It is true for us to say: "God is Good, and I am not," but we don't leave it at that and give up on having a relationship with Him. Rather, we thank Him for sharing His goodness with us, through His Son. Here are four examples (in Paul's words) of God's goodness in his life outside of the garden and orchard, plus one in the garden.

A Morellian Year

On Friday, April 15th 2020 I went up to visit Paul and take a few pictures. When I pulled up, Paul was not back from an in-town appointment. However, two young people were knelt down on the surface of the orchard. They were weeding on this cloudy, breezy, but dry Sequim day. One of Paul's helpers was Nick Ager, a fellow from

---

120 Not knowing the fatherhood of God leaves us living an unnecessarily messed-up life with an orphan spirit.

Maryland. I had heard about Nick from Paul and a mutual friend in Florida named **Don Blizzard.**

As Nick was up close and personal on the orchard surface, he noticed a startling growth! There was one, then another mushroom becoming visible as he scanned the area. Actually, he and I stopped counting at fifteen morel mushrooms.

Why is that a big deal? Because Paul and Carol love morels, and he had been asking God for them to grow on his property. Now, they had shown up overnight. Paul hadn't seen them yet, so I got to be there when Nick announced that there will be a morel mushroom harvest soon.

Paul was thrilled! This was a clear answer to prayer. A year prior, Paul brought some morels into the garden, crushed them with his hands and broadcasted them over the woodchips. Now, they had proliferated to fifteen-plus! Either way, it was a clear gift from above. "Every good gift and every perfect gift is from above, and comes down from the Father of lights, with whom is no variability, neither shadow of turning." James 1:17

The verse that came to Paul's mind was Psalm 37:4 "Delight yourself also in the LORD; and He shall give you the desires of your heart."

Part of Paul's life that so many wish they had are the continual surprises the Lord weaves into Paul's daily existence. It keeps things fresh, holy, vibrant. All the while, it bolsters an already amazing life of faith. He knows that we cannot out-give God: out-bless, or out-love.

STRANDED

"The first winter we were in Sequim [1978], we needed firewood, After I got off work, I loaded the family in the truck, and we drove up a mountain to gather wood. We loaded it until it was getting dark. I was trying to back the truck out but couldn't see that well. I almost backed over a cliff! Thankfully, I stopped in time, and we sat there—practically teetering on this ledge. I had Carol and the kids get out of the truck, while I pondered what to do. Easy: Cry out to God to rescue us."

"Now, we were in a remote mountain location. We didn't see anybody going up there. But lo and behold, a few minutes later, a couple of guys in a VW bug came upon us. They were way out there smoking pot because they didn't want to get caught. They stopped and offered to help. As ridiculous as it seems, that little excuse of a car was able to pull my [all steel] 1954 Dodge pickup [loaded with wood] out of harm's way and back on the road. We were so thankful that night. It was a huge lesson for us."

STUCK IN THE MIDDLE WITH YOU

In the summer of 2017, Paul was driving on Highway 101 in his trusty 1954 Dodge when the heater hose blew out. He was stuck in the middle of the highway and didn't have a cell phone with him. A gentleman came that had a cell phone, but that stretch of Highway 101 was a dead spot for cell signals, and the phone didn't work. Paul was pretty concerned about what to do. He sent an arrow-prayer[121] to Heaven: "God, what do I do?" Next thing he knew, a state trooper pulled up right behind him and gave Paul a safe push off the road. Now, he was out of danger. Then the trooper drove Paul to his house! This was such a blessing from the Lord. Paul was able to take another vehicle to get a new hose and coolant. He was dropped off, repaired the hose, topped off the fluid, and drove it home. Paul says, "You couldn't have orchestrated that any better." He views it as God's favor and it was such a blessing.

UP IN SMOKE

One cold and windy winter day, Paul was doing his routine morning chores: emptying out the overnight woodstove ashes into a metal bucket and hauling it outside. This day, he set the bucket down on the wooden porch as he went to attend to the dog and cats. He came back and dumped the ashes in the chicken yard, as was his custom. While he had been away from the full bucket, the wind had blown some ashes out of the bucket, and at least one glowing ember had landed on the padded doggie bed on the porch. Paul did not notice that when he took the bucket away nor when he crossed the porch going back into his house.

A while later, he was looking out his window and saw smoke, low smoke, not the kind from a woodstove chimney. He wondered what that was about. As he went out his door to the porch, he witnessed his neighbor putting out a fire on Paul's house with an extinguisher. After the embers had come in contact with the doggie bed, the wind had fanned them into flames and spread both to the floor of the porch and the log exterior of Paul's house.

The neighbor is a doctor and normally would have been at work on that Wednesday morning, but this day he wasn't. He told Paul, "I went into my kitchen for no reason. While I was there, I looked out the window and saw six-foot flames on your porch." Paul tells me this man is very organized, with many smoke detectors and multiple fire extinguishers in his house: upstairs, downstairs, garage, etc. So, the neighbor grabbed one of his extinguishers and ran across the street to

---

121 A quick prayer with few words.

put out the flames. He was successful, and Paul was so blessed. Paul told me: "David, you know how slow I walk. I would have had to use a bucket of water and would need to go back and forth to fill it. There's no way I could have put out that fire." If the neighbor hadn't come as well equipped as he was, the whole house could have been destroyed. Indeed, to this day, you can see the charred wall of his porch, as Paul decided to leave it there as a testimony to others and reminder to him of God's unmerited favor he received that morning.[122]

When you look for these things, they seem to show up all the time, but when you ignore them, you miss the feeling of utter gratefulness to the Lord for His grace and mercy. That is, we steal our own joy by being oblivious to the love and goodness of God. When our joy is stolen, our strength is lost because the joy of the Lord is our strength.[123]

French mathematician **Blaise Pascal** said: "He that takes truth for his guide, and duty for his end, may safely trust to God's providence to lead him aright." Paul has learned to look for the providence of God in even the small things. It is a constant source of vitality and wonderment to him.

---

122 After that, he no longer leaves the bucket on the porch, but takes it right out to the chicken yard.
123 Nehemiah 8:10c.

TOPPING THE CHARTS

When *Growing Food God's Way* first came out as an eBook in 2015, I had the pleasure of informing Paul that it immediately climbed to #1 in three Amazon categories (including young adult nonfiction). Paul said, "See, David, that's the favor of God. He favored the [*Back to Eden*] video, and He is favoring this book too."

Paul reminds us: "You have a loving Father, who's awesome and who knows how to upgrade things [like your garden or orchard]. Pray: 'Father, I dedicate this place to You, and I want to be a good steward. Father, I need Your help. I've got some depleted soil, and I need You to upgrade it and speed things up.' God says: 'You have not, because you ask not.'"[124]

Paul continues: "God calls those things which are not, as though they were! He'll call out your funky soil to a higher realm of existence because He can. I'm just telling you walk in that place of faith because faith pleases God. Even if you are wrong at times, it's still the safe place to be because faith pleases Him.

"Consider this kind of prayer: 'Father, I bless this [soil, seed, or plants] in Jesus's name. I ask for productivity. Thank You, God, for overcoming all the issues because You're God.'

"Just be in faith and watch things happen. He loves it when we come under His authority and follow His design."

---

124 James 4:2.

CHAPTER 8

A Generational View and Earth Stewardship

Only take heed to thyself, and keep thy soul diligently, lest thou forget the things which thine eyes have seen, and lest they depart from thy heart all the days of thy life: but teach them thy sons, and thy son's sons.

– Deuteronomy 4:9

LEGACY: ANYTHING HANDED DOWN FROM THE past, as from an ancestor or predecessor.[125]

Indicative of American consumerism were bumper stickers in the 1990s that proclaimed: "He who dies with the most toys wins." A decade later, aging parents proudly pasted on expensive RVs: "I'm spending my kids' inheritance." The concept of purposely leaving good things for your children and your children's children has been swallowed up by the me generation and those since. Yet providing a good garden as a sustainable food source can surpass inheriting a nice bank account.

The legacy element of relational permaculture is two-fold:

1. you pass on a thriving garden to someone, and (Lord willing)

---

125 *Webster's New Universal Unabridged Dictionary*, 1989, Dilithium Press Ltd.

2. you pass on your faith and love relationship with the Creator to those closest to you: family, friends, and even neighbors.

There are many men who either solely tend the family garden or who, at least, do the more aggressive things like tilling the ground and pulling weeds. The older male relational permaculturist takes comfort in knowing that if something were to happen to him, his wife's or children's labor to maintain their garden will be minimal. In other words, *they're covered*. With the proper soil covering in place, they can easily plant, almost not have to water, easily weed, and uncommonly (in a good way) harvest. The peace of mind that comes from establishing a healthy backyard food bank and knowing that it, with God's blessing, will provide good food for years to come is priceless.

If you are a giver and practice Effective Habit #7 (explained in the next chapter), there is joy in knowing that, even after death, you will still be giving precious, healthy gifts to your loved ones, friends, and neighbors. That is your legacy; plus the love of the Savior and better stewardship of the land could be your legacy as well.

EARTH STEWARDSHIP

On this topic, Paul is typically passionate: "God's economy and inheritance [are] huge. My children will have something much superior to what I had starting out. They will be able to stand on my shoulders and go so much further, versus a farmer that leaves depleted soil to his children to try to raise food."

Humanists have co-opted medicine, co-opted education, and co-opted the American conservation movement, resulting in an Earth-first, humans-second mentality. Moreover, in the public discourse of earth stewardship, they have relegated the believers in God as either pretenders or non-starters in this vital area. Some professing Christians have given plenty of fodder to feed such impressions, as Joel Salatin shared in his foreword. The inference is that one cannot be God-focused and earth-friendly at the same time. It simply isn't true.

As you listen to Paul's heart on this, don't miss the fact that those who don't believe and love God cannot truly sense accountability to Him for earth stewardship nor fully benefit from the best practices that emanate from Him. Paul says, "This is My Father's world, my Dad's. I need to respect what is His. It is required of a steward that he be found faithful, to give faithful care and stewardship.[126] God will destroy those who destroy the earth. It is a revelation of Him. When man corrupts it, he is also corrupting the Creator."

I could not remember a Bible reference about God destroying those who destroy the earth, until I found it in the last book of the Bible. Revelation 11:15 says: "The kingdoms of this world are become the kingdoms of our Lord, and of His Christ; and He shall reign forever and ever." Okay, okay, that's a pivotal stanza in **Handel's** *Messiah*, but three verses later, it declares: "Thou shouldest give reward unto thy servants the prophets, and to the saints, and them that fear Thy name, small and great; and shouldest destroy them which destroy the earth."

Believers in God (in all denominations) should not only be participants in the stewardship of creation, but also be stalwart pacesetters in matters of responsible use and care of earth, sky, and water.

In critical areas of life (like getting a job or accepted into a university), the age-old saying holds: "It's not what you know but who you know." Similarly, when it comes to relational permaculture, it's not what you know, but Who you know.

---

126 "Moreover, it is required in stewards, that a man be found faithful." 1 Corinthians 4:1.

CHAPTER 9

7 Effective Habits of Relational Permaculture

Trust in the LORD with all thine heart; and lean not unto thine own understanding. In all thy ways acknowledge him, and he shall direct thy paths.

— Proverbs 3:5-6

1. CONNECT

Without a relationship with the Creator, you would have just plain permaculture. Relationship is the absolute key to relational permaculture. It is connecting with the Creator; hearing His voice, His promptings, His Word; receiving all the cues He has prepared for us in His Word and in nature; and then acting on those revelations. Connecting benefits your life in and out of your garden. He promises visions and dreams.[127] Like Paul and countless others, you and I need to repent before we can connect.

2. OBTAIN

Find, or set aside, some land for gardening. If you don't have enough space, maybe you know someone who does. Ask the Lord

---

[127] "And it shall come to pass afterward, that I will pour out my spirit upon all flesh; and your sons and your daughters shall prophesy, your old men shall dream dreams, your young men shall see visions." Joel 2:28.

where you can start a garden. Put your need in His lap. Consider how to protect the garden from natural foragers, like deer, chickens, rabbits, moles, and others. Make sure you can get the woodchips to it handily. "Ask, and it shall be given you; seek, and ye shall find; knock, and it shall be opened unto you: For everyone that asketh receiveth; and he that seeketh findeth; and to him that knocketh it shall be opened." (Matthew 7:7-8)

3. COVER

For the first-time planting, cover the soil or grass with three or four layers of newspaper. If you can afford it, paint and home improvement stores carry paper on rolls for construction and painting crews. It is quicker to roll paper over than laying sheets of newspaper down again and again.[128] A thick layer of leaves can be used with success according to some leaf-spreading practitioners.

---

128 20% discount code available from your local paint supplier (Sherwin-Williams) at: www.growingfoodgodsway.com "Resources" tab.

Paul cautions against using cardboard because its stiffness may leave air pockets for grasses and weeds to grow. If you can, cover the newspaper with about two or more inches of compost material. Things like animal manures can make for great compost if they do not contain weed seeds. Cows process their food via four stomachs, so weed seeds aren't an issue with their manure. Woodchips that have been in a pile for a year or more may have decomposed into compost and are suitable for your garden's compost layer.

In my case, we got woodchips from a city stockpile of woodchips and leaves. Over the years, the city workers just kept dumping load after load of fresh chips upon the older chips. So initially, we hauled out the dark, moist, and dense organic matter below the surface chips to cover our newspaper layer. Paul also adds woodstove ashes to his compost, which recycles his heat-source waste and benefits the soil.

Afterwards, cover your compost with four to seven inches of woodchips or partially composted chips. This, to be brutally honest, is a lot of work and effort up front, but the investment of time, shoveling, and raking and the calluses are worth the future returns. After exhausting the city's woodchip stockpile, I contacted the local public utility company because it contracts with Asplundt to trim trees all over the county. You can also contact Asplundt directly to get information about your region. A reader of the first book registered with ChipDrop. com to let their member tree services know she was willing to take a load. **Bonnie** finished registering at about 8 p.m. and around 8 the next morning she got a call from a driver that was parked in front of her driveway and said she needed to move her car to dump the load! Finally, I have acquired a few loads of woodchips from independent tree service companies. The last company that came by my place was called Blessed Tree Service. Mostly, I'll see a chip truck working by the side of the road and stop to (carefully) talk with the person in charge to let them know where they can dump their load for free.

DO NOT TILL the woodchips into the soil. You should know by now that the tiller is an enemy combatant to you garden. Also avoid using bark dust or sawdust. Those do retain moisture but can rob your soil of needed nutrients and air. Finally, you may want to broadcast quality nitrogen-rich material like mushroom compost, weed-free animal manures, and/or mineral dust over the woodchips once they are down and allow nature (or your hose) to water the top surface and let the good elements percolate to the soil.

4. PLANT AND PRAY

When the weather is suitable, place your seeds in the soil about one-quarter-inch deep, no matter what the seed packet says. PLEASE do not plant into the woodchip layer. Your seeds need real soil to germinate properly, so push the woodchips (and/or rocks) aside to plant in the direct soil and compost layer.

Paul makes a valley through the woodchips with the end of his hard rake. He quips: "Anytime I want to plant, I just come out and get my rake, rake it out, make a little groove, drop seeds, cover it, and I'm done." With relational permaculture, you sow seeds in the earth and sow prayers to Heaven. Ask God to bless your soil and plants that your soil would yield her strength.[129] Thank the Lord for the privilege of being a sower, the honor of being a tender, and the blessing of being a harvester.

5. WATER

Initially, you may need to water after planting to break down the seeds so they will sprout. The moistness of the soil will be your best advisor. If moisture is already evident, you don't need to water at all. After the plants begin their growth above the soil line, it is time to gently rake the woodchip covering around them. Let sunlight reach the leaves or pods. Unless things are harshly dry in your area, you should not have to water again. Be sure to observe the leaves as they will let you know if watering is warranted.

If you plant in a low spot, you should not have to water at all in that it receives subterranean and surface (runoff) water. Covered gardens tend to be overwatered the first year, when we are so accustomed to needing to water. As a result, we water out of habit, and that habit can easily work against us. Like to water? GET OVER IT. Water your grass, flowers, or your neighbor's conventional garden, but your covered garden will do just fine without this repeated practice, thank you very much! If you pay for your hose water (to the city or water district), using less water helps you save money each month.

---

129 Genesis 4:12.

6. Reap

Again, the key to harvesting is proper timing. Resist the temptation to pick early. Ripeness is the time to cash in on the fruits of your labor (and that of others in some cases). "But this I say, he which soweth sparingly shall reap also sparingly; and he which soweth bountifully shall reap also bountifully." (2 Corinthians 9:6)

Reaping is a joyful and fulfilling time. Savor it! Once you reap you are ready for effective habit #7.

7. Share

God is a Giver, not just of life and time but also of many good gifts. It helps to realize that each passing day is God's gift of twenty-four hours to us. We exhibit His nature when we give to others. After all, aren't other bodies craving for real, live food too?

We give out of thankfulness to the One who has given to us. Paul loves to quote 1 Thessalonians 5:18: "In everything give thanks, for this is the will of God [in Christ Jesus concerning you]." He adds: "It's not for God's benefit." Clearly, we benefit by being thankful.

Of the five laws of stratospheric success found in the bestseller *The Go-Giver*,[130] the law of value states: "Your true worth is determined by how much more you give in value than you take in payment." More poignantly, Jesus made the profound assertion that "it is more blessed to give than to receive."[131]

---

130 Bob Burg and John David Mann, *The Go-Giver: A Little Story about a Powerful Business Idea*, New York: Portfolio, 2007.
131 Acts 20:35.

REAL FOOD IS GOOD FOOD

Paul encourages visitors to sample the things that grow there. Many a parent tells Paul their kids probably won't eat much of anything, only to stare in disbelief as their kids unabashedly eat and eat and eat Paul's fruits and vegetables. Then they try to admonish their kids to stop or slow down, and Paul smiles and says, "There's plenty," and "There's no harm in eating live food." Quite possibly, it may be their first time getting to do so.

The fact is—real food is beguiling. It entices with its healthy looks and often aromatic smells. As far as scintillating goes, a sprig of Paul's fennel takes no back seat to Channel No. 5˚. His celery stalks seem like arms raised in a classroom, with each stalk enthusiastically saying, "Pick me, pick me!" The carrots and beets are stealthier. They, of course, are underground and thus appear to be as kids playing hide and seek. Half of the fun is discovering what exactly you'll get when you pull one up. Next, you seek out someone else there to hold it up and say, "Look at this!" The apples in season are like delicious ornaments on a Christmas tree, as are his pears.

Who Does Not Seem to Be Getting It?

Paul has had many experiences with naysayers. He mentions, "I have all these farmers come in here and tell me I can't do what I'm doing." After the *Sunset* magazine article in 1990, a team of Washington State University professors just showed up in a Chevy Suburban. As Paul recounts, "They walked around, ate some of my fruit and produce, loved what they ate, but in the end, the main professor declared that 'It won't work' and that 'All the apple trees will die' because I had placed woodchips ten inches along the trunks. Then they drove off." That was thirty years ago, and Paul's only problem with the trees is that they produce too much.

Linda Chalker-Scott PhD

In all fairness, **Linda Chalker-Scott**,[132] a WSU associate professor and author of *The Informed Gardener*, *The Informed Gardener Blooms Again*, and her latest co-authored work, *Gardening with Native Plants of the Pacific Northwest*,[133] visited Paul's garden in the summer of

132 http://gardenprofessors.com/author/linda-chalker-scott/.
133 https://www.google.com/books/edition/_/aLKMDwAAQBAJ?hl=en.

2013 with her husband (who also has a PhD in horticulture), along with their son and daughter. The two-hour tour left a greatly positive impression upon the whole Scott family. For months, I had hoped Paul and Linda would meet because she has been touting woodchips for landscaping and soil remediation for about ten years. Indeed, they were tracking nicely the whole time. At the end of the garden tour, she actually told Paul, "I wouldn't change a thing," followed by telling her husband, "See, there is someone else that talks about woodchips as much as I do." He smiled, as though she was reading his mind.

On another occasion, Paul tells, "I had a biologist come to my place, and he's looking at foliage and the color of my celery and says, 'There's no way you get that without fertilizer.' I said, 'I don't fertilize.' He said, 'There's no way. I'm going to come back, and I'm going to test your soil.' So, he came back and tested my soil, and it blew his mind. You know what the pH in my soil and woodchips is? Woodchips, they tell you, are acid-forming. You know what the woodchips tested (with pine in it)? Seven.[134] The guy was in such shock he tested in three different places, and it was 7.0. 'Let God be true and every man a liar.'"[135]

Paul continues: "Here's the thing about God; He didn't miss a thing, and what He's put in nature is the most amazing design to break it all down and to make it totally neutral: 7.0 across the board. That's why He can grow everything in the same place and we're out there adding lime, doing all this stuff to adjust the pH, and God just balances it, puts it dead center so everything's happy. *I love Him.* He's just so genius smart. He designed this incredible landscape so He'd never have to show up to work. I love that! You know how hard you and I work to do stuff? God has this amazing landscape on millions of acres, that no one has to show up to work. He thought this up, and they're telling me this isn't intelligent design?"

> *There are none so blind as those who will not see.*
> – Matthew Henry (1662-1714)

If you are willing to see, then please charge into to the next chapter, "Mystery Revealed."

---

134 A 7.0 indicates perfectly neutral, or pH balanced, soil. Readings above 7.0 indicate alkaline, and readings below 7.0 are acidic.
135 Romans 3:4.

CHAPTER 10

Mystery Revealed

If thou shalt confess with thy mouth the Lord Jesus, and shalt believe in thine heart that God hath raised him from the dead, thou shalt be saved. For with the heart man believeth unto righteousness; and with the mouth confession is made unto salvation.

– Romans 10:9-10

IT MAY SEEM A BIT OUT OF CHARACTER for a biographical gardening book on sustainability and healthy foods to dare take on the weighty subject of who Jesus is and what His existence means to us, but He is central to Paul's life of growing food God's way, and I would be defrauding you if I didn't at least dedicate a chapter to introduce, or reintroduce, the Messiah to you.

If I had to summarize Jesus in one word, it would be love.[136] His was not an ethereal, philosophical love but was a love that was lived out in His role in Creation, His earthly birth, His childhood, His ministry of teaching and miracles, His suffering and death, His resurrection, and His ascension and will be in full display at His second coming to Earth.

---

136 The Apostle Paul prays for the Ephesian believers to "know the love of Christ, which passeth knowledge, that ye might be filled with all the fullness of God." (Ephesians 3:19)

It's Greek to Me (Too)

The Greek language uses different, more specific, terms than the English language offers to describe the various attributes of the word "love." In English, we often run into exact same words that carry different meanings. For instance, if we were at a restaurant and you told me the Thai food was "hot," you could be saying the physical temperature of the food may burn my mouth, or you could be warning me that the spices in the food are capable of burning my mouth. Even more confusing (if you are a single guy), you might also tell me that the waitress is hot. That one word has three connotations.

To avoid confusion in discussing love, the Greek language differentiates between brotherly love, an endearment kind of love, a romantic love, and a giving, selfless, **Mother Teresa**–type love. The latter form of love is (in Greek) known as "agape," pronounced *ah-GOP-ay*. It is the only form of love that is selfless and not dependent upon our feelings and emotions.

So, what does *that* look like?

The Real Deal

Can you imagine with me that it was not natural (at first) for Mother Teresa to touch and hold the lepers she had a heart to minister to? If that is remotely true, then her faith in God and the acceptance of His grace (to exhibit His love) mentally vetoed any natural feelings of freaking out about the condition of the lepers. Unlike the general populace, to her, leprous people were not repulsive; they were (and are) God's creatures, formed in His image and imbued with an eternal spirit.

Mother Teresa had to know that Jesus loved and cared for lepers because one day He healed ten of them at one time! All she had to read was the seventeenth chapter of Luke (an Apostle of Jesus and a Greek-trained physician), verses 11-19, where it says:

> And it came to pass, as He [Jesus] went to Jerusalem; that He passed through the midst of Samaria and Galilee. And as He entered into a certain village,

there met Him ten men that were lepers, which stood afar off. And they lifted up their voices, and said: "Jesus, Master, have mercy on us." And when He saw them, He said unto them: "Go show yourselves unto the priests." And it came to pass, that, as they went, they were cleansed. And one of them, when he saw that he was healed, turned back, and with a loud voice glorified God, and fell down on his face at His feet, giving Him thanks: and he was a Samaritan. And Jesus answering said: "Were there not ten cleansed? But where are the nine? There are not found that returned to give glory to God, save this stranger." And He said unto him: "Arise, go thy way: thy faith hath made thee whole."

Mother Teresa said of her work with the Missions of Charity in Calcutta, India, and around the globe, "Many people mistake our work for our vocation. Our vocation is the love of Jesus."

When I say Jesus can best be described by the word *love*, I am only talking about pure agape love. His 24/7/365 life of love on earth was one with "no reservations, no retreats, and no regrets."[137] It is because of His example for us to follow that I paraphrase 1 John 4:19, a seminal scripture: We (unreservedly) love Him because He first (unreservedly) loved us. Jesus was, and is, the world's best example of loving others, even if they don't love back, even though the world requited His love with jealousy, hate, personal humiliation, and torment.

He suffered and died for my sins, for Paul's sins, and for yours because we were unwilling and incapable of dying to ourselves to put God first. If there was a recipe of good works we could follow to earn our way to Heaven, then Jesus would not have been needed as our once-for-all sacrifice. "Neither is there salvation in any other: for there is [no] other name under Heaven given among men, whereby we must be saved." (Acts 4:12)[138] If there was some other spiritual path to reach God, then God would not have had to send His Son to this evil and cruel generation. "For God so loved the world, He gave His

137 A quote by William Whiting Borden (1887-1913). He was a Yale, then Princeton alumni and a millionaire-turned-missionary.
138 "None" changed to "no."

only begotten Son, that whosoever believes in Him shall have eternal life." (John 3:16)

Do you appreciate irony? Isn't it ironic that the Roman soldiers jammed a crown of thorns on Jesus's head?[139] The very symbol of the curse upon man (thorns) was taken to the cross as our Messiah became a curse for us.[140]

Agape love is a giving love. All the other Greek expressions of love have a sharing element at best and a taking element at worst, but agape rises above all that in its purity, practice, and consistency. Here's how the Bible describes agape love, which is called "charity," in 1 Corinthians 13:4-8:

> [Love][141] suffers long, and is kind; love envies not; love [exalts] not itself, is not puffed up,
> Doth not behave itself unseemly, seeks not her own, is not easily provoked, thinks no evil;
> Rejoiceth not in iniquity, but rejoiceth in the truth;
> Beareth all things, believe[s] all things, hopes all things, endureth all things.
> Love never fails."

IF GOD'S SO SMART . . .

Why would an omniscient (all-knowing) God create a people that would reject Him and His Son? Why should the Son suffer at the hands of sinful, jealous, arrogant religious rulers and government officials? One word, love, and its next of kin, joy. "Looking unto Jesus the author and finisher of our faith; Who for the joy that was set before Him, endured the cross, despising the shame, and is set down at the right hand of the throne of God." (Hebrews 12:2)

Jesus knew how His actions in the present would indelibly affect eternity: yours, mine, all nations', the earth's—everything's.

---

139 John 19:5: "Then came Jesus forth, wearing the crown of thorns, and the purple robe. And Pilate saith unto them, Behold the man!"
140 Galatians 3:13: "Christ hath redeemed us from the curse of the law, being made a curse for us: for it is written, Cursed is everyone that hangeth on a tree:"
141 Love used rather than "charity."

"For He [God] hath made Him [Jesus] to be sin for us, who knew no sin; that we might be made the righteousness of God in Him." (2 Corinthians 5:21)

This "love every soul to the Cross" persona of the Messiah was foretold by the prophet Isaiah in 53:2-12.

> For He [Jesus/Yeshua] shall grow up before Him [Yahweh/YHWH] as a tender plant, and as a root out of a dry ground: He hath no form, nor comeliness; and when we shall see Him, there is no beauty that we should desire Him.
>
> He is despised and rejected of men; a man of sorrows, and acquainted with grief: and we hid, as it were, our faces from Him; He was despised, and we esteemed Him not. Surely, He hath borne our griefs and carried our sorrows: yet we did esteem Him stricken, smitten of God, and afflicted. But He was wounded for our transgressions, He was bruised for our iniquities: the chastisement of our peace was upon Him; and with His stripes we are healed.
>
> All we like sheep have gone astray; we have turned everyone to his own way; and the LORD hath laid on Him the iniquity of us all. He was oppressed, and He was afflicted, yet He opened not His mouth: He is brought as a lamb to the slaughter, and as a sheep before her shearers is [silent], so He openeth not His mouth.
>
> He was taken from prison and from judgment: and who shall declare His generation? For He was cut off out of the land of the living: for the transgression of my people was He stricken. And He made His grave with the wicked, and with the rich in His death; because He had done no violence, neither was any deceit in His mouth.
>
> Yet it pleased the LORD to bruise Him; He hath put him to grief: when Thou shalt make His soul an offering for sin, He shall see His seed, He shall prolong

His days, and the pleasure of the LORD shall prosper in His hand. He shall see of the travail of His soul and shall be satisfied: by His knowledge shall My righteous servant justify many; for He shall bear their iniquities.

Therefore will I divide Him a portion with the great, and He shall divide the spoil with the strong; because He hath poured out His soul unto death: and He was numbered with the transgressors; and He bare the sin of many, and made intercession for the transgressors.

As Paul would say, "Do the math." The prophet Isaiah wrote this about seven hundred years before Jesus was born. Today, if Jesus (Yeshua) was brought to trial for being the Messiah, the Jewish prophet Isaiah would be on the witness list for the prosecution team. In a sense, that is the current state of this book: to present you evidence of the glorious reality of Jesus Christ and let your own spirit judge whether He is guilty of loving you to death (His death) on your behalf.

Isaiah declared, "He hath poured out His soul unto death,"[142] but how did that come about? What was the catalyst for such devotion and sacrifice? Forgiveness. Though he was "despised and rejected," Jesus not only forgave His hateful tormentors and false accusers, but also His substitutionary death on the cross and His empty tomb[143] paved the only way for future generations (that's us) to be forgiven as completely and lovingly as the hardened Roman soldiers and the hardhearted Jewish (religious) rulers.

WHO CARES ABOUT FORGIVENESS?

We don't hear the word "forgiveness" too often in our modern conversations. Years ago, I had an unexpected encounter with **Amy Van Dyken**,[144] one of the top US women swimmers at the Will Rogers Airport in Oklahoma City, Oklahoma. At the time, she had just won the most (six) Olympic gold medals of any American woman, except speed skater **Bonnie Blair** and swimmer **Janet Evans**. As Amy and

---

142 Isaiah 53:12.
143 Mark 16:1-6.
144 Now, Amy van Dyken-Rouen.

a friend were boarding the same plane I was boarding, I introduced myself and told her that my whole family had watched the Summer Olympics a few months before[145] and how we had cheered her and her U.S. teammates.

Next, because I had just come from a conference on character at the Character Training Institute,[146] I handed her a pocket guide of forty-nine character qualities as a gift. Later (after the seatbelt lights went out), another institute attendee on board (**Tim Coe**) asked her which character qualities were the most applicable for her as a gold-medal Olympian. He handed her one of his pocket guides and asked her to circle those specific qualities. She circled thirteen of the forty-nine. There were no-brainer ones any athlete would likely circle—determination, initiative, and thoroughness—but there were some surprises like humility and forgiveness. The character pocket guide has operational definitions for each of the forty-nine qualities. Humility is "acknowledging that achievement results from the investments of others in my life." She readily agreed with the definition and admitted that key "others in her life" were her parents and swim coaches. More importantly, the operational definition for forgiveness is "clearing the record of those who have wronged me and not holding a grudge." The classic 1996 version of the guide also uses antonyms to help the seeker of good character to understand the terms better. The antonym given for forgiveness is rejection.

The nonsectarian character training I received points out that the whole purpose of forgiving (that boss, that peer, that one who reports to you at work) is to restore the relationship. The hurtful, unkind, or downright dastardly thing someone did to offend you blew a hole in your relationship with that person. What the relationship was the day before is not what it is today, is it? Why? Because your feelings were hurt, your pride was offended; you may even have received some physical abuse and pain. Once the gauntlet has been laid, we have to decide to do our part to restore the damaged relationship. If we make no attempt to forgive, then we have rejected the relationship, willing to let it die a natural but awkward death.

---

145 We had a working TV back then but have since removed it from our household.
146 Now known as Strata Leadership and Character Core. See https://characterfirsteducation.com/ and https://www.strataleadership.com/core.

Enter Jesus (the) Christ.

The relationship Adam and Eve (humanity) had with the Father was badly damaged. Time did not heal all wounds in that, even with the giving of the Mosaic Law. Generations later, there was (and is) rampant failure to keep even the Ten Commandments.[147] The relationship between God and the mankind He created was in a death spiral. At this critical point, God's sacrificial love kicked in, and He sent His only Son (born of the Spirit) to Earth to call all men and women, boys and girls, to repentance, the fear of the Lord, and Kingdom authority. However, both the sons of perdition[148] and the religious establishment joined forces in opposing the Savior of the world. That culminated in a sham trial, physical beatings, and then the shame (and curse) of being hung on a wooden cross.[149]

Paul shared with me a definition of forgiveness that came not from his pastor or an evangelist but from the renowned American author **Mark Twain**: *"Forgiveness is the fragrance the violet sheds on the heel that just crushed it."* Think about that. The last act in the life of the flower was to bless its enemy with the very essence of the violet itself. Can you see that is exactly what Jesus did for you and me? My prayer is that you will come to grips with His agape love for you.

Jesus bled and died for our sins. He had to; there was no other sacrifice acceptable whereby men and women, boys and girls, could be saved.

> Neither by the blood of goats and calves, but by His own blood, He entered in once into the holy place, having obtained eternal redemption for us. For if the blood of bulls and of goats, and the ashes of an [sic] heifer sprinkling the unclean, sanctifieth to the purifying of the flesh: How much more shall the blood of Christ, who through the eternal Spirit offered Himself without spot to God, purge your conscience from dead works to serve the living God? (Hebrews 9:12-14)

---

147 (1) Have no other gods, (2) make no graven images or serve them, (3) take not the Lord's name in vain, (4) remember the Sabbath Day (keep it holy), (5) honor father and mother, (6) do not kill, (7) do not commit adultery, (8) do not steal, (9) do not speak falsely (lie), and (10) do not covet (desire) the things of others. See Exodus 20:1-17.
148 Evildoers.
149 Deuteronomy 21:23.

Jesus was beaten (cruelly) but not to death. He was stabbed by a spear, crowned with thorns, and mercilessly whipped, yet He did not bleed to death. He was suspended by His hands, being nailed to a wooden cross-piece behind Him, which greatly restricts breathing, yet He did not die of asphyxiation. So, what would a coroner's report have said? He died as a result of being crushed by the weight of the sins of all humanity (present and future) that He willingly took upon Himself.[150] He paid for my sins and yours on a hill outside Jerusalem called Golgotha (Hebrew for "the place of the skull"). For a time, God the Father could not look upon God the Son as He became sin for us.[151]

But it doesn't stop there. Jesus's death on our behalf would have limited significance if He had not risen from the dead. It was foretold in prophecy-and came to pass three days and nights after He was buried.[152]

Why is that so important? Because it validates that He was truly the Son of Man *and* the Son of God, that He exercised dominion over death. The fact is, if He is not Lord *of all*, then He cannot be Lord *at all*. Also, He promised His believers that they would be resurrected to live in glory with Him.[153] What better way to validate that promise than by doing it Himself?

Life does not end with our body's last breath. Listen to the Apostle Paul as he addressed the Greek philosophers of his day:

> Then Paul stood in the midst of Mars' hill, and said, 'Ye men of Athens, I perceive that in all things ye are too superstitious.[154]
>
> For as I passed by, and beheld your devotions, I found an altar with this inscription, TO THE UNKNOWN GOD. Whom therefore ye ignorantly worship, Him declare I unto you.

---

150 John 10: 17-18: "Therefore doth my Father love me, because I lay down my life, that I might take it again. No man taketh it from me, but I lay it down of myself. I have power to lay it down, and I have power to take it again. This commandment have I received of my Father."

151 2 Corinthians 5:21.

152 Matthew 12:40.

153 2 Timothy 2:12.

154 The Greeks were largely pantheists; believing in many gods.

God that made the world and all things therein, seeing that He is Lord of heaven and earth, dwelleth not in temples made with hands;

Neither is worshipped with men's hands, as though He needed anything, seeing He giveth to all life, and breath, and all things;

And hath made of one blood all nations of men for to dwell on all the face of the earth, and hath determined the times before appointed, and the bounds of their habitation;

That they should seek the Lord, if [possibly] they might feel after Him, and find Him, though He be not far from every one of us:

For in Him we live, and move, and have our being; as certain also of your own poets have said, "For we are also His offspring."

Forasmuch then as we are the offspring of God, we ought not to think that the Godhead is like unto gold, or silver, or stone, graven by art and man's device.

And the times of this ignorance God winked at; but now commandeth all men everywhere to repent: Because He hath appointed a day, in the which He will judge the world in righteousness by that Man whom He hath ordained; whereof He hath given assurance unto all men, in that He hath raised Him from the dead. (Acts 17:22-31)

So, is that the mystery? Not quite. We have to check in with the Apostle Paul and his letter to the Colossian believers to find the key. Paul declares that he was made a minister to fulfill the Word of God,; even the "mystery which hath been hid from ages and from generations, but now is made manifest to His saints; which is Christ in you, the hope of glory."[155]

BIBLICAL ONENESS

Did you get it? The true believer in Jesus doesn't go it alone. Unlike any other person or deity that mankind has paid religious

---

155 Colossians 1:27.

homage or devotion to, only Jesus declares to His believers that He will not only be with them but dwell in them as well (spiritually). An expansion and clarification of this mystery was again revealed by the Apostle Paul as he wrote, by inspiration of God, to the Jewish believers in Ephesus:[156]

> How that by revelation He [God] made known unto me the mystery . . . which in other ages was not made known unto the sons of men, as it is now revealed unto His holy apostles and prophets by the Spirit; **That the Gentiles should be fellow heirs, and of the same body, and partakers of His promise** in Christ by the gospel: Whereof I was made a minister, according to the gift of the grace of God given unto me by the effectual working of His power. Unto me, who am less than the least of all saints, is this grace given, that I should preach among the Gentiles the unsearchable riches of Christ; And to make all men see what is the **fellowship of the mystery**, which from the beginning of the world hath been hid in God, who created all things by Jesus Christ. (emphasis added)

> Galatians 3:6-8 explains it further:

> Even as Abraham believed God, and it was accounted to him for righteousness. Know ye therefore that they which are of faith, the same are the children of Abraham. And the scripture, foreseeing that God would justify the heathen through faith, preached before the gospel unto Abraham, saying, In thee shall all nations be blessed.

Not only would Christ indwell the Messiah-receiving Jew, but also He opened the door for Gentiles (all people that are not Jews) to enter into God's fullness as well. THIS IS HUGE!

Why? Because Paul Gautschi is not a Jew by birth, thus Jesus, as the Son of God, opened His salvation to Paul, as He does to

---

156 Ephesians 3:3-9

"whosoever will."[157] Jesus is the bridge between a sinful Paul and a righteous God. He is our bridge (and much more) if we will accept Him by believing, and receiving, Him by faith.

A WORD ABOUT GIFTS

The salvation of our souls is a gift *from* God, not *to* God. Scripture makes this very clear: "For by grace are ye saved through faith; and that not of yourselves: it is the gift of God: Not of works, lest any man should boast."[158] Awesome! And His major gifts come in order:

1. The Gift of Life (to everyone born)
2. The Gift of Love (to everyone living)
3. The Gift of Salvation (to all who believe and receive Him)
4. The Gift of Glorified Life on Earth; (to active believers)
5. The Gift of Glorified Life in Heaven (to all believers who hold fast to the end)

Because you hold the first gift (life),[159] you are qualified for the second (love).[160] If you respond to God's love (personified by Jesus) and make Him Lord and Master of your life, you receive the third gift (salvation).[161]

Having salvation, you begin as a babe and grow in Christ to experience the fourth gift (glorified life),[162] which is your title to your fifth gift (eternal glorified life)[163] in God's presence *if* you do not deny Him on earth.[164]

WHO'S YOUR MASTER?

By the time President **Abraham Lincoln** issued the Emancipation Proclamation, in 1863, there were about 3.9 million African-American

---

157 See Matthew 16:25, Mark 8:34-35, Luke 9:24, and Revelation 22:17.
158 Ephesians 2:8-9.
159 Job 33:4; John 1:4, 6:38, 20:31.
160 John 3:16, 15:9,12.
161 Acts 4:12, Romans 10:10.
162 Romans 8:30, 2 Thessalonians 1:12.
163 1 John 2:25, 5:11, 5:20.
164 Matthew 10:33, 2 Peter 2:20-21.

slaves in the United States according to Wikipedia.[165] That source also indicates that a total of six hundred thousand African men and women were transported to America for the purpose of indentured servitude.[166] Slavery stands as one of the greatest sins of America, and if you do the math (as Paul likes to say), it's very evident that the vast majority of slaves were *born into slavery*. Their parents were slaves, so they automatically were slaves of a master. They did not get to choose who that master was because it was predetermined by who the parents served.[167]

That is important to wrap our minds around because it reveals a spiritual truth: **We are all born into slavery**. Our initial progenitors (Adam and Eve) went from ultimate freedom and a relationship with God to become slaves of the devil and estranged toward God. We were born into that, which is why Jesus told a man named Nicodemus that he must be born again.[168] This is not a second physical birth but a spiritual one. We would be wise to note that in each birth, *all* the effort was made by someone else, not us. We cannot birth ourselves. It is Jesus who delivers us. The truth is, if we are not running to Jesus, we are dancing with the devil (and he is doing all the leading, even though you may think you are the one doing it.)

Thus, we must all face this question in life: *Who's my master?* It is the one you serve, think about, fuss over, and devote your time, money, and attention to. Be honest with yourself. Is God your Master, or is it the enemy of your soul?

A slave cannot free himself or herself. A slave's freedom must be bought (or gained via conquest) by a greater Master. Through God's providence, He sent His Son to redeem you back unto Himself. "If the Son therefore shall make you free, ye shall be free indeed." (John 8:3)

It was this freedom relationship God designed us humans to live in the first place. Jesus bought us with His blood, and our old master cannot deny the price was paid once and for all. Thus, he can only try

---

165 https://en.wikipedia.org/wiki/1860_United_States_Census.
166 https://en.wikipedia.org/wiki/Slavery_in_the_United_States.
167 Ephesians 2:3 "Among whom also we all had [lived] our [lives] in times past in the lusts of our flesh, fulfilling the desires of the flesh and of the mind; and were by nature the children of wrath, even as others. (Emphasis added)
168 John 3:3-7. Also 1 Peter 1:23: "Being born again, not of corruptible seed, but of incorruptible, by the word of God, which liveth and abideth forever."

to persuade you it never happened and that you are still his. Don't believe him!

DEARLY BELOVED, WE ARE GATHERED HERE TODAY

In Holy Scripture, Jesus is referred to as "the bridegroom" ten times. The bride is His beloved, His followers who believe in Him. In traditional US wedding ceremonies, the minister (or judge) asks the groom if he will take "this woman" to be his lawfully wedded wife. Everything is on hold until the groom responds. If he says: "Yes, I do" or "I will," the officiate turns to the bride to ask her if she will take the groom to be her lawfully wedded husband. The point is, *he* is asked to make the commitment first and then *she* has what amounts to veto power over everything up to that critical and exciting point.

So you see, in history, in the present, and in the future, Jesus said, is saying, and will say, "I do," to redeem us of our sins, to be our Groom, and to love and care for us; and we, the intended bride, are the ones to either return His love or reject Him. To receive Him is to abandon everything less than Him and pour our lives into our Groom.

Jesus is offering you an eternal love relationship with Him. Won't you say, "I do?"

> *If any man will come after Me, let him take up his cross daily, and follow Me. For whosoever will save his life shall lose it: but whosoever shall lose his life for My sake shall save it." Jesus of Nazareth (Luke 9:23, 24)*
> *He is no fool who gives what he cannot keep,*[169] *to gain what he cannot lose.*[170]
>
> – Jim Elliot

IS GOD TRUSTWORTHY?

Paul shared how God rescued him from the drug culture of his day, but the following is another true personal account of an

---

169 His physical life.
170 Eternal life with God. Martyred missionary Jim Elliot's life is depicted in the book Shadow of the Almighty by Elizabeth Elliot (New York: Harper Collins, 1979) and the movie The End of The Spear (2006).

American, twenty-nine-year-old **Jesse**, and the drug culture he was into as a late teenager. He emailed me this directly:

> I was so lost . . . hopeless; in constant misery and torment of heart. Longing to find peace and purpose but looking in all the wrong places left me feeling . . . [more] empty and down than I can even describe to you . . . to the point of constantly just wanting to end it all, disappear, take my own life to escape the misery of my selfish heart.
>
> I remember sitting at the edge of a 100-foot tall water tower in the middle of [the] night in the forest. The weather was freezing. I was so ready to jump. I had made up my mind and that is why I climbed all the way up there. The two feet of snow on the ground would [in] no way be enough to break my fall so I wouldn't [have] survive[d] if I had succeeded in jumping.
>
> [In] many situations similar to this I remember something supernatural holding me back. It was not a fear of death. I did not fear death; I wanted it badly. It was something more. I know it was my heavenly Father. But with no hope in life, I turned to drugs day and night (with no stopping) to keep me as far away from [my] miserable reality as possible. Many nights I wandered the streets all night long even through the freezing cold of winter . . . lost but not knowing where to go or what I was looking for.

I could go on, but I want to get to the good part now: He never left me! Through it all He [God] held on to me. When I thought life was meaningless, He knew that He had a special purpose for me . . . and in [spite of] my stupidity and blindness His mercy abounded. My family prayed for me; not losing hope, though I abandoned them and treated them badly . . . they were ready to receive me back when I was ready. God called me out of darkness into His marvelous light.

In the middle of an intense drug overdose I cried out to my heavenly Father to save me, His Spirit came and led me to freedom. In the middle of a drug culture, I became transformed and born again. I stayed there not knowing what to do and often falling again, until on the hospital bed [September 9, 2002] staring death in the face. Again, I cried out to Him and He heard me. I surrendered my life and future to Him if He would give *one more chance,* and He took me up on it! Through this journey, [this] wild ride of life, I am thrilled to be with Him daily. He *can* use me!

I was expelled from school; a street kid panhandling all day to buy pot. I knew that there had to be something more, but I couldn't see it. Now I [have] found it and am filled, and I know there is even so much more. More of Him to be had, tasted and experienced, in this love relationship.

Now He has put His love in me for the people of the world; the ones who are still lost as I was. He has given me His light to shine for them.

Are you a reflection of God's "marvelous light" to others?

We cannot be a reflection unless we are pointed to the Source; otherwise, we are reflecting something else (usually ourselves). The moon has no light in itself, but it gives us light as it reflects the light of the sun to us at night. For the moon, the sun is the source of light, but for the believer, the Son of God is our source of light and truth.

Jesse had to repent and surrender. He had to take "Jesse" out of the equation and replace himself with Jesus, not a mental assent that "He existed" or that "He was a good man" but a real relationship with the Messiah in the here and now. To the believer in the Lord Jesus, eternal life doesn't start when the body is dead and buried, but when one surrenders (dies to self) and begins a new life "hid in Christ."[171]

---

171 Colossians 3:2-3: "Set your affection on things above, not on things on the earth. For ye are dead, and your life is hid with Christ in God."

CHAPTER 11

Humble Beginnings, Exalted Endings

I call to remembrance the unfeigned faith that is in thee,
which dwelt first in thy grandmother Lois and thy mother
Eunice, and I am persuaded that [is] in thee also.

– 2 Timothy 1:5

GETTING A START

PAUL GREW UP AS THE FIRST BORN of **Charles Harlan** (he went by his middle name) and **Helen Gautschi**. Though his last name first struck me as Italian or Sicilian, he tells me that Gautschi is a Swiss name. A quick internet search revealed that the name dates back to the late 1700s and primarily came from the canton (county) of Aargau in Switzerland. Paul's dad worked in the Los Angeles, California, area. Harlan Gautschi was raised by a strict father. The legacy of strictness carried forward with Harlan to the raising of Paul and his brother. Paul's deeper parental relationship was with his mother, whose nurturing was a welcomed complement to his dad's firm expectations, but she was also strong and inspiring.

Paul recollects: "My mom was a natural evangelist. Her whole heart was to tell people about the Lord. My parents were diligent to have us memorize the Word.[172] We would have daily devotions[173] and would write Bible verses down and recite them as a family." Also, young Paul was inspired to think that all mountains in life are surmountable. He affirms: "My mom did not have the word *can't* in her vocabulary." That strong character was an extension of her mother. Helen Wagner-Gautschi's father died when she was young, and Helen's mother raised her and her three siblings during the Great Depression on a farm near Lake Michigan.

Paul spent his formative years in the Highland Park neighborhood, a suburb of Los Angeles, California. "I grew up before TV. Back then, kids and grownups went from house to house in the evenings—playing board games or just talking with each other. Everybody knew everyone in the community, and there was a sense of togetherness. But when people started getting TVs, we'd stop by, and they couldn't come out to the porch because a TV show was coming on that they wanted to watch. TV ruined our neighborhood. My parents didn't get a TV. In little time, there were no neighbors to go and visit with on their porch."

Paul's introduction to gardening came early. "My mom and my grandmother were avid gardeners," he recalls and credits the garden-fresh food they ate for their never being sick or missing a day of school. Though he learned a lot in the Gautschi garden, he attended regular classes as well. Paul recounts: "I went to public school there [Highland Park] and did well grade-wise. I would get high grades and good marks for participation but tended to get marked for 'unsatisfactory cooperation.' My dad made it a point to encourage me to be a thinker, to question everything, and pursue truth." It may have made his dad proud, but it did not please Paul's teachers when he challenged the veracity of their statements or questioned their sources while documenting his own from the local library.

GOOD MORNING, VIETNAM

Paul graduated from Franklin High School in June of 1967 and was drafted in the United States Army in October of 1968. He served in the 101st Airborne as an infantryman on the ground. He

---

172 The Holy Bible.
173 A family time of reading the Bible. Some families also sing and pray for others.

recalls: "I was a kid [eighteen years old], and my parents were patriotic, and I felt I was doing my government a service. Once there [in Vietnam], I realized I was lied to. I watched incredible, wonderful people get killed."

A certain Jewish private was inducted the same day as Paul. Though they were of somewhat different faiths, they became buddies. His buddy's parents were faithful Jews and blessed their son on every Sabbath[174] as he was growing up. "You could see the life and potential of this young man, who received a spoken blessing from his dad fifty-two times a year." Paul continues, "One day, I put him in a body bag and placed him in a helicopter. I had seen other men killed and maimed, but he and I went all the way back to induction at Fort Ord. It totally impacted me . . . it was totally unjust and not right. We are putting body bags on airplanes to go home, and I am getting angry, thinking, 'This is not right. We are fighting a war with no intent to win.'" Paul returned to California in 1970.

"What was [strange] about that war was that when we came home, we were totally rejected," Paul painfully recalls. I need to point out to younger readers that in the late 1960s and early 1970s, when returning Vietnam soldiers (in uniform) arrived at airports in many U.S. cities, they were greeted by people staring at them with indignation, some verbal booing, and even chants or posters that (wrongly) declared they were baby-killers. Paul's reflection of that time speaks for countless Vietnam vets: "No other society rejects their warriors. I was told to go. It wasn't my choice." Can you imagine risking your life for your country in a dangerous foreign land, with death and disease all around you, and then being made to feel un-American when you came home?

Purple Haze

Paul continues: "I got bitter, and bitterness is not good. As human beings tend to do, it is not a good thing, but when you see an error, in trying to find the balance, you flip over to the other side because the error is so bad you just go all the way to the other extreme. I came to the place in my mind that I was lied to by my government. I

---

174 Usually the seventh day of the week, Saturday.

also thought I was lied to about God, so I threw it all out. I began to try out psychedelic drugs. I took LSD,[175] mescaline, and [daily used] marijuana. With the use of those drugs, I destroyed my memory. Psychedelic drugs will take out your brain. I lost everything I learned in school. I was a basket case.

"Do you know what was amazing? I could not clear my mind of the scriptures I learned as a child! I came back to God out of sheer exhaustion. I had these philosophies in my mind that there is no god but me; then scripture would come in and just destroy the whole thing. I just could not keep up. I could not get away from it. So, I said, 'God, I am going to go after You with everything I've got!' All my friends were smoking pot, talking about Eastern religions and all this stuff they are doing. I mention Jesus and everybody gets uptight. I said, 'I am going to find out why.' You see a reaction from people when you mention that name. *There is power in that name and I am going to find out why.* I could not avoid what I was seeing."

Paul remembers how "God had come to me and convicted me about smoking pot. I told Him, 'There is no way I can get free from this; I love it too much. *You* will have to take it away from me.' Because I offered it to Him, He totally took away the pleasurable effect—so I stopped doing it." By then, the LSD use was casual, but smoking pot was his lifestyle. So, when Paul quit smoking pot, he quit all drugs. "*When you have those kinds of encounters with God, you're changed,*" Paul declares. That is how he got off the "doing drugs" grid.

Paul adds: "Because my parents had the Word planted in my heart (it says, 'Train up a child in the way he should go and when he is old he will not depart from it').[176] I had that Word, and God used it to bring me back. I am so thankful. I went after God with everything I had, and I have been there since. I love God! He is so faithful."

But what about his bitterness? Paul relates his Vietnam anger and indignation by saying, "I sensed that the only way to get free (the Holy Spirit helped me) is to forgive. I forgave the US government who put me through that. You overcome evil with good, and forgiveness is good."[177]

---

175 Lysergic acid diethylamide, or "acid" for short; a hallucinogenic.
176 Proverbs 22:6.
177 "Be not overcome with evil but overcome evil with good." Romans 12:21.

College Daze

In his zeal to "follow God with all he had," Paul enrolled at Prairie College[178] in Alberta, Canada in 1971. He showed up with his long hair and some attitude and still lacked normal memory. Losing memory has a major impact on a person's life. It is one of those things that most folks take for granted until they no longer have it. Memory loss leaves you feeling an emptiness that comes from not being able to find years of life's moments and experiences that were so faithfully stored in your mental vault.

Paul's long-term memory was wiped out, but short-term memory (like, what day is it?) was functional. Yet he had just enrolled in a Bible college! He says that came about because "my aunt and uncle gave me the book *Expendable!*" This story by **W. Philip Keller** was about **L. E. Maxwell** and the founding of Prairie Bible Institute (now Prairie College).[179] They encouraged Paul to apply at Prairie, but the prospect of going to a Bible school was so daunting to him that he says he "sent in an application that was so obvious that I didn't want to go there." Nonetheless, he was accepted.

In his evangelism class, the students had to memorize many Bible verses each week. The teacher was **Paul Maxwell**, the son of Prairie's founder. As a freshman, Paul reacted to Maxwell's inviolable rule of students memorizing his notes and giving them back verbatim on a test. This reaction was fueled by a bit of defiance, coupled with the frustration of his memory loss. To expect that of him seemed insensitive at best and cruel at worst. God used the situation to refine Paul with a spiritual challenge: "If you cannot obey one you can see, then how can you obey Someone you can't see?"[180]

This challenge was a turning point with Paul and an early lesson in God's amazing amalgamation of mercy and truth. Paul reflects: "I repented [turned my attitude around] and prayed, then agreed with God, and committed to my original purpose; to follow Him.

---

178 https://prairie.edu/.
179 Prairie Press, 1966.
180 Similar to 1 John 4:20: "If a man say, I love God, and hateth his brother, he is a liar: for he that loveth not his brother whom he hath seen, how can he love God whom he hath not seen?"

Afterwards, God gave me my memory back as I memorized His Word. It was gradual, but obvious. The Word will renew your mind."[181]

You may be asking, "How can this be? No meds? No psychiatric treatments?" It's simple: God promises to bless those who meditate on His Word.[182] Meditation in America has become more and more popular, but it rarely involves meditating on the right things. They may sound like good things, but they fall ingloriously short of the Holy Bible, and you will not get the blessing God has committed to give. God-less meditation acts like a form of idolatry.

When the Going Gets Tough . . .

Paul is a metabolically healthy seventy-one-year-old (2020). That fact is validated by his blood tests, overall strength, and vigor. Yet, for some time now, he has a physical limitation with his hip and legs. Some Vietnam veterans with exposure to Agent Orange[183] have had similar challenges with mobility. I don't know the details of Paul's limitation, other than it is inoperable nerve damage, but I do know that he is expecting the Lord to give him a victory over it someday and many pray that He shall.

Paul wills himself to be very active and industrious. The only point in bringing up Paul's physical challenge is that the blessing of his low-maintenance garden lets us know that God understands people need to grow food His way (naturally, with less effort, less stress, less cost), whether they are healthy, have specific physical damage, or are just slowing down as they get older.

Paul is definitely off the woe-is-me grid. His physical difficulty seems to propel him onward and upward. His life is characterized by hope and joy, not by regret and defeat. Paul is leaving an awesome living legacy for his wife and children; but through this book, the *Back to Eden* documentary, various guest-filmed YouTube videos, and his garden tours, he is leaving it for us as well.

---

181 Romans 12:2: "And be not conformed to this world: but be ye transformed by the renewing of your mind, that ye may prove what is that good, and acceptable, and perfect, will of God." And Hebrews 10:16: "This is the covenant that I will make with them after those days, saith the Lord, I will put my laws into their hearts, and in their minds will I write them;"
182 Psalms 1:1-3, Joshua 1:8.
183 An extreme defoliant used by the US Army in the jungles of Vietnam.

A Family Man with a Family Plan

No one's biography would be complete without sharing about the spouse he or she married, the children they brought to this world, and how things went along the way. Paul's story requires no less. After his service in Vietnam, he met **Carol Tuney** because, as Paul explains, "Carol's brother and my younger brother were good friends. When I got back from Vietnam, her brother asked her if she would go out with me. She did, but it did not go too well, so things were pretty much over before they began."

Paul continues: "I went to Prairie Bible, then to Wisconsin's Camp Forest Springs[184] as a counselor. [Carol and I] had a mutual friend named **Duane Dill**. One day, Carol asked Duane, 'What ever happened to Paul?'" He told her about Paul going to a Bible college and that he was now at a Christian camp in Wisconsin. Later, Carol started writing Paul at the camp, and he responded. The two shared the awesome experiences in Christ they had had since that first (and seemingly last) date. Paul gleams: "I started pursuing Carol because I was very attracted to her. I was very tenacious, and eventually won her over." They were married at his parents' beautifully landscaped backyard in Los Angeles.

Paul and Carol raised five daughters and two sons. Their practice was to spend time with the babies before they named them, and each

---

184 https://forestsprings.us/.

one's character guided them accordingly. In birth order, their names are **Rebekka, Terah, Aaron, Lael, Devorah, Isaac,** and **Havilah**. Knowing they aren't Jewish, I asked why the names are Hebrew in origin. Paul explained: "We have an affinity to the Hebrew culture, which seems to be a very special thing to God."

HOME'S COOL

The Gautschis chose to raise their children in a homeschooling environment. I asked Paul about that, and he said, "We were starting to see the control of the school systems over each student, and we wanted to better their learning environment. I love home education in the Bible: You put things on the wall [scripture, maps, the alphabet, timelines, etc.] and then talk about it. When you start relating God's word to life, it becomes a lifestyle. *God's word is the last word.* Heaven and earth will pass away, but His word will never pass away."[185]

The curriculum they used[186] began with scripture [Matthew 5] and added knowledge through it, as opposed to starting with academics and sprinkling Bible verses in secondarily. They learned about medicine, history, language, math, and science as brought out from the Owner's Manual. They wisely took the liberty to pick the meat of the curriculum meaningful for their family and leave the bones. That is, they did not allow the curriculum to become a yoke to be slavishly followed. It is one of the advantages home instruction has over government, private, and charter schools.

Paul and Carol believe that everyone is gifted in one or more areas. The key is to discover and apply those gifts in young people, and their home education environment allowed their kids to discover personal gifts on their own. Once the gift, or bent, is known (music, art, sewing, animals, mechanics, serving, problem-solving/engineering, etc.), then studying a subject through that looking glass becomes more delight-directed.

---

185 Luke 21:33.
186 Advanced Training Institute. See https://atii.org/about/.

Carol Cares

Carol (or Mom) is a world-renowned midwife. The births of her first two babies were stressful, horrible experiences. After the second, she exclaimed, "I'm not coming back to a hospital ever again!" Later, she was featured on the **Sally Jesse Raphael** show in the 1970s to share those experiences. Beginning with the third baby (Aaron), they used the personal services of a midwife named **Joan Dolan**. At the birth, Paul was with Carol and recalls: "I was there; it changed my life. The midwife was so relaxed. When you see a professional, they make it look easy. I caught the baby, we washed him in the sink, and he smiled."

Carol was later mentored in midwifery by Ms. Dolan and became a proficient apprentice. She also worked with a popular California doctor, **Nial Ettenhausen**. It is Carol's passion to spare other women the pain and humiliation she first experienced by OB/GYNs of both genders. For forty-two years, she has loved, counseled, and prayed over hundreds of couples, having delivered over one thousand babies. Carol is a CPM, LM[187] and works alongside clients[188] to prepare their whole spirit, soul, and body for the birthing experience. That includes eating foods that boost their bodies, so she often loads them up with items from Paul's orchard and garden.

Paul tells of Carol's early experience in midwifery. One day she was driving to a birth event and was asking God, "I need an assistant that knows as much as I do because this is too much responsibility for me by myself." She arrived at the home to deliver the baby. The birth had complications because the baby's shoulder was lodged in the birth canal. It's called shoulder dystocia. Eventually, Carol had to incise the mother to accommodate the shoulder and allow the baby to get through. The baby was born, and Carol stabilized the little boy. She went back to the mother to suture the cut. When she looked to where the incision had been made, it was gone, completely healed— as if there had been no cut at all! On the way home, Carol heard the Holy Spirit say: "I just wanted you to know I was there." Since that amazing God moment, she has approached every birth event with the assurance that the heavenly Father was present with her because

---

187 Certified Professional Midwife, Licensed Midwife.
188 She doesn't call them "patients" because she says "they aren't sick."

He's always there. She processed that as Him saying: "Carol, I'm the midwife and *you* are the assistant."

At a subsequent birth, a baby boy came out and was not breathing and started to turn blue."

Panic filled the room, and someone called 911. Carol calmly and confidently picked up the baby and said, "In the name of Jesus, breathe right now!" Immediately, the baby coughed and began breathing (and continues to breathe to this day).

Another time, Carol had a client going through a very long labor. The consulting physician advised Carol to break the water, but Carol clearly sensed that God said, "Do not break the water." The birth continued, and the water broke on its own. The baby was born immediately (which is unusual). The miracle is that the baby had a very short umbilical cord and was staying up high in the womb to save its life. Had Carol broken the water too soon, the baby would have died from lack of oxygen. But when the water broke naturally, he was thrust through the birth canal and born with no cord attached, as it stayed with the momma.

After the birth, the doctor asked Carol, "How did you know not to break the water?"

Carol said, "I just heard 'Don't break the water.'"

Currently, Carol travels all over the world to share her midwifery knowledge and experiences to all kinds of caregivers and audiences. She can be reached via **gentlebirths.net**. My favorite Carol Gautschi quote is: *"Faith is to believe what we do not see, and the reward of this faith is to see what we believe."*

Before pruning.

After pruning.

CHAPTER 12

Tending to Unintended Consequences

Be not deceived, God is not mocked; for whatsoever a man soweth, that he shall reap.

– Galatians 6:7

ONE CANNOT OBSERVE PAUL GAUTSCHI'S LIFE without concluding that what he does day by day has a purpose. Some people call that a purpose-driven life. We'll call it *intentionality*. In a way, it is a play on words, because we all know that Paul is intense (passionate at what he does) and that it has become no small part of his personality (intentionality). He has a laser-focus on his goals.

What was his main goal? To raise healthy food for his family.

Did he arrive at that goal? Yes!

Why? Because he saw the end result in his mind, observed how God grows things in nature, and fashioned his garden and orchard according to the blueprint of covering (working), praying (communing), and trusting (having faith in) God for the intended results.

Far too many of us (myself included) live lives of unintended consequences. We didn't intend to:

- have an overweight body;
- be estranged from a child, sibling, or parent;
- be a carnal or unfruitful believer in Jesus;
- be low on finances;
- grow old;
- have vehicles and tools that break down;
- lose our zest for life and learning; or
- live in a food desert.

The list goes on and on. Unintended consequences hit us in the present and the future. It's when we are forced to face the music and own up to our past actions or inactions.

If we are brutally honest with ourselves, we have to admit we are:

- overweight because of the foods we ate and the sugary beverages we drank;
- not talking with a close relative because of bad things we said to the person in the past or because of good things we didn't get around to saying to him or her when we should have, like "I love you" or because of an offense we took from what the relative said or did and we have not forgiven the person; made a good-faith effort to let him or her know we've let it go, and asked for forgiveness for holding a grudge for so long;
- unfruitful in God's field of harvesting souls for Jesus because we don't put ourselves in the position of engaging the unsaved, or we do engage, but chicken out (not share even our testimony of gaining peace with God or what the Word says about repentance and forgiveness.),
- in a rat-race existence of trying to make ends meet because of missed opportunities, poor investment decisions, unwisely being a surety for someone who later defaulted on a loan, got overwhelmed by medical bills, or lost a judgment in court (when we could have settled for less if we weren't greedy);
- feeling old because we believed the lie that we need to slow down as we get older and deserve an end-game of luxury and going from amusement to amusement (while eating and drinking acidic things that contribute to aging);

- continually having to fix vehicles and tools because we didn't maintain them properly from day one (regular oil changes, checking tire pressure, not leaving tools in the rain, etc.);
- passionless for life by defining ourselves by our circumstances and ignoring the blueprint of love, peace, and prosperity[189] that God has drawn for us, or we stopped growing because we chose to stop learning;
- stuck in a food desert because we never took the time and effort to designate a place to grow healthy food or we made a minimal effort to grow food (man's way) and the results were disheartening, so we gave up.

We can't avoid the law of sowing and reaping.[190] What we are experiencing today is clearly a direct result of our actions (and inactions) in the past. It's a real thought and may be a depressing one. For some, it's a real depressing thought, but we can choose to wallow in our own pity-pool about life, or we press on towards a better day.

Just like in nature, it can be cloudy all day. The sun is still where it should be, but the clouds obscure it to a gray dullness from our earthly perspective. However, as the clouds move away (or burn off), the sun shines on us again. In this illustration, your destiny, or life goal, is the sun. The clouds are the limitations to seeing your goal. As weak humans, after months (maybe even years) of not seeing the sun (the goal), our eyes and our resolve atrophy, and we lose heart for the vision. Living a sun-less life becomes the new normal.

Somehow, we have empowered the clouds to become our intrepid prison guards. Is it a lack of education? *Get educated!* Is it a lack of faith? *Step out in faith!* Do you need to grow nutritious food? *Start planting!* The more we exercise our faith, the stronger our faith gets. Before Moses was told by God to part the Red Sea, he had many opportunities to practice his faith with the same staff in his hand. He

---

189 Beloved, I wish above all things that thou may prosper and be in health, even as thy soul prospers. (3 John 1:2) The Greek word for "prosper" means "get to where you're going." It is not limited to wealth generation.

190 "Be not deceived; God is not mocked: for whatsoever a man soweth, that shall he also reap. For he that soweth to his flesh shall of the flesh reap corruption; but he that soweth to the Spirit shall of the Spirit reap life everlasting. And let us not be weary in well doing: for in due season we shall reap, if we faint not." (Galatians 6:7-9) So, let's "faint not" by being intentional.

saw it become a snake and eat the Egyptian magician's two snakes, and he saw it dipped in the Nile River and all the water turned to blood. These were stepping-stones to a greater faith, so that when it came time to call upon an ocean to part, Moses had firsthand experience with God's power and perceived that as completely doable!

Whatever your cloud is, deal with it on your terms. Fire your prison guards (in the name of Jesus!). If your clouds are feeling old, what can you do (besides read this book) to educate yourself on feeling younger? What physical or mental exercises can you do to build up your body muscles and faith muscles? Are you consumed by a fear of death? That means you lack faith muscles because fear and faith can't co-exist! Remember what the Lord says: "Perfect love casts out fear,"[191]

Take stock of your current life, feel the warmth of your sun (life goal), and move away your clouds—toxic friendships, unforgiveness, fear, regrets, traumatic experiences, pauper and orphan mentalities, believing that you're not worth anything to anybody. Find one or more people to bless and inspire. Invest in their lives and help them achieve *their* goals.

Don't you see? That is what Paul is doing for all of us. He could be content to live by himself and eat amazing food every day and share it only with his immediate family. Life would be good. But he'll tell you it is so fulfilling to reach out to the world and share his testimony (and his food) as he can. The *Back to Eden* documentary and the *Growing Food God's Way* books fit into Paul's intentionality to get his life messages to us.

Put yourself in Paul's place about twelve years ago: You are in your early sixties, don't use a computer, and don't know anything about videography. So how are you going to get your message out? It must have seemed hopeless to Paul. His clouds were very thick at that point. But what happened? Out of the blue, a guy named **Michael Barrett** (from Louisiana) comes along and hires **Dana** and **Sarah** (from California), and the *Back to Eden* video is filmed and produced, prior to going viral in the worldwide web. A few years later, I show up (from Oregon at that time), tour with Paul in August, and get Paul's blessing to write a biography that is self-published two years later. In the meantime, a local

---

191 1 John 4:18 There is no fear in love; but perfect love casteth out fear: because fear because fear hath torment. He that feareth is not made perfect in love..

prepper guy nicknamed **Thatnub** starts videoing Paul's tours and winter pruning times. Now, he has sixty thousand subscribers.

This is how Paul related it in a 2019 tour: "I'm not a woman. Women are amazing beings. They can be on the phone, fixing a meal, taking care of the kids—doing all three at once—with full cognizance and total function. I can't do that! I'm not a multi-tasker. 'So, God if I got to write a book, I can't take care of my garden and orchard. So, could you help me?' Then God sends this guy from Louisiana, who hires these [women] to do this film, and the film's created. Next, God brings David Devine and his wife here on a tour, and then he tells David to write a book for me! It's just been so fun working with God."

Let's recap:

- If you offered Paul one thousand dollars to build himself a website, he wouldn't do it. He doesn't know how; yet he has the benefit of the *Back to Eden* website. It is super popular.
- If you offered him one thousand dollars to write a book, he wouldn't do that either. It's not that he couldn't, but he views the time commitment as detrimental to his main goal. Yet, his biography has gone out to over two hundred US cities and shipped to over a dozen countries. Thus far, many more eBooks than printed books have been acquired around the globe. For a long time, his book was in the Top Five in three Amazon book categories. In the winter of 2020, it had 4.7 out of 5 stars in customer ratings!
- If you offered Paul to finance a YouTube channel, he wouldn't do that as well because he lacks the expertise. Yet the L2Survive YouTube channel has thousands of subscribers who are fed the wisdom Paul has acquired over "years of doing things the wrong way," as he puts it.

Most recently, **Nick Ager** (from Maryland) made a "Growing Back to Eden" Instagram page, and he gets Paul's message out to thousands of subscribers too!

The clouds that kept Paul from making a video, writing a book, and being active on YouTube and Instagram were all blown away by the Lord. Because that happened, his sun (goal to share what he has learned) shines brightly and will get even brighter with more time. I have to give a shout-out to the many talented men and women who blog about what Paul does and produce podcasts or vlogs. They are how this all stays bright and gets brighter. I can't do justice to everyone out there but let me at least share a representative list: **Wranglerstar, Katz Cradul, Justin Rhodes** Great American Farm tour, Dr. Joseph Mercola, **Karina Lovett**, and **Leann Jasper**.

Okay, now it's time to take some needed steps towards intentionality. On a sheet of paper, list the unintended consequences you are now living in. Some will be difficult to change, like "being a widow" or "lack of children or grandchildren nearby" or "finding the right spouse." Others will be more surmountable challenges like "twenty pounds overweight" or "three dress/pant sizes too big" or "no college degree" or "can't speak a second language." Perhaps you wish you had a better job or an advancement where you are. Just get them listed.

Next, imagine what your preferable future would look like. Try to see it in your head. Why? Because that will be *your vision*. When Paul prunes a tree, he looks at it first (the real tree). Then he considers what it should look like when he's done pruning (the desired tree). Once he has the end result in mind, it is just a matter of (systematically) making the right cuts (or choices) to get to the desired results. From time to time, he may have to step back and view the progress and course correct his cutting, but that is how he achieves his goal. On occasion, you step back and look at the big picture (the forest) for direction and then get back close into the trees. The concept of visualizing outcomes also comes to us by one of the world's most famous artists:

> *Every block of stone has a statue inside it, and it is the task of the sculptor to discover it.*
> – Michelangelo

Why can't we apply Paul's pruning process to pruning our lives?

Rather than looking back on your life and getting filled with regret for the lack of intentionality in previous years, focus on the present. Your tree is overgrown in certain areas. Now what can make it better in the future?

For each item on your list, pray and brainstorm a solution. Envision your preferable future in that area of your life, and then GET TO IT! Break that vision into small enough steps that you can accomplish with intentionality and with faith. There's little or no true success without faith. Each success builds enthusiasm for the next challenge.

INTENTIONALITY IN PRAYER

Paul's prayers are intentional as situations arise. Many are short and sweet, like:

"God, talk to me."
"God help me with this."
"God speak to this lady."

Paul is very familiar with this intentional Old Testament prayer in 1 Chronicles 4:10: "And Jabez called on the God of Israel, saying: 'Oh that thou would bless me indeed, and enlarge my coast, and that thine hand might be with me, and that thou would keep me from evil, that it may not grieve me!' And God granted him that which he requested." This man was intentional. He knew what he wanted, and he knew Who had it to give. His mother named him **Jabez** (Hebrew for sorrow). His was not a destiny of success handed to him on a silver platter. In fact, it was so much the opposite that he was desperate for God to rescue him from the curse of his name and take him farther and higher.

The young Hebrew king **Solomon** had a unique God-moment. In a dream, he was praying to God because he was overwhelmed with the task of taking over his father's kingdom. This was his intentional request: "Give therefore thy servant an understanding heart to judge [T]hy people, that I may discern between good and bad: for who is able to judge this [T]hy so great a people?" God was very pleased he didn't ask for what most would request: long life, riches, the removal of his enemies, and so on. Rather, Solomon asked for understanding and to judge with discernment (wisdom beyond his years). The request was a reflection of his heart, and his heart was to serve the people and honor his dad. Solomon intended to not be a failure, but he recognized that failure was inevitable without God's intervention. As a result, God gave him what he requested plus riches, long life, and rest from his enemies.

We must learn to ask God for things, no matter how independent we pride ourselves as being. Like Paul, Jabez, and Solomon, we must learn to be *master askers*. Beyond asking, we must always give God thanks with gratefulness. God is not our personal drive-thru; where we pull up when we want to and order this and this and that. However, in Matthew 7:7-8, Jesus did instruct us to ask: "Ask, and it shall be given you; seek, and ye shall find; knock, and it shall be opened unto you: For every one that asks receiveth; and he that seeketh findeth; and to him that knocketh it shall be opened." There is a caveat in James 4:3: "Ye ask, and receive not, because ye ask amiss, that ye may consume it upon your lusts." At a minimum, that means alcoholics shouldn't pray for booze, greedy people shouldn't pray for money, and prideful people shouldn't pray for fame. Finally, praying without faith is a waste of time. Let's look at James 1:5-7: "If any of you lack wisdom, let him ask of God, that giveth to all men liberally, and upbraideth not; and it shall be given him. But let him ask in faith, nothing wavering. For he that wavers is like a wave of the sea driven with the wind and tossed. For let not that man think that he shall receive any thing of the Lord."

INTENTIONALITY OF EFFORT

Paul will tell you that faith motivates his efforts. To hear from the Lord is motivating and encouraging. The tests come when what we hear does not line up with our feelings, book knowledge, and practicalities. When the Hebrews were being oppressed by their Midianite enemies, they needed a miracle to get out of the lifestyle of oppression and defeat. Enter a man named **Gideon**. A warrior? Absolutely not. A local hero? No. In fact, he was a local zero. A man born from a brave warrior pedigree? Nope. Just a meek farmer, yet God chose him to lead the battle to defeat the Midianites. First, they gathered twenty thousand men, but God said that's too many. Gideon reduced it to ten thousand. Still too many. Finally, God allowed him just three hundred men!

So, you see how God's way is often contrary to man's way. We would have wanted more than twenty thousand, not less than two percent of that many to go into battle. But God did not want the size of Gideon's army get the glory for the victory God was handing them. Indeed, 120,000 Midianites were conquered by those three hundred men of Gideon's army![192]

I love the account where three of King David's warriors overheard him say, "Oh that one would give me drink of the water of the well of Bethlehem."[193] It was not a demand, just a wishful thought. The big problem was that Bethlehem had been overtaken by the enemy Philistines, who had a garrison there. Nevertheless, three of David's men, with extraordinary intention and devotion, risked their lives to enter the enemy camp and secure a cruse of water for their weary leader. Against all odds, they were able to skirt through enemy lines and return to the Israelite camp to present David's favorite water to him. All this was done in secret. He didn't know this was coming.

When David realized they were telling the truth and the water in his hand was from the very well he pined for, David was so overcome by their devotion and willingness to risk their lives for even a whim of his that all he could do was pour out the water to the Lord as an offering to Him. It was enough for the men to please their king. David realized that such a level of devotion should only be given to the King of Kings, so he wisely took their offering to him (a man) and transformed it to an offering to YHWH (the Lord). David multiplied the value of their sacrifice one-hundred-fold by not taking a sip and by pouring it out to God. The utter holiness of giving a drink offering far surpassed the refreshment of drinking that water.

WHAT IF YOUR GARDEN WAS A REFLECTION OF YOUR HEART?

There is an aspect of Paul's garden that doesn't get caught on cameras. If you look, you can see it in his facial expressions and how he engages with the folks there—how he models dignity and caring. It comes from his love for people. It comes from the empathy he has for those who are caught up in the treadmill of trying to grow food with

---

192 Judges 6-8.
193 2 Samuel 23:15 And David longed, and said, Oh that one would give me drink of the water of the well of Bethlehem, which is by the gate!

failed and unnatural methods as he was. He loves to liberate experienced gardeners and inspire brand-new gardeners.

A phenomenon I have noticed since writing the original *Growing Food God's Way* is that some people start out with great results and excitement. Then, something happens in their personal life, and their love for God, family, and their neighbor wanes. Somehow, that seems to have a profound effect on their gardens. They suffer. They lose the power of love that seems to catalyze the woodchips, soil, and seeds. Also, the lack of prayer and straying from relational permaculture can have catastrophic consequences on our gardens. Believe me, I know we think the solution to it all is more woodchips. Well, that can't hurt, but why not start loving more and see what happens to your garden? God is Love. When we show unfeigned love for others, we are honoring God. Trust Paul's life example; God will honor you back and multiply your love in creative ways.

CHAPTER 13

What Became of the Curse?

*Cursed is the ground for thy sake; in sorrow shalt thou
eat of it all the days of thy life.*

– Genesis 3:17

GETTING IT STRAIGHT

T HE CURSE UPON MAN was declared by God to Adam the day after
he broke off his relationship with God.

Excuse me? Wasn't he cursed because he disobeyed, ate from the
tree he was forbidden to? Not exactly. The act of eating was only an
outward expression of an inward desire or motivation.

We know from the Genesis 3 account what Eve's inward motivation was: to be as God, to know good from evil. That desire was all
Satan needed to tap into, and he used it to deceive her into thinking
that disobeying the Creator was somehow a good thing. Guess what?
It was a good thing *for the enemy of their souls* but a really, really bad
thing for Eve and Adam.

Imagine you and a spouse have all the beauty and productivity of the best garden the planet Earth has ever seen (Adam and Eve
did). Now, image you are in harmony with every living creature you
encounter (they were). Also, imagine you have such pure innocence

that it is of no account that you're not clothed (they weren't). Finally, imagine you don't need to be clothed because God has even given you harmony with the environment; it would never cause you to shiver or profusely sweat (they had that too). Now that you're there, in something more beautiful and wonderful than Utopia, isn't it unimaginable that you would crave for anything else? Adam and Eve had everything, yet somehow, that wasn't good enough.

Before we get done with the two humans we all came from, there is another question: Have you ever made a dedicated effort to do something, to give or show something to someone, and that person lets you know it isn't good enough? Maybe it was a gift, an extra effort to clean your room, or to mow the lawn, make a special meal, or draw a picture. You couldn't wait for the person to see it, and your anticipation was so thick you could cut it with a knife. Finally, the big moment came, and the response to it was so poor that the needle on your appreciation meter barely moved. So, in the end, it was your heart that was cut deeply, and it was all too easy to conclude, "If *that* isn't good enough, then *I'm* not good enough." Ouch.

Just know that this is what God must have felt like with Adam and Eve. He moved Heaven and Earth to make heaven and earth, just to have His created man and woman say (in their hearts and by their actions), "It isn't enough for us, God; we want more," or worse, "We have *a right* to more."

Thus, Eve wanted to "be like God," so she ate of the forbidden fruit. Adam, being a man, did not want his wife to have something he didn't have, so he ate too. No one wants to live with a know-it-all, right? Now, they both disobeyed, and the (literal) pain train is on the tracks: She would have pain in childbirth, maybe one to six times in her life, and growing food to live on would be a pain for him every year of his life.

To solve the question of the curse, we need to jump to Genesis 5. It comprises thirty-two verses of A begat B, B begat C and so on. Only hard-core genealogists get excited about texts like this, but there is something significant there to all of us. Even if you consider yourself a Bible scholar, you may have totally missed it. Verses 28 and 29 read: "And Lamech lived a hundred eighty and two years, and begat a son: And he called his name Noah, saying, This same shall comfort us concerning our work and toil of our hands, because of the ground which the LORD hath cursed."

There are three main things to grasp here:

1. The baby was named Noah, and Noah means *rest*.
2. His father speaks a prophetic life-purpose over his son. It isn't to build an ark but is to "comfort us" concerning all the pain and effort they are expending to grow food out of dirt.
3. This statement is plenary evidence that the curse, which began in Genesis 3, is in full force nine generations later.

You can't help but want to inquire of the Lord when you've spent much time with Paul Gautschi. It is such a driving force of his life, and the results of hearing and obeying God are unassailable. So, having spent hours and hours with Paul (in person and watching him in videos), when I read Genesis 5, I had some questions for God:

1. Wasn't Noah's life purpose to build the ark and survive the worldwide flood, so he and his family could repopulate the earth?
2. What would have to happen when this baby boy grew up for him to teach his dad and brothers how to grow food without all the toil, thorns, and thistles?

God gave me a series of spontaneous thoughts that revealed His truths: Yes, his earthly father had a vision of Noah's contribution to the family, and his heavenly Father had a greater (though not conflicting) purpose for him. They were both accomplished.

But how did Noah discover the key to relational permaculture so he could share it with Dad?

God took my attention to the sixth chapter of Genesis. There, we find more clues as to who Noah was and the condition of the world in his day. As a backdrop, God had had enough with the utter depravity and wickedness of man by this time. Verse 6 tells us it "grieved His heart." At this point, God purposed to destroy it all. In verse 8, we find: "But Noah found grace in the eyes of the LORD." Why did he find grace? The latter part of verse 9 explains it: "Noah was a just man and perfect in his generations, and Noah walked with God."

I thanked God for showing me this, but it produced another question to ask Him: "God, what does it mean to walk with You?"

Maybe you know the answer to that already, but I seriously didn't, even though it had become a cliché in Christian circles.

Immediately answering, the Lord directed my attention to more scripture (more truth), specifically, Isaiah 55:8-9:

> For My thoughts are not your thoughts, neither are your ways My ways, saith the LORD. For as the heavens are higher than the earth, so are My ways higher than your ways, and My thoughts than your thoughts.

After reading that, the spontaneous conclusion was, because Noah was just and his heart was right (perfect) before God, Noah's thoughts were more like God's thoughts, and Noah's ways were more like God's ways.

That's it! That's the answer! Because Noah was tracking with God so well that he "walked with God" means God revealed to Noah what He later revealed to Paul: to cover the soil and not to till it!

Beyond that, there is the wise practice of taking (even seemingly mundane) things to God in prayer for His direction and/or blessing. This lifestyle is based on Proverbs 3:5-6: "Trust in the LORD with all thine heart; and lean not unto thine own understanding. In all thy ways acknowledge Him, and He shall direct thy paths."

Remember, all means all, and that's all . . . all means.

So, I believe (but cannot show you chapter and verse) that Noah did apply the covering and that he taught his father and brothers to do the same before his dad died (five years before the flood). The reason I'm so sure goes all the way back to Genesis 2:15: "And the LORD God took the man, and put him into the garden of Eden to dress it and to keep it."

It didn't seem fair to me that God made this awesome garden for Adam and Eve, at the beginning of the Earth, but did not make a garden for Noah and his family after the destruction of the Earth's surface.

"What's with that, God?" I enquired.

The answer was: "I didn't need to make Noah a garden because he already knew how to grow food My way." That hit me, like . . . duh!

Of course! God did not have to show Noah how to make a garden any more than He had to show a duck how to swim.

We zoom past Genesis 7 (the flood) and pick it up in chapter 8. There, the rains have stopped, the ark has run aground (on a mountaintop), and all are still inside the ark. After many days, the waters subside. God instructs Noah that all should disembark. The great door is opened, and the birds, animals, and reptiles (with perhaps, the grandest case of cabin fever) make their way out and head into the world, except one of every "clean" species. Noah offered them as burnt offerings to the Lord. I call it *The Mother of All Worship Services*. What happens next is absolutely critical: The curse is withdrawn! Yes. You read it right. It was voided, not renewed!

Verse 21 says, in part, "And the LORD smelled a sweet savor; and the LORD said in His heart, **I will not again curse the ground any more for man's sake**; for the imagination of man's heart is evil from his youth; neither will I again smite, any more. everything living, as I have done." (Emphasis added.)

Did you get that? When God flooded the earth, He hit the *reset* button, meaning the ground He cursed in Genesis 3 is not the same land Noah and his family set foot on in Genesis 8. Therefore, God had a decision to make: either re-curse the ground or not. Obviously, "I will not again" means He didn't, nor will He in the future.

The implication of this for our day is staggering. If the land curse is off the table, then our prospects for growing food have vastly improved. This revelation led me to another question: "God, if you removed the curse, why do I have an occasional thistle and lots of blackberry briers to deal with on my property?" The answer that came was "Because the land you live on had the cover removed in the past."

This is absolutely true for our properties in Washington, Oregon, and Arizona. Beyond my personal impressions, look at Paul's garden. It is Exhibit A that covering not only prevents thorns and thistles but also alleviates the need to till. It is not under the curse because he is following God's way of growing things; His order and way of doing it in nature.

In the past, we struggled to grow things because we believed we were under the curse. Sure, there are those who fastidiously worked and worked (and still work) at their gardens and have impressive results, but that just served to overwhelm the rest of us. But now that we know *we are no longer under the curse*, we don't have to live as though we are. It's no longer hopeless. We can reorient our ways to God's and receive all the benefits of *not* being under the curse. *That is a game-changer* (if you will wrap your mind around it).

Hopefully, by now, you are asking yourself, "What other curses are detracting from my life that shouldn't be?" If we conclude that God did not renew His Genesis 3 curse upon the ground, then the thought that the ground is cursed today is a lie! Therefore, the problems with our soil are not curse related but, rather, the result of biological cause and effect.

The real question, especially for the believers like Paul, is, "What other lies are sucking the resurrection life out of me that have no right to assault my identity in Christ?" These are some of the lies that the enemy of our souls uses to make feckless Christians:

- The signs and wonders we read of in the Gospels and the book of Acts all ended when the last Apostle died.
- Demons don't exist in the twenty-first century.
- Speaking in tongues was necessary only on the day of Pentecost.
- You must confess your sins to a man and not to God directly.
- Only an ordained minister can baptize a believer.
- Once a sinner, always a sinner.
- People who are heavenly minded are of no earthly good.

From the instant you truly experience salvation, the evil one begins the process of zapping the strength Christ earned for you - away from your new life. Jesus likened it to weeds choking out the life of the wheat. The Apostle Paul was very sensitive to this when God had him write to the brethren in Galatia and Ephesus: "Are ye so foolish? having begun in the Spirit, are ye now made perfect by the flesh?"[194] Here, the Apostle Paul addresses the fact that gentile believers in Galatia were defaulting to Greek pragmatism and not the "hearing of faith." He goes on to say:

---

194 Galatians 3:3.

> This I say therefore, and testify in the Lord, that ye hence-
> forth walk not as other Gentiles walk, in the vanity of
> their mind, Having the understanding darkened, being
> alienated from the life of God through the ignorance that
> is in them, because of the blindness of their heart:[195]

Paul the Apostle confirms that Christians are to look, sound, and act different from worldly people. Our understanding has been enlightened, we have appropriated the life of God because our hearts can now see and discern the things of God as He reveals them to us and to Paul Gautschi in the word of God.

Finally, Genesis 8:22 concludes: "While the earth remaineth, seedtime and harvest, and cold and heat, and summer and winter, and day and night shall not cease." Life is a series of contrasts, and that's what makes life so special. Our own observations in life validate verse 22. We see the seasons and know there is a time to plant and a time to harvest; we experience days and nights, cold and heat.

Referring to pain in birthing, my wife asked, "What about the woman's curse?" I passed that one up to the Lord as well. He informed me that the ground had changed in the cataclysmic flood but that the female parts of Noah's wife and his three daughters-in-law hadn't. Physical changes lead to physical outcomes, but no physical change retains the way it has been (the status quo). Thus, the pain in child-birthing remained, so much so that, many years later, the Hebrew prophet Isaiah refers to it "like as a woman with child, that draweth near the time of her delivery, is in pain, and crieth out in her pangs; so have we been in thy sight, O LORD." (Isaiah 26:17)

Now, one might read Genesis 8:21 and see the very opposite being said, that is, that God didn't need to renew the original curse because He knew that men's hearts hadn't changed: "for the imagina-tion of man's heart is evil from his youth." Thus, we have a matter of interpretation between *God did* and *God didn't*. Looking to the con-text, we see the issue of the ground curse was tied in with the curse of the flood. Concerning the latter, God essentially says, "I'm done doing catastrophic global flooding." Based on that, a reasonable para-phrase of verse 21 would be: "Even though My created humans are

---

195 Ephesians 4:17,18.

still bent on sinning, I will not curse the Earth's soil again, nor will I flood the whole Earth as I did."

An old wealthy man with dementia may live like a pauper if he forgets he has millions of dollars in savings. It is a self-imposed curse that doesn't have to be. That is what it's like when we try to grow things as though we were still under the Genesis curse. It is so unnecessary. Just stop it from now on! Repent of that defeatist attitude and move forward with His blessings and favor instead:

> "Oh, Father God, please forgive me for believing a curse was in place when it truly was not. May You lead me to cast off any curse (in Jesus's name) that would cause me unnecessary hurt and defeat. I desire to walk in Your victory, Jesus. In Your holy name, Amen."

> *You can't go back and change the beginning but you can start where you are and change the ending.*
> – C. S. Lewis

CHAPTER 14

How Did We Get Here?
Where Are We Now?

*Before destruction the heart of man is haughty, and
before honor is humility.*

– Proverbs 18:12

GOD BEGAN REPLENISHING THE EARTH with a man who knew
about God's covering. So, how did we get to where we are now?
How is it that tilling and plowing is the norm when the initial post-
flood means of tending the ground was to keep a cover on it?

First, let's remember that, from Adam on, men broke God's natural coverings in their efforts to grow food. Thus, when God sent
the flood, He re-covered the Earth over a period of eighty-plus days
and nights. That is, when God hit the reset button, He undid all the
uncovering of successive generations to give Noah and his family a
clean slate of covered ground, not pine needles just yet, but likely volcanic ash and tons of debris, sand, and riverbed-like soil because the
whole Earth was a riverbed (under water) for a time.

It can only be inferred that one or more of Noah's sons rebelled
and went back to the over-self-important way. I call it the Cain-sian
method of gardening. Just as economics has a flawed model called

the Keynesian model,[196] the sons of Noah—Shem, Ham and Japeth—must have adopted the flawed practice of Cain. We read about Cain in Genesis 4:2. Eve had two sons (Cain and Abel), and we're told what they grew up to be: Cain was a "tiller of the ground," and Abel was a "keeper of the sheep."

The following verses go on to explain that each man brought a present for God. Cain "brought of the fruit of the ground an offering to the LORD," and Abel "brought of the firstlings of his flock, and of the fat thereof."

God's response? "And the LORD had respect to Abel, and to his offering: but to Cain and to his offering He had not respect."

Now understand that God made Adam and Eve to eat of plants and herbs. That fact causes many (including Paul) to believe that a vegetarian diet is God's way for humans (and animals) to eat. Let's not conclude that this incident of rejecting Cain's produce was a paradigm shift from plant-based eating to eating the flesh (and fat) of animals. No, that was not the issue at all!

The problem was pride and living apart from God's revealed truth. Cain learned to grow food from Adam, his dad. He did not learn it from his heavenly Father. Thus, Cain's offering was all about Cain. It was an arrogant offering, and there is no way God could accept it. It was corrupted by Cain's efforts. Whereas Abel's offering was a proper blend of faith and skill. In essence, it was a sacrifice.

To grasp why God was so severe with Cain, God took me to Exodus 20. It is the first chapter where the Ten Commandments are recorded. However, there is a huge lesson for us to learn at the end of that chapter, beginning with verses 24 and 25. God is instructing His people how to make Him an acceptable altar. Let's see what He says:

> An altar of earth thou shalt make to Me, and shalt sacrifice thereon thy burnt-offerings, and thy peace-offerings, thy sheep, and thy oxen: in all places where I

196 The Keynesian model comes from John Maynard Keynes, a British economist teaching, among other macroeconomic theories, that governments can spend their way out of struggling economies. It is a top-down approach, as opposed to bottom-up practices of supporting small business growth and expansion by reducing tax burdens. The Cain-sian method of gardening is thinking you can use chemicals and supplements (and extra toil) to get nutrient-dense, natural fruits and vegetables. It may seem to work, but there is a better way: bottom-up soil regeneration via the covering.

record My name I will come to thee, and I will bless thee. And if thou wilt make Me an altar of stone, thou shalt not build it of hewn stone: for if thou shalt lift up thy tool upon it, thou hast polluted it.

The Hebrews could make an altar only with natural (made-by-God) stones. The minute they use a tool to chip at just one stone, the whole thing becomes corrupted to God. So we see that, when we put too much of our effort into gardening, we have polluted the results, both in God's eyes and in (often) metabolically compromising the food value. Be honest with yourself, when you sweat and toil over multiple tillings, labor over multiple fertilizations, vigorously pull weeds, remove rocks, and obsessively fret about bug control, and you happen to get a good-looking garden, you can't help but say, "Look what I've done!"

When Paul gets a bounty in his garden or orchard it's always: "Look what God has done." We can't wear red *Make Gardening Great Again* caps and do it Cain's way and expect God's blessing. The fourth chapter of Genesis blows that concept out of the water.

Remember the catalyst for Cain-sian gardening is pride. Write this in your calendar today: GOD HATES PRIDE. God has blessed Paul because he has learned (by a lot of mistakes) to be humble. Take a moment and look at the cover of this book. It is a biography of Paul Gautschi, right? He didn't even want his name on the cover! I had to make an appeal to him by saying, "It can't be a biography if it doesn't have the name of the person on the cover." The book cover was the result of negotiating with Paul, and he finally consented to his name being in small letters that blend in with the blue sky.

Finally, I spoke to a no-till Christian farmer in Illinois years ago. He farms one thousand acres. His friend from Maine had shared the *Back to Eden* video with him and his wife felt the message was for them. When he went with a covering (by leaving the remains of harvesting corn and soybeans), he was able to sell most of his equipment, and he didn't need to spend so much of his time in the fields. Afterwards, having more money, less debt, and more time, he was pleased to see his crop yields stay just as productive over the years since he switched.

As if that isn't enough benefit, the U.S. Soil Conservation Service (now the Natural Resources Conservation Service) pays him to *not* disturb his soil. That alone landed him fifty thousand dollars a year. I was amazed and asked, "Why would any of your neighbors continue farming the old way when they can make $150,000 (on three thousand acres), have zero risk, and still grow a sellable soy crop?" His reply: "Boys love their toys." Seriously? Men would go into insane debt, damage the soil they depend on, and run the risk of crop failure for the joy (and pride) of sitting in the air-conditioned cab of a 400 hp John Deere 8400R tractor they don't need? Wow. Cain would be proud of them.

CHAPTER 15

A Day in the Life

Trust in the LORD, and do good; so shalt thou dwell in the land, and verily thou shalt be fed. Delight thyself also in the LORD; and He shall give thee the desires of thine heart. Commit thy way unto the LORD; trust also in Him; and He shall bring it to pass.
– Proverbs 37:3-5

I WAS CURIOUS TO SEE what a full day looks like for Paul. Thus, my wife and I spent a Thursday night at his place so I could chronicle his life the following day. Although it was after the summer rush of visitors, folks called him basically every day and still asked to stop by, "if it's okay." Every year is different, but his public tours cease from September through May. Beginning the first Sunday in June, he has public tours every Sunday afternoon (2:30 p.m.) through summer harvest (last Sunday in September).

On this day, there were planned visitors from the country of Chile. Carol was out of the country giving midwife lectures.

Friday, October 19, 2012

7 a.m. Awakens.

7:30 a.m. Builds fire. Feeds and waters cats, dog, and chickens. Personal breakfast grazing (three or four plums and one apple).

8:30 a.m. Phone calls and some house chores.

10 a.m.-3 p.m. Host garden tour with Chilean grape grower. (No lunch.)

3 p.m. Restock firewood (located way out by the pasture).

4 p.m. Phone calls (in and out bound) and dinner prep.

6:40 p.m. Dinner (huge salad and baked potatoes for three of us).

8:30 p.m. Dishes and reading.

10:30 p.m. Off to bed.

It is amazing to watch Paul engage with the folks he is showing around. He doesn't carry a water bottle and just doesn't seem to stop for any personal reason. He consistently outlasts the vast majority of the guests, who need a drink, to sit down, to find some shade, or to make a bathroom stop.

Eggs-Ample

On occasion, Paul starts his day with his own breakfast drink consisting of one quart of raw cow milk or almond milk, three raw eggs, one-third cup B-grade organic maple syrup, which is blended to a delicate frothiness. A quart of milk seems like a lot for one person, so when my wife brought home some B-grade maple syrup she found in Arizona, I settled for one raw egg, one tablespoon of maple syrup, and about eight ounces of raw milk. It's pretty tasty, and I didn't feel like **Sylvester Stallone** in *Rocky 1*.[197] Paul insisted I use B-grade maple syrup because, as he puts it, "the A-grade takes too much good stuff out." Each day, Paul usually eats two to three apples (either fresh from the orchard or stored in his cooler). He eats four apples a day on workdays when he goes into town. Also, Paul drinks kombucha every day (that he makes with a starter scoby).

---

197 In the movie, Rocky Balboa is training for the title fight and swallows six raw eggs from a glass for breakfast.

Paul comments on the complexity of the American diet, how "we've been taught to live with food groups and such is way too much, too unnecessary, way too complicated. The whole concept of three meals a day is the living-to-eat [as opposed to *eating to live*] mentality."

DRIVEN TO HEALTHY EATING

One visitor to Paul's garden was a cancer survivor and NASCAR driver named **Jerrod Sessler**. He wrote a book called *5% Chance: Winning the Cancer Race*.[198] His doctors had said Jerrod's prospect of surviving the cancer he had was only five percent, yet he did survive. On page 165 of his book, Sessler says: "Knowing that God made us, and that He made food for us, and that He designed a way for us to be able to exist and enjoy that food with little or no effort on our own, should increase your worship of Him. I know it does for me!"

198 Published in 2008 by ToDoBlue Press. Jerrod had advanced melanoma at age twenty-nine. See www.FivePercentChance.com.

Quality versus Quantity

Getting back to Paul's day, did you mentally add up his food intake? At best, three apples, four plums, no lunch, two baked potatoes for dinner, and as much fresh salad as he desired (my talented wife Phyllis gathered it and delightfully put it together). Nonetheless, you may have concluded he was way below the threshold of proper diet in terms of volume (I know I could reach that conclusion pretty easily). However, my bent has always been *quantity over quality*. His is just the opposite; he doesn't need to eat as much, as long as what he does eat is quality food. That's just it; he could have eaten almost whatever, whenever, but a little quality food goes a long, long way.

It reminds me of the time my family opted to save money by buying a huge white sack of generic dog food for about eight dollars for our golden retriever. The quality of the food was so poor that the dog needed to eat more volume to maintain her energy. Extra eating meant extra waste in backyard piles - and extra work for us! Conversely, when we fed her expensive (quality-blend) dog food, she didn't need to eat as much, left fewer waste piles in the yard, and the piles that were there were not so disgusting.

One day in October 2013, Paul shared his food intake with a visitor:

> Breakfast – one avocado
> During the day – some cilantro and an apple or two
> Dinner – some zucchini

Paul comments: "I'm shocked at how little I eat. Because this stuff is so nutritious, I'm satisfied. I'm totally satisfied; I'm not hungry. It's blowing my mind, but real food works like that; you don't need a lot."

Paul walks the talk: eating *raw, local, fresh, and in season*. Showing others his garden is not strenuous activity to Paul. Rather, it energizes him to testify of the goodness of the Lord.

CHAPTER 16

Ask Paul How to Get Started

Wherefore seeing we also are compassed about with so great a cloud of witnesses, let us lay aside every weight, and the sin which doth so easily beset us, and let us run with patience the race that is set before us.

– Hebrews 12:1

THIS CHAPTER FEATURES COMPILED QUESTIONS from various sources that may address a question you have for Paul. All responses are his; only comments in brackets are mine.

How costly is it to add woodchips to my garden?

"I asked God for them, and He provided. I never needed to buy woodchips; they were delivered to me for free, and many others have gotten them free also or chip their own brush and tree limbs. I used to buy compost, which (in my area) runs from ten dollars to thirty dollars per yard, depending on quality. [Having them] delivered would cost you more." [On February 8 of 2016, I did a Facebook post on getting chips. At the time, I suggested trying Craigslist.org (for your area) and a service called Chipdrop.com.[199] Their 2020 website claims they've arranged for tree services to deliver more than eighty thousand

---

199 https://getchipdrop.com/?ref=chipdropcom.

deliveries of woodchips across the US, UK, and Canada. On a visit to Phoenix, Arizona, I queried the local Craigslist for woodchips. I found a wonderful ad from a tree service in Mesa that not only delivers free woodchips but gives you a ten dollar gift card as well. *Sheesh!*]

How do you get your chickens to lay in winter?

"Having the right breed. I get Red Star chicks from Murray McMurray Hatchery[200] in Iowa. **Martha Stewart** and the **Emperor of Japan** buy their chicks there as well. Also, I do not use lights at night."

Were you to do it over again, would you still plant dwarf apple trees?

"Yes, for a variety of reasons: The apples don't fall far to the ground and it is easier to reach the whole tree for pruning or picking.

"If you plant dwarf root stock, make sure you space them adequately, more than the books say, because the trees that grow in compost will grow better, so allow at least fifteen feet between them and eighteen to twenty feet for semi-dwarf trees.

"When you buy to plant, make sure you buy bare root, not container trees. As they come to your supplier in February or so, show up as soon as they get in to buy the best stock." [Paul's trees vary from thirteen to fifteen feet apart.]

Do you use any type of weed killer or insecticide?

200 http://www.mcmurrayhatchery.com.

"No, but it is necessary in my climate to use an organic spray (a fungicide made of lime and Sulphur, which are natural, organic elements) to treat for apple scab; nothing in the garden." [By 2017, God's favor eliminated Paul's need to spray the orchard at all. Apple scab disappeared.]

If you could grow and eat only one thing, what would it be?

"Russian kale. There is not a close second, but apples would be next, followed by cilantro.

"Russian kale is prolific (grows easy and is vigorous). It is biennial, meaning it bears through the winter and into the next spring. [Paul likes its special cleansing properties and explains.] After a free radical penetrates the cell walls, the anti-oxidants can't reach it, but the phytochemicals in kale go in and eat the free radicals within the cell."

[Paul told some visitors one day: "Just to give you the power of this food, I had two people come here who were unable to go to sleep at night without pain medication because of the incredible pain. All they had were several leaves of kale, went back that night, took no pain medication, and went to sleep. It is powerful."]

"Also, because my chickens are more connected to nature, I observed that when I bring excess lettuce and kale into the chicken yard for feed, the chickens scratch the lettuce aside and always eat the kale first. They know which has the maximum food value.

"I had a nine-year-old boy come here last Sunday [October 14, 2012] who was totally allergic to apples. When he eats an apple [from the store], he just totally swells up in big lumps and turns red. He is telling me this. So I just share with him, 'Nothing is wrong with your body; it is telling you the stuff you are eating is poison. You can be thankful for that. You are welcome to eat these apples. It will be okay.' It was so cool. He walks over to these beautiful red apples, and you watch his eyes, and he was so . . . can I trust it? . . . and he went for it and he ate one. There were sixty people here, and this kid, he starts yelling, 'I'm not reacting! I just had an apple. I'm allergic to apples, and I'm not reacting!' And I said, 'Whoa, God.' I love it. It was so special how it impacted his spirit. I looked at him and said, 'You are fearfully and wonderfully made.[201] There is nothing wrong with your body. Your body is telling you the [store-bought] apple you eat is poisonous. It is good that your body could sense that. He was so blessed. He loved [my] apples.

"Then the next week, a woman comes from New York. Same thing: 'I'm allergic to apples. It's the chemicals; if you will look on his website (Dr. Mercola in 2012), the first on the list of things you should not eat were apples. They wax them and seal in all the toxic chemicals.' She tried one of my apples; no reaction. So she ate another one (just to be sure) and was still fine. She left with an armload of apples to take back to New York.

---

201 From Psalms 139:14.

"Cilantro is the best source of natural vitamin C there is.[202] Also, it is a natural chelator.[203] It can also be [eaten] in the winter.

"One Sunday, a man from Bainbridge Island [Washington] skipped the last day of a Permaculture Convergence in the area and came here. He ate one apple, two kale leaves, one celery stalk, and said he was 'content.' He was overweight and claimed he's always hungry but was amazed that a small amount of live food satisfied him. [Looking over at Paul's pasture and seeing the sheep all lying down], he said, 'I feel as contented as those sheep over there.'" [Paul said God reminded him of the 23rd psalm: "He maketh me to lie down in green pastures."]

"Moreover, the man said it had been months since he could breathe through his nose, but after he ate here, he was able to breathe through his nostrils and was marveling at that. . . . Months later [April 2013], he comes back with his wife and tells me that he has been eating good, raw foods since he met me. He had obviously lost weight and was so excited about all these benefits that they were planning to quit their jobs and grow CSA[204] food for a living."

202 You'll find other foods with higher levels of vitamin C, so Paul must be referring to naturally assimilated vitamin C.
203 Pronounced KEY-lay-tor. It gives our bodies the ability to better assimilate minerals via the amino acids, proteins, and polysaccharides in natural foods.
204 Community Supported Agriculture. See https://www.localharvest.org/csa/.

Do all the people in your neighborhood garden the same way?

"No. Some still do it the old way, but the other day, a neighbor brought over a friend of his who has done organic gardening all over the world. This man couldn't believe his eyes when he ate full-sized carrots that I had planted just two months prior [August]. The neighbor was so impressed he said, 'I'll have to bring my wife over next.' I have a neighbor who uses woodchips for his fruit trees, but still tills his garden." [Paul has been there, done that.]

Do you sell any of your fruit or vegetables, or enter them in fairs?

"No."

Most people build up mounds for potatoes, so why does your potato area look flat?

"The problem with mounds is that because they are exposed, they dry out quicker. I don't need to hill my potatoes because the woodchips inter-connect, so when the potato grows, [it] can rise and maintain the cover. The easiest and best way to do potatoes (if you can get seed) is to find the nastiest, grassiest place in the garden; then put the [whole] potato down on all that grass. Put them in the rows [each potato] a foot apart, with the rows three feet apart [from each other], and then bury the whole thing with ten inches of woodchips, even a foot if you have it. All the grass dies, and next spring, you have the most amazing potatoes.

"With eight or more inches [of covering] you suffocate the grass and weeds. It is only at the four-inch level that the grass will come through. So you see, I never did newspaper because I did eight inches or more. When I started out, I didn't know any better; I was putting it down en masse. I was covering it ten inches deep and I had great results."

[By 2017, Paul began planting potatoes under his trees.] "I plant potatoes in the root ball of my apple trees, and I'm experiencing abundance there. Never cut your seed potatoes. Each eye grows a shoot, and that shoot needs to feed on the potato around it. If you cut your potatoes, you're starving your shoots of needed food and guaranteeing a smaller harvest. *Plant the whole potato* because the more eyes, the more shoots, and more potatoes will grow for you. When you harvest, leave the best potato in the ground for your next crop. God says, 'If you give Me the first fruits,[205] I will bless you with abundance.'"

---

205 Numbers 18:13.

What feedback or observations have you gotten from folks who watched *Back to Eden*?

"People watch the film, men and women alike. Because it's so related to God and His Word; they are connecting with their spirit. That's where it's all coming from, the spirit, and when they watch it, they sit there and say, 'Well of course, that makes sense; that's simple.' Then because the women are cool (they are more spirit-oriented) and don't have the hang-ups, they say, 'Of course!' The men go home, they start looking at their hard dirt, and they are right back to 'well you have to till it; you have to break it up.'

"See, they immediately go back to the mind telling them to till it more and deeper. But the women say, 'Didn't you see the movie? Just put a covering on it,' because they got it and they are not going [back] to the mind. I watch this all the time. Finally, I get to the guy and say, 'Why don't you just be an honest scientist? You know how scientists, when they come across a new thing, they will do what they have always done—that's the standard—[and then] they will compare it to the new thing; they do a comparison. Do your tilling, but take a small section and let your wife cover it with woodchips and do her thing there. Then you compare how much time you are spending over here and how much time [she is spending] there: water, weeds, all the stuff. Just keep records.'

"They will call me back in a year and say, 'I can't believe my wife's garden is so great. I mean she has no weeds; everything is growing great; she's not watering, I can't believe the effect. It's overwhelming. I get it.' I'm saying, 'Well, it works!'"

[There are exceptions to the norm of women trying the covering and men sticking with the status quo, like our friends in central Washington. They are the ones who sent us the *Back to Eden* link. When they first watched it, the husband was gung-ho about covering all three of their garden areas. However, the wife was the one who had put the most effort into the plots, and the thought of dumping inches of woodchips over it all seemed like sacrilege. So they compromised and only dressed one of the three gardens with a covering. At the end of the season, she observed how superior the produce was from the woodchip garden and really regretted that the other two plots weren't covered as well.]

How do you bring dry, poorer soils around?

"If you start growing things, you'll create an environment for things to grow in. Start planting things with a cover. Israel was a beautiful land originally, a land flowing with milk and honey. After the Israelites were kicked out and they lost it, the Crusaders came in and burned down everything and made a desert out of it. It became a desert because there is nothing growing there. Today, as it says in the Bible, it's thriving with all this stuff growing, some of the best in the world. This is what I love about God. As soon as you repent and restore the natural order, nature and everything comes in and cooperates and blesses it."

Won't I need to regularly water because I live in a warmer climate?

"*Weather is secondary to soil condition.* My question is 'How does oxygen get to the tilled ground?' You see it compacts so hard there is no air space in it, where my garden is full of air. I will get people here, point to the surface of my garden, and say, 'Now I want you to compact this,' and they will be pounding it, and it is bouncing. They bounce up and down, but the ground will not compact. You can drive a truck on this, and it will not compact, whereas with dirt, when you pound, it compacts. And you see, compacted ground has no air, and so this is why I say to people who always water their garden, 'What a waste. That water's not going to your plants because there are no roots. The roots can't spread out because the ground is so compacted. So you are wasting your time watering plants.'"

How about places where it freezes a lot?

"Track with me; everything in people's farms when it freezes gets killed. And yet in nature, where no one's taken the cover off, nothing [in ground] is ever lost in the winter. Are you getting it? The cover acts as an insulator. In my garden, the beautiful carrots and beets and rutabagas will be there all winter, no matter how cold the ground gets, even when it freezes hard, because it's insulated. It's not killed. You know who thought this up? God is awesome!"

Who are your human heroes, past and present?

"Past would be a former pastor of ours named **Arthur Corey**, a really special man here in Joyce, Washington. As a young man, he smoked a pack of cigarettes a day. Do you know how he got over his cigarette habit? The Holy Spirit told him to get a Bible the size of a cigarette pack and put it in his front pocket. Every time he went for a cigarette, he got into the Word. That man had the Word so memorized to break that habit of cigarettes; he was an amazing guy. He raised ten children; his life was a whole life of miracles. At ninety-two, he was still preaching. He was humble, simple, not flamboyant, yet had a walk with God that was so amazing, so dynamic and real. He had such simple faith. He was a major hero. I was really inspired and blessed by his life.

"He was our pastor. Everyone in his church was in ministry, everyone. We are here to be salt and light and he [Pastor Corey] demonstrated that to his people. He was a shepherd and an example. Whole groups of motorcycle people could come through and feel comfortable because he was so real and so honest. When they wanted truth, they could go to him and not be judged. He walked out his faith. It was not just something he spoke about on Sunday; it was a lifestyle. It was powerful, and you were drawn to that because it works. It was evident: this is how we are supposed to live.

"It's a sad thing so many people in the ministry don't live it. [For them,] it is a profession and not a lifestyle, not practicing what they are preaching, not living it out. Most of his children are missionaries.

Several still live down there on his property in Joyce, and most are still in ministry.[206]

"Present would be **Dr. Runar Johnson**, pictured above, our dentist in the Sequim area. He remembers everything he ever read or heard. He is knowledgeable, a genius with an incredible heart, kind, generous, and thoughtful. He goes well beyond the norm for his patients when they are in a bind. For decades, he was a good dentist, but was professionally limited to treating mouths when there were other things that he desired to treat patients for. At age seventy-two, he went back to school to earn his ND [naturopathic doctorate] degree and is now licensed to treat the whole body and person."

The Bible says to not plant and harvest once every seven years. Do you practice that?

"Everything in Scripture relates to a fallen culture. I asked God about that by saying, 'I see in the Word You have the Israelites, every seven years, put the land into rest. Now, how do I put my trees to

---

206 A recent book about Arthur's wife Margaret is called Pots, Pans and Peace, by their daughter Eleanor Corey. https://www.amazon.com/dp/B085H719LT/ref=dp-kindle-redirect?_encoding=UTF8&btkr=1.

rest?' It was so cool. He says, 'Paul, that was written for a people who were under the effect of the curse, who were tilling and cultivating. And because their ground was stressed, they needed to let it rest every seven years. I [God] never let anything in nature rest every seven years; it's in a constant state of rest, and so is your garden. It's not under stress; it's always resting. How do you make it rest any more than it's resting? It's only written for those who are under the curse.'

"People give me that Scripture,: 'Break up that fallow ground,'[207] and I always ask, 'How did it get fallow?' Someone [in rebellion or foolishness] took the cover off, and it got fallow. You realize that this is what people did, so He's relating to a fallen culture with cultivated ground, and they're so disconnected in the spirit that He has to come down to their level."

Jesus told the parable of the sower that speaks of three types of soil: shallow, thorny, and good. Could you elaborate?

"[Seed in] shallow came up quickly because it couldn't have roots because it hit hardpan [roadside]. Then it fell on the thorny stuff, which choked it out. Then it fell on good ground, and it produced really well. Even with that good ground, there were levels: thirty, sixty, a hundred-fold; different degrees [of success], but it's all there. This was talking to a culture that had hardpan. They had weeds because they cultivated because of the curse [thistles and thorns would compete with you[208]]. And then there were those that had done their work and had good ground that they're working (you know); they maintained it, and there were levels of production.

"That's what I'm seeing here. When I first came, I had a garden, and when I tilled it was good, but it was not like *this*. When you're connecting with God, it's like there's compounding interest levels. It gets better every year, and you do no work. It's so cool."

How can I speed up the benefits of a covering?

"By adding blood meal [on the soil around the planted seeds]. I'm seeing the heart of God. He's so quick to restore and give back what was originally ours. You wouldn't believe the calls I get from folks in their first year. God is redemptive, forgiving. Seek Him. Go and look at what

---

207 Hosea 10:12.
208 Genesis 3:18.

He has created. Go to nature and see what works. Nature is giving us revelation, and it is parallel with Scripture because God is the Author of both. You are trying to connect with the Spirit. It is a walk of faith. If you cannot get out of the mind and into the heart, you won't get it. The Word says, 'The natural man cannot receive the things of God.'"[209] Blood meal infuses critical minerals quicker than any soil supplement I know.

Do you recommend dethatching aggressive grasses before placing the newspaper, compost, and woodchips on top?

"Over in my garden in Sequim, I had quack grass, and quack grass is a nightmare. If you leave one little piece in the ground, it spreads like crazy. Well the place in Sequim, the whole pasture was quack grass, so I thought I would be fighting this stuff forever. But I put the woodchips a foot deep (we're talking twelve inches), and I was in shock. Nothing came through. A foot deep suffocated all that quack grass, and it totally died.

"You see, the whole idea is that whatever you have growing, if you take oxygen away from it, it dies. Anything deprived of oxygen dies. It's the bottom line in all of life. So if you cut out oxygen, whatever plant material you have there will die. You just have to find a way to cut it off. You have to use newspaper under the four-plus inches [of covering] so when it gets wet it lies tight to the ground and suffocates [what's underneath], takes away all the oxygen so [weeds and grass] dies."

Why do we have weeds?

"Weeds on the ground are like scabs on our skin. When skin is broken, your body is vulnerable. When man takes the cover off the soil, it is vulnerable to wind and erosion, so the weeds cover it to protect it from washing and blowing away. All creation groans and travails.[210] *Everything in nature, except man, is in total connection with God.* Weeds are organic plants I can feed my chickens before the garden has produced an excess of food plants to feed them, so weeds are a blessing!"

---

209 1 Corinthians 2:14: "But the natural man receiveth not the things of the Spirit of God: for they are foolishness unto him: neither can he know them, because they are spiritually discerned."
210 Romans 8:22.

Have there been any relevant experiences that resulted from eating your live food?

"A woman came [to stay here] from Minnesota with two little boys; one was two and one was four. The four-year-old's body[211] was covered with eczema because the body tries to get rid of toxins through your skin. My blueberries were at eye level, and this kid was on them. His mom said, 'I can't keep him out of your blueberries.' I said, 'Leave them alone; they are okay.' I'm thinking their bodies must need this nutrition.

"She said, 'I feed my kids organic; they eat well.' I said, 'Well it can't hurt them.' The next day she comes and says, 'I've gotta take my kids to the bathroom all day long, and now they are in your carrots!' 'Well it's not going to hurt them; leave them alone.' They were here for three days.

"On the fourth morning, she comes running into the house and says, 'Paul, Noah's skin is totally clear!' In three days! [After going home,] she was smart, and she went out and borrowed a refractometer so she could test the food in the organic store that she was buying [in Minnesota] and was shocked. The refractometer shows the nutritional value of food.[212]

"She's testing this organic stuff, and this thing is hardly moving. She was thinking, 'Is this thing working?' I had given her some garlic to take home, and she tests my garlic, and it pins right to the top! Even the organic farmers are not putting minerals back. They are only putting nitrogen, phosphorous, and potassium (N-P-K) but not minerals. In woodchips, all the minerals needed are present. God is all about healing us and showing forth His love and power."

In the winter, do you grow things like tomatoes in a greenhouse?

"I grow tomatoes in the summer. Can I tell you about tomatoes? They are a nightshade,[213] and you should NOT eat them all year long. You know why they come in the summertime? They have a phytochemical in them that protects your skin from exposure to hot sun. Many people are too young to know this, but when I was growing up, no one had skin cancer. It was totally nonexistent because when I

---

211 Legs, for the most part, according to the mother I interviewed.
212 Specifically, the degrees Brix, which indicates sugar content.
213 A plant from the Solanaceae family, which includes potatoes, eggplant, and most peppers.

was growing up [in a desert], everyone ate tomatoes that were grown outside in full sun.

"Today all tomatoes in the store are grown in greenhouses, and skin cancer is rampant. Let me tell you why: They did tests on tomatoes that were grown in full sun. If you look at tomatoes grown in the sun, the skin is no thicker than yours. It takes 100 degrees[214] temperature, just blazing on it all day long, and it never blisters. The skin on it is totally thin and beautiful.

"There is a phytochemical that keeps that skin from blistering. Sun-ripened tomatoes were tested and found to have three hundred phytochemicals. Testing the heirloom tomatoes grown in a greenhouse, they could only find fifty phytochemicals. Two hundred fifty were lost with light going through glass because the glass interrupted photosynthesis.

"You notice when tomatoes get ripe? It is in August[215] when the sun is the hottest. Do you think that is an accident? Do you think God missed that? That's when you need maximum protection. You know He is just so awesome! Just check with Him and see what He's like. He's amazing.

"So far as greenhouse tomatoes go, your taste buds tell you they are worthless; they are tasteless and mushy. In paying attention to your senses, they are saying, 'This is not real.' We [tolerate] it because we are trained to. This is what everybody does.

"People talk about going to the store and say we [raw-food and live-food eaters] are living such a boring life. [The fact of the matter is] you get the same stuff, put it in your refrigerator, and eat this same boring stuff all year long. I am living at a quality of life that billionaires don't even approach. I will explain why: In ten minutes, after fruits and vegetables have been picked, they [can] lose up to 80 percent of their metabolic properties. In ten minutes! Now imagine the food value you are getting from the stuff coming from South America, from China, and from Mexico. Come on folks!

"When you pull a carrot out of the ground [in my garden], the whole air will fill with the aroma. Everyone will smell it. You go to the store and buy a carrot, there's no odor, so something is not there

---

214 100° F equal to 37.8° Celsius.
215 Not true in the Southern Hemisphere, but tomatoes still ripen in the hottest month in your part of the globe.

anymore. Something's not present, and this is why God put man in the garden up front. It was not an experiment. He did not issue a stove and refrigerator. Did you think about that? It is not like He couldn't or didn't know. He's omniscient, omnipotent; He can do anything. It's just that we were never designed to take healthy live food and put it in the refrigerator and let it die and then cook it and kill the [remaining] enzymes. We don't get it."

What has God shown you to do about moles, shrews, and field mice (voles)?
"I have cats; they are so efficient. The secret is to not overfeed them. Their hunger motivates their hunting skills. I haven't had to set traps for a long time." [Paul prepares one bowl of cat food for their three cats and one big bowl for the dog, as opposed to continual feeders that, while convenient, would allow them to overfeed.]

I heard you shot a crow to keep crows out of your orchard. What if a bald eagle was a threat to your chickens?
"I actually had an eagle that had killed several of my chickens. I asked God about it, and He indicated I should put [my dog at the time] Tova in with the chickens. I said, "God, Tova is a bird dog by species. She could do much more damage to my chickens than that bird of prey.' The Spirit took me to Isaiah 55: 8 and 9: 'For my thoughts are not your thoughts, neither are your ways my ways, saith the LORD. For as the heavens are higher than the earth, so are my ways higher than your ways, and my thoughts

than your thoughts.' So I yielded to this truth, and it was so comical when it came time to let Tova into the chicken yard. There I was, telling her not to be mean to the chickens, but to protect them.

"I took her in, the chickens were immediately on edge, but she went over to the far corner of the yard to [lie] down. She stayed there the entire day. Then the eagle flew in and perched on a tree limb near at the edge of the yard. Tova saw it and ran to the middle of the yard and started barking. The eagle fixed its eyes on Tova for a long time. Finally, it gave up the stand-off and flew away, and it never returned."

Do you process and eat your chickens after their egg production goes down?

"No. They die a natural death, and I bury them."

If my soil is a bit acidic, should I put lime down?

"When I came to this place [Craig Road], it was sterile. Nothing grew, and now I put woodchips. Everybody said it was acid-forming. A PhD biologist came out here and tested three times in three different places, and every single one came out 7.0 [pH]. So, my mentality is God is amazing; get out of His way. Put the stuff down there and don't mess with it. *Realizing Who you are dealing with, coming under His authority, and getting out of the way is what it is all about.* He does it perfect."

Do you only plant seeds, or do you use starts?

"I mostly plant seeds but use starts for tomatoes and peppers. My experience with other starts has been that they don't perform as well as what I grow with seeds. Typical greenhouse starts look good to begin with but are too suited to the controlled temperature of the greenhouse and do not handle real outdoor temperatures and other factors. They just seem to linger rather than grow. My seeds come from my own stock, Johnny's Seed Co.[216] and Fedco.[217]

"As to my greenhouse [about 4x5 feet], we tried starting plants all over, on the porch and stuff, and they just don't grow like they do in there. I empty it for the winter and won't have anything there. I never have to water it, but [with traditional] greenhouses you have

---

216 https://www.johnnyseeds.com/.
217 http://www.fedcoseeds.com/.

to water. Mine is completely no maintenance, no fans. With having the open roof, no issues." [In a recent phone call, Paul explained to me that he only uses his greenhouse to grow basil in the ground. The surrounding panes serve both as a means of additional warmth, and as a needed wind break.]

"I told you how I read that article [about tomatoes grown in hothouses]. I did not get it, and God had to blow that thing [greenhouse] over and break four panes of [roof] glass so I would get it because it was what He wanted me to get. I felt that taking out all your nutrition from your food from the lack of photosynthesis is not healthy. And again, God did not create greenhouses! He would have created them in nature if we were supposed to have them, but He didn't. My sense is that everything in nature, all those animals out here are not developing greenhouses. They are fine living where they live with what is available in nature.

"So my sense is that *wherever you live, God is supplying everything you need there.* There is no lack. Everything in nature is living very healthy and well. We are always trying to improve and make things better, thinking like we are smart, and I am not sure that they are better. Again, look at the nutritional quality of store tomatoes with everybody having skin cancer that they never had before when we were not growing in greenhouses.

"In the beginning, God did not have it rain. It was subirrigated underneath, feeding the roots. That was His original idea. The rain came after the Fall. The sub-irrigation was the ultimate, and my pond was the demonstration of it. [Paul points towards his pond.] Look at the size of that seventeen-year-old cherry tree down there. You don't get a cherry tree that size in seventeen years. Because it is subirrigated, the water coming up underneath there feeds that thing. Everything now just thrives amazingly well because of the sub-irrigation. Read Psalms 1.[218] When you go by rivers, the trees by the rivers are the biggest most beautiful around because of that subirrigation. So, that is the ultimate irrigation." [Paul subsequently chopped the tree down, so it is not there to see on a tour of his place.]

"That's what I love about having low spots that you couldn't use before; but with the covering now you have a major resource that is really advantageous to you. Find low spots where water is hanging

---

218 Verse 3: "And he shall be like a tree planted by the rivers of water, that bringeth forth his fruit in his season; his leaf also shall not wither; and whatsoever he doeth shall prosper."

out; cover it, and you got it. You never have to water it because it is low. All your minerals are collecting there, so it is a major reservoir, a valuable resource. [Before], you did not know how to deal with it because it is a muddy area; it was a negative. But once you have the cover on it, it's incredibly awesome. This is what I so love about the covering; it changes everything. Where it used to be negative, now that you have the covering, it is a major asset."

What kind of water do you drink?

"My own well water from the tap, but the best water is in produce. That is the most potent, clean water that exists. And again, this all goes back to God. He set this all up. When you think about it—how the roots all filter that out—you start thinking about it and, yeah, of course, it is. This is the cleanest, most nutritious, water you can drink."

[I noticed the Gautschis have an Enagic[219] water ionizer. As a midwife, Carol routinely invites her pregnant visitors to drink water from it.]

I take it you don't can your produce. Is that true?

"No, and you know why? Ninety-five percent of the food value is lost in canning.[220] If you want to preserve food, dry it. Drying is the most amazing way. You maintain 95 percent of your food value when you dry."

---

219 www.mywaterwellness.com.
220 This is a broad and firmly held belief of Paul's. I have not found independent validation, other than a study that noted a 67 percent loss of vitamin C from fresh peas to blanched and canned.

Do you freeze?

"No, I eat everything fresh in season because God did not issue the human race a refrigerator or freezer or a canner. Can I tell you my example? The Sermon on the Mount is a powerful statement from Jesus (Matthew 6:26). I love this statement He makes: 'Consider the birds of the air.' (Consider . . . look at them . . . that includes all the animals because they did not separate, they didn't fall, they didn't rebel toward God, and they stayed connected.) 'Consider the birds of the air; they don't sow, and they don't reap, and they don't store food in barns, but your Heavenly Father takes care of them.' Then He poses a question to get us to think: 'Aren't you of more value than they?' What He's trying to say is 'I planned on taking care of you the same way; you disconnected, they didn't. They get everything they need.'

"I love the bear. When there's no food, the bear just takes a nap in the winter and wakes up in spring. They live incredibly healthy lives. They eat food fresh in season, don't store anything. They don't have health insurance, don't go to doctors, and live incredibly healthy lives. *Excuse me, human race?* And we're supposed to be intelligent beings?"

There are rocks mixed in with the free manure I got. Should I screen them out?

"I'll tell you the insanity of the human race. You know what rocks are? Rocks are concentrated minerals, and we remove them from the ground . . . *duh*! My place in Sequim, if you look closely, it's 85 percent rock (riverbed). I cover the rock with woodchips over it, growing everything great. All the rocks are a benefit, a major resource, a major asset to the ground. To take them out is like cutting your throat. God never removes rocks. When you drive by a mountain and you see trees growing out of rock, yay, God.

"He knows what He's doing. We've got to adjust our totally dead minds, you know. It's not what I see; it's God. And I've got to pay attention to what He does and don't go back because I try to figure it out. It's simple faith and believing. You believe, and it pleases God, and you get these incredible benefits."

Do you eat Swiss chard raw?

"Yes. When you cook food, you kill enzymes."

Does the dog eat only vegetables too? She looks really healthy.

"Tova (our dog) eats three raw eggs every day [with her dog food]. Then in the afternoon, she goes into the orchard and picks up a pear and [lies] down in the grass and eats it, or apples, whatever. You know what's interesting? If I go to [the store[221]] and buy an apple, my dog won't eat it. She knows it's toxic.

"My wife will go out to the store and buy organic carrots, the small ones you put in salads. I offer one to my dog, and she won't eat it. Here, she goes out and eats my carrots any day. The health store carrots are raised organic, but [too often] they corrupt it. They spray it to maintain shelf life. You see, God never created things to be on shelves. They're supposed to be eaten fresh in season."

Isn't it unlikely that I can obtain the benefits you have since the Olympic Peninsula has extraordinary weather patterns and growing season?

"[In June] a woman called me from Montana. She was whining and complaining about her short growing season. I said, 'It is 53°F at my place and in the mid-70s at your place, and you are whining about your short growing season?' I am already in my second planting of arugula, spinach, lettuce, and cilantro in this kind of climate! It has nothing to do with temperature but everything to do with soil health and vitality."

Can I get by with cheap tools?

"You buy quality things, and they will last. They will serve you for life. We are supposed to be good stewards. That is clear all the way through [the Bible].[222] To waste money on junk stuff is just not good stewardship. So, from the stewardship perspective, I think it is wise to invest in some good quality things, maintain them, take good care of them, and get the pleasure.

"My lawnmower is incredible to use; it works so beautiful. It has a hydrostatic drive, no belt, no gear. It is the most incredible, wonderful machine. It has served me so well for these **twenty-nine years.** In my condition, I still do all the walking behind, and it is an

---

221 Paul does not want to discredit the store by revealing its name, but you would likely recognize it.
222 Consider 1 Corinthians 4:2.

incredible investment. It's a Honda. It has hydrostatic drive, like a tractor. Nothing on it has failed. Our yard was a pasture, and I just started mowing. Clippings go to the chickens. All the birds out in nature are out eating this stuff [grass]; it is their food, so to me it is a very wise thing to take this to our chickens."

Why are your plants so chock-full of minerals?

"First off, the woodchips help a lot in supplying plants, but I have gone to my local sand and gravel operators, and they have a rock-crushing machine that runs all day long. As it is crushing rock, a fine powder comes out the side or bottom of the crusher. That powder is concentrated minerals. They freely let me fill my five-gallon bucket with the powder, and I broadcast it over the top of the woodchips. In little time, the minerals leach into the soil around my plants, and the plants get a huge benefit. They look and taste superior, and they are so much more healthful than anything out there."

[As of the end of the 2013 season, Paul no longer broadcasts rock powder on his garden, respecting that he doesn't see God doing that in nature. Certain Oregonians and southwest Washingtonians well remember how, in 1980, God sprinkled (or dumped, rather) powdered minerals on their soils in the form of Mount St. Helens volcanic ash. Thus, I would advise adding the mineral powder the first one or two seasons and then not fussing about it in the future. Speaking of ash, Paul used to put his wood stove ashes in the chicken yard, but now he spreads them over the top of the orchard, as wood ash adds beneficial elements including potassium, calcium, magnesium, and phosphorus.[223]]

What do you do with your strawberries?

"I have found that God thins strawberries better than I do, so at the end of the season, I cover all the strawberry plants with more woodchips before the winter weather hits. During the cold months, the weaker plants die and decompose, while the stronger plants survive. Next spring, the remaining plants exhibit fantastic, hearty growth and bear wonderful tasting strawberries in abundance. When God does the thinning, I don't have to show up for work!"

---

223 Per Oregon State Extension Service Fertilizer Guide, FG61, revised May 1982.

CHAPTER 17

Dear Paul

And he wrote a letter after this manner . . .
— Acts 23:25

FOLLOWING ARE EXCERPTS OF LETTERS Paul has received over many months. He insists on not having an email account (or much to do with computers in general), so inquirers and well-wishers communicate with him by letter (snail mail) or by phone. People's initials are primarily shared in deference to the confidentiality of the letter writers. The first letter is from a medical doctor.

Dear Paul:

I just finished watching *Back to Eden* for the second time! My eyes are filled with tears because the film was an answer to my prayers.

I'm a novice gardener . . . toiling and trying new ideas and spending tons of money. [Her summer water bills came to four hundred dollars a month!]. *Back to Eden* has relieved all stress! I know "the blessings of the Lord makes rich, and He adds no sorrow to it."[224] The woodchip method of growing ameliorates all worries. Thank you!

I plan to use my garden for a greater purpose . . . [to] help transform my community by offering healing and wholeness. My responsibility

---

224 See Proverbs 10:22.

is to follow Him and let Him manifest His desire through me. Many thanks to you for sharing His system with the world.

R. W., MD
Tennessee

Dear Paul,

I am a pastor, seasonal East African missionary, church planter, and wanna-be farmer. I started a farm on the Serengeti in Kenya and will be implementing your (God's) system there, in a famine plagued area. Our farm has little water and our well drilling machine just broke. Now it may not matter. I can't tell you how important your work is to me.

J. M.
Keene, New Hampshire

Dear Paul,

As a long-time backyard organic gardener, I loved the *Back to Eden* film and follow-up videos featuring your divinely inspired method of growing remarkable vegetables and orchards! My grandchildren helped me spread forty yards of woodchips throughout our quarter acre last spring.

I am very grateful to you for contributing to our expanded and improved garden last summer—and have shared your knowledge with neighbors. The place where we obtain our woodchips now calls them their "Eden" woodchips.

For all the heavenly inspiration and knowledge you have shared to benefit all of us who reverence the land—we thank you from the bottom of our hearts!

J. N.
Orem, Utah

Dear Paul,

I watched your video[225] this past week for the first time and wanted to jump up and down and sing after watching it.

Our three-year old daughter had a cancerous brain tumor removed a little over a year ago and I have been so burdened ever since to change how we eat and care for my family's health the best I can. It has proven to be overwhelming at times and very expensive. It has meant buying organic and seeking the best ways to get the healthiest foods in my family, and having a garden that works is essential to helping me do this for reasonable costs.

So again, thank you! I'm starting my garden this spring and I'm so excited to watch it work. I'm telling everyone I know about this gardening method.

D. V.
Coggon, Iowa

———————

Dear Paul,

Thank you so much for all the time you have spent sharing all the great information on your garden. I started to use woodchips in January 2012 after watching *Back to Eden*. This year I can really see what has happened. I had Swiss chard in my garden last year and never pulled it out for winter. It survived in the wood chip garden through very cold New Jersey winter days and, at one point, I thought it had died. It came right back in spring and now in May [2013] looks so dark green, big and healthy just like one of your plants. I did nothing to it too. This completely convinced me of this method.

Thank you again and much blessings to you.

With . . . woodchips . . . I thought about all the work and products that are rendered null and void:

- Drip irrigation systems, pipes, valves, timers
- Worm bins and vermicomposting
- Compost piles, compost tumblers, turning, and containment

———————

225 Paul gives credit to Michael Barrett and his friends for making the Back to Eden video and the website. As of 2013, the Back to Eden producers (Dana Richardson and Sarah Zenz) received control of the website and the video rights. https://www.backtoedenfilm. com/watchfreeorganicgardeningmovie.html.

- Compost tea brewing in buckets, aerating bubblers, molasses, sprayers
- Soil pH testing and testing kits
- Expensive organic fertilizers and amendments; lime, colloidal phosphate, greensand—you can't even get this stuff and have to special order, drive far, or have shipped
- Green manures and cover crops to till under, seed for all this, rototillers, gas, maintenance
- Big garden sheds to house all this equipment, bags, buckets, pipes, hoses, etc.
- Digging water catchments and swales using heavy digging equipment
- Spending money and time reading garden books [*Growing Food God's Way* is not a garden book.]

You are the one person in gardening that I can believe since you are not selling anything. I hope to see your garden in person and taste one of your apples.

D. R.
Delanco, New Jersey

Dear Paul,

I have recently been introduced to your gardening techniques through the video, and then watched all the videos on You Tube.

I live in British Columbia on a property on the edge of a forest. I have taken to bringing back buckets of soil from the forest floor, in the hopes of bringing my garden up to those standards, but you have obviously simplified that. We embrace your methods totally.

My great grandfather was a horticulturist for the B.C. government, and I have a book that is the minutes of the meetings in Parliament in 1906; arguing in Parliament against the adulteration of fruits. I feel in watching your film that you are taking gardening back to a time when it was much better.

I see your techniques as something world governments should be taking on instead of GMOs to deal with world starvation.

Thank you so much for all you do, and for my part I am sending your video to everyone I know to try to get gardening back to what it should be.

J. B.
Scotch Creek, British Columbia, Canada

Dear Paul:

Yesterday I saw the *Back to Eden* film. It was an answer to prayer! Currently, I teach a wonderful gardening method, Square Foot Gardening (SFG), and last year I approached a local homeless shelter with an idea. They were so enthused that we are now working together on a three-phase garden project:

Phase I – I gave them a small 2'x2' SFG and the residents had a blast with it and took it upon themselves to make a few more raised beds. It was so successful, that one resident even made pickles with his harvest. He was so proud!

Phase II – We hope to reduce the . . . [shelter's] operating expenses by having them grow much of their produce.

Phase III – [They] have a plot of land and we hope to turn it into a garden and use the garden as an income stream, where they sell their excess vegetables, herbs, and flowers.

Initially, we were going to use the SFG method, but after seeing the film, perhaps your (rather God's) method would be less expensive and ultimately be better. . . .

We are so excited! Thank you so much for your sensitivity to God's word and for sharing it with everyone.

K. R.
Glen Burnie, Maryland

Paul Gautschi,

I want you to know how very much I appreciate your sharing the revelation that you received from God. Not too many people would take the time to [share] a video that could transform lives and give it out for free.

Not only have you helped me with my gardening techniques and clarified several key aspects of gardening for this novice, but you have also made a major impact, through God, in my spiritual life.

I have received so much from this, and that is why I wanted to write this letter. I want you to know that it won't stop here (the knowledge/revelation) that you have shared with me. My spiritual walk is manifesting great fruit, and I know my garden will do the same.

You are truly a man who walks out a life in Christ, and you show me that it is possible for me to do it too. Oh, how I thank you Paul, for allowing God to use you!

Brandon J.

———————————

Paul,

A friend of mine sent me an email a few weeks ago with a link to the *Back to Eden* film.

In August, I wanted God to bring something to me that would help people spiritually and physically, so when He said "Why not do something with your love of gardening?" I thought "Yes!" I could start a garden that would provide lifesaving, nutritious food in this nutrient desert we live in.

So, I set out this winter reading books on organic gardening and made big plans to expand and renovate our current garden. In addition to toying around with the idea of giving healthy food to those in need, my family has also been challenged with some health issues that could benefit from better nutrition. Partner that with our financial goals to be thriftier, a garden of food that is better than what you can get at any grocery store appeared to serve all purposes.

I spent most of the time . . . this spring toiling in the soil, hand digging beds to prepare our gardening space. I even enlisted the help of six chickens a few times to scratch up the soil. The whole time, all I could think was "How am I going to be able to provide any benefit to my family, let alone others, with the amount of labor this is consuming?" I am only thirty-one years old, but a previous car accident has limited me somewhat in my activities. It just didn't seem possible.

Seeing the movie and the accompanying videos on the internet has literally been a Godsend. The truth of Matthew 11:28-30[226] keeps on repeating itself in my head every time I am harvesting in the garden at sunrise, thanking God for His blessings. Seeing your garden and hearing your wisdom has shown me the reason why covering is truly a gift from above.

Lastly, I wanted to thank you for sharing your story and wisdom with strangers like me. I'm sure others have told you that you have blessed them richly with your gifts, but in case [not], let me . . . humbly say you are blessing me and my family already in innumerable ways.

Blessing to you,
R. K.
Ramsey, Minnesota

Dear Paul,

Your gardening techniques were just what I was looking for to feed our family at a cheaper cost, without having to worry about where the food came from or what is in it.

I am a Type-1 diabetic since the age of two years . . . and have thus been insulin dependent for the last 24+ years. This is very expensive and requires me to take serious action to wean myself from insurance to avoid the high cost of living. We have a home with a small yard that I have started growing some food successfully, for the most part, and I have been eating a raw, vegan "diet" the last nineteen days with the help of a vow I made to my unborn son—to do this until his birth. It's been a lot of vegetables (mostly leafy greens), sprouted seeds, buckwheat, almonds, fruit, and fermented items (all of this stuff bought raw and prepared by myself).

I have already seen significant improvements in blood sugars but have little doubt that I will not reap the full benefits until I can grow my own food and eat it fresher and more alive than I am currently able to. Love,

S. M.
Springfield, Missouri

---

226 "Come unto me, all ye that labor and are heavy laden, and I will give you rest. Take my yoke upon you and learn of me; for I am meek and lowly in heart: and ye shall find rest unto your souls. For my yoke is easy, and my burden is light."

Dear Paul,

Around the end of June [2013] . . . I came across your video and wow! What an inspiration. I stayed up until 4:00am watching it and it stirred something within me.

I had been growing vegetables but found myself working too hard. The hard labor caused friction between my husband and me. I felt that I was left alone with so much work. After watching the video, I realized God's order is needed in every aspect of our lives. It all made sense. I got a vision for my garden.

Next day, I told my husband about *Back to Eden* and asked him to watch it (he has no passion for gardening) and he got excited and involved. He has watched the video four times. He helped me build five 4x8-foot raised beds and we are also planning on making space for an orchard. We have covered all [raised beds] with woodchips.

It is a miracle to me that he is involved in the garden, but when you applied principles from the Word of God, his eyes were opened as well. I am very thankful for you sharing that revelation with us. [It] came in a time I really needed it. I am no longer working that hard or fighting with weeds.

I wanted to let you know that the principles stated in the Bible and spoken by you were inspirational, refreshing, and eye opening. I was losing hope with my garden, not understanding why I had to labor so hard. Be aware that my garden will be an extension of yours here in (clay soil) South Carolina.

Thanks again,
O. and D.
South Carolina

Hi Paul!

Thank you so much for sharing what God taught you! The film has blessed me tremendously! I started to garden, after buying my first house, a year ago and found it a very tiresome, expensive experience with no great result.

I know God wants me to garden, so I asked Him to make it His garden and teach me how to tend it on behalf of Him. Know how He answered me?!!! The *Back to Eden* film! It not only taught me God's way of gardening, it also taught/encouraged me to take my stuff to God always and first.

God . . . told me to garden, but I didn't ask Him how. I asked my Mom, YouTube, Google, but not God. When I finally did, God answered. It is wonderful to experience the way God cared for us.

Thank you again for sharing a God-centered life, [and] demonstrating it without restraint [or fear] while expressing God's nature so clearly.

M. L.
California

———————————

Dear Paul,

I just finished watching *Back to Eden* and I just wanted to tell you how truly blessed I was . . . my spirit lifted by your words.

I too, am an avid gardener. I loved how you used scripture and your garden to testify of the goodness and abundance of our God. I was very down when I began the film, but by the time it was over, I felt that God used you to remind me how "the earth is the Lord's and the fullness thereof."[227] He has everything in control. He is the sovereign God!!

About the garden . . . I knew mulch was my friend, but I never thought to garden in it! I am already planning my "new" garden using woodchips.

God bless you and your family, and your garden.
In Christ,
L. O.
St. Michael, Minnesota

———————————

Mr. Gautschi,

I really want to thank you for sharing your story through the documentary video and L2Survive videos on YouTube.[228]

I found a link to *Back to Eden* while doing some research on my first vegetable garden . . . [and] smiled knowing I had found what I hadn't known I was looking for.

Hurricane Sandy rolled in a couple of days later, and I knew for sure I had watched it when I was meant to. We had tree services

227 1 Corinthians 10:26 (quoting Psalms 24:1).
228 www.L2survive.com.

working up and down the street who were more than happy to dump two loads of woodchips in our yard. [Spreading the woodchips] was an incredible amount of work, but I'd gladly do it again.

The more I learn about our food and food system, the less stressed I've become; and have desired nothing more than to provide my family with healthier, safer food.

My garden this year was beautiful. Had I been better prepared to fight the voles and squirrels, we would have eaten more from it, but I learned a lot and next year will do better. I know [that] without the woodchips, we would have lost our tomato plants to all the rain (like everyone else did around here this year).

I sincerely thank you from the bottom of my heart for your generosity . . . and your part in my great attempt to keep my family healthy through safer, better, food . . . especially my three children.

God used you to share this information so that those of us (who were not listening close enough) could still learn and change.

I'm listening now. Many thanks and best wishes,
A. Z.

———————————

Greetings Mr. Paul,

I came across *Back to Eden* . . . and I absolutely loved every minute . . . of the documentary, and how everything was explained. I love how the garden and God are [connected] and how effortless it becomes once one has done the initial work.

Thank you, Brother Paul.

As I write this letter South Africa and the world [are] celebrating the life of a man who brought hope . . . to many; former president Dr. Nelson Mandela.

My vision, Paul, is to be a woman who teaches other women how to nourish the home, children and husband, heal her kids with everything in the garden; from the fruits to the herbs and bark. I believe that for every illness there is a cure in the Garden. [We need to be] re-educating the taste buds with REAL FOOD.

Your "Sistah" of the Light,
K. I.
Midrand, South Africa

Dear Paul,

I wanted to write you a letter so I could tell you how blessed I am that I have seen the movie *Back to Eden*. Every time I walk through my garden, it brings a smile to my face and peace in my heart. I hope more and more people will take over this way of growing food, so we can make the world (little by little) a better place for our children. ♥

In my garden, I have a very small shed and on the door I painted: "In nature, nothing happens without a purpose," so every time I have an issue in my garden and I am thinking of a solution, there is a moment that I see those words and I know that God has a purpose for everything. I only have to ask Him!

God bless you and your family,
M. de R.[229]
Netherlands

Dear Mr. Gautschi,

I absolutely love the *Back to Eden* film! It was a huge answer to my personal prayers. Honestly, my garden felt so labor-some that for the last two years, I have been studying Matthew 11:28-30[230] and asking God what it truly meant.

I have been canning for years. It is very labor intensive, and now I have two grandbabies helping as my daughter and I work together doing the gardening and the storage. Then God showed us how to dehydrate foods. Honestly, my daughter and I are laughing with joy. Everything just became so easy and we cannot credit anyone but the Lord, Creator/Master Gardener. But also, thank you for sharing what you have learned.

My husband and I do missions work in Haiti. We are presently working with a doctor in Cap Haiten . . . his vision is to have a garden large enough to support his family so that he can provide medical care for free in his community.

---

229 This is the woman who translated the documentary into Dutch. Paul was amazed at her labor of love.

230 "Come unto me, all ye that labor and are heavy laden, and I will give you rest. Take my yoke upon you and learn of me; for I am meek and lowly in heart: and ye shall find rest unto your souls. For my yoke is easy, and my burden is light."

So, I just wanted you to know we are bringing the [covered] garden to Haiti and will have to see what that looks like with Haitian resources. Thank you for sharing the blessing God has given you,

K. M. K.
South Grafton, Massachusetts

Dear Paul,

Hello from over here in Chelan [Washington].

I want to give you a wood chip update—more than just how it changed my life; and I'm not going back to weeds and watering, because woodchips have certainly done that. They have changed my life and I'm not going back.

First—results

Black beans – the biggest plants are twice as tall as the as the ones planted last year in the soil. The largest of all plants had 99 pods on it.

Tomatoes – Great harvest. Most dirt-grown heirloom tomatoes end up with a rough and scaly skin, but my tomatoes were smooth and luscious, more so than ever before.

People in the garden are in for a life-changing treat—gardening is easy—what a wonderful world we have to learn from. Blessing to you and your family,

L. C.
Chelan, Washington

Dear Paul,

I am a mom to four kids and over the past few years, I have grown very concerned about the food that I feed them, and the future of food in general. I have been prompted to get a garden going for my family.

In the late summer of last year . . . I bought some cold-hardy greens seeds (kale, spinach, collards, beets, etc.) and got them in my poor clay ground. The ground was hard, and the seeds weren't germinating, and when I watered, all it did was run off and erode and make a muddy mess—until it hardened up again into a rock that no seedling could push through.

I had pretty much given up . . . when I happened upon a short YouTube video about [your] gardening method, with a link to the documentary. I watched it immediately. It made complete sense to me, and I knew this was an answer to prayer. I feel so much hope about the future. We will be OK. Yes, maybe the food in the grocery stores is poison, and maybe our country is falling apart before our eyes, but God loves us and wants us to be happy and healthy and thrive, and there is a way! Thank you for helping me find that hope.

K. S.
Ammon, Idaho

Paul,

I learn something from each and every one of your videos. My family has auto-immune issues and we are making lots of effort to eliminate toxins and eat a better diet.

I am fifty-eight years old and have some slight mobility issues, so am happy to see how easy your method is. The Eden method will enable me to continue doing my favorite thing, gardening, for a long time to come.

I am a certified master gardener in Michigan and have been interested in and studied different methods most of my life. Your advice has been the most helpful to me and makes the most sense.

D. D.
Saginaw, Michigan

Paul,

First, I want to thank you for returning my calls. I tend to rush off the phone because I imagine you get millions of calls. Trust me I would love to keep you on the phone and ask many questions, so I limit myself to just a few.

My life has changed since watching your film. My husband was a firefighter captain in New York City . . . and soon after 9/11 was forced to retire due to illness. I was convinced if I could grow more cultivars and 100% organic I could help assist in getting authentic nutrition back into his body. The challenge was that I just didn't know how I was going to maintain a 5500 square foot garden, work, and at the time I knew we wanted children. Because of your film, my prayers were answered. WOODCHIPS!

As the neighbors watched [me spread the woodchips] instead of applying [some too], I laughed because it is so true that most people have to see to believe. This was year two and what a difference. From the bottom of my heart I thank you for your generosity with your experience, information and most of all, your time!

We love you here . . . and my 8-month old loves the food mommy is now able to grow that I was not able to before the woodchips. My husband hopes to get well so we can take a trip over to your place. You are so immensely appreciated by us! Thank you and your wife for letting us all take your time from her. XOXO

K. L.
Bristol, Connecticut

[In 2018, K. L. sent an update to her letter.]

Seven years ago, God blessed us with Paul Gautschi's film *Back to Eden*. It arrived in my email shortly after its launch. Little did I know what was in store for my family and [me].

My mom asked me to please just try the woodchips on a small area first, to see if it works. I laughed and said, "Works? This man is 40 years into this, and the forest has done it for thousands of years, I'm pretty certain it works!!"

130+ dump truck loads later, our entire backyard has been transformed into an edible landscape. We are swimming in an edible jungle of nutrient dense food and soil that has developed into what I call 'black gold!' Every year I'm blown away by the flavor and water content. The size and productivity are particularly noticeable. I remember calling Paul saying: "We harvested 35 pounds of strawberries it's so amazing." The following year, it was approximately 60 pounds next thing you know it's 100, and this year 160! We harvested 460 pounds of potatoes from six 25ft. rows. I was beside myself. It has gotten to the point where I ask people to come see for themselves because it comes across like I'm exaggerating.

Even year One was a harvest I never saw in my life (300 lbs. of watermelon from three plants and 400 lbs. of squash from four plants).

You can imagine I never foresaw the blessings ahead. I had to call Paul to tell him all about it. His response to me was a giggle and with profound words of wisdom: "God only knows multiplication and will continue to blow you away . . . Yay God!"

Even Paul continues to have results he has never witnessed before. So my sense is that the show has only begun, and we all have so much more to anticipate. Woohoo!

My husband eats our nutrient dense food to assist in regaining his health from the NYC 9/11 attacks. Through the struggles, we realized how important raw nutrient dense food is for recovery as well as maintaining our health. Our observation is, "Organic" does *not* mean nutrient dense, flavorful, or even chemical free (which is not an option for us). Eden gardening has been instrumental for us on so many levels. Our bug issues are 98% gone and weeding/watering are minimal. My time in the garden is more allocated to harvesting, where it should be. It is our main source for health—second to prayer.

I would have never dreamed that seven years ago, a gardening video would have cultivated a sincere friendship and mentor Paul has become for me.

Imagine someone becoming one of your best friends yet have never met them in person. One day, hopefully soon, my family and I will have the opportunity to meet Paul face to face. I have many times expressed how grateful we are for his kindness, time, generosity, wisdom , friendship, knowledge and (most of all) his prayers.

[To Paul]:

I am spreading the word. You have inspired me more than I can say or write. Our family is forever grateful to you. We pray and think of you and Carol often.

I love you my friend, you are the salt of the earth.

[*In November 2019, Paul and Carol traveled to New Hampshire. While they were there, K. L. drove over from Connecticut, and they finally got to meet face to face. Paul's view of that meeting: "It was great to finally meet K in person. She even helped me prune the apple trees of the pastor who took Carol and [me] in."*]

Hello Paul,

We are so blessed to receive the wisdom you got from God in the . . . simplest things that God has shown you of His nature.

My family and I have incorporated your garden method and it has worked for us, which has been our second year.

Many have ridiculed us for not going the traditional method, but the fruits in the end speak volumes.

I will be praying for you; that you will continue to serve our Messiah Yeshua (Jesus) for His will. Numbers 6:24-26[231]

M. G.
Ontario, Canada

Dear Paul Gautschi,

I have been thinking for some time that I would like to grow some of our own food, but I never saw it possible. . . . Now I do! I saw the *Back to Eden* movie back in April and it blew my mind! Before that, I saw a lot of videos and read info on different types of gardening—and although they were organic—they were very labor intensive. So, with a part time job and two children under five, I could not see myself doing that at all.

We live in [the] south of Norway (northern Europe), and we have similar climate as you, so planting under fruit trees is definitely happening in the future . . .!

You are truly a man of God. Thank you for sharing your time and wisdom with us all.

H. E.
Mandal Municipality, Norway

Hello and greetings from Poland,

I . . . heard about the *Back to Eden* movie two years ago and as soon as I have watched it, I started to prepare my . . . small garden. It has been a true revelation to me and inspiring beyond belief (I have never garden[ed] before!).

---

231 "The LORD bless thee and keep thee: The LORD make his face shine upon thee, and be gracious unto thee: The LORD lift up his countenance upon thee, and give thee peace."

I have doubled the area with woodchips and I hope next year will be way better.

... I'm also planning to establish a small orchard as soon as I get more woodchips.

I would like to express my gratitude . . . Paul for sharing [your] knowledge, for encouragement and motivation.

Kind regards,
W. R. G.
Warsaw, Poland

———————

Hi Paul,

[I] . . . wanted to say thank you for all the information you have made available . . . through the YouTube clips posted by Thatnub.

I have never thought to invite God into my garden and to teach me through nature. I have now, and I know I can ask Him for guidance on anything that is puzzling me.

I . . . have a lot of . . . work to getting my garden in shape, but you have given me confidence to go ahead and try without worrying what others may be thinking.

Thank you!
R. H.
Diamond Creek, Australia

———————

Dear Paul,

Thank you, a thousand times over, for sharing your garden, and how it helps the land; how it encourages healthy plant growth, and how it helps me feed my family.

I have raised beds, but even still, it made my garden tons better.

I always wanted to thank you for talking about God, and sharing that aspect of everything. It was a healing thing for me.

Thank you,
A. J.
Hollister, California

———————

Hi,

I am a single mom from Ilderton, a small town in south western Ontario.

I have two small boys and seeing the movie *Back to Eden* was life changing.

I could do a garden too. It would be impossible to have a conventional garden in my situation . . . your videos on YouTube are amazing.

We, who are not able to go in person, feel like we are there. Keep up the great work, we really appreciate it!

H. R.
Ilderton, Ontario

Hello Paul,

[I am] grateful for the information you have shared.

Although it took . . . some considerable effort to get the woodchips into place, it has saved me hours of time each week in weeding and watering. I watered my main garden area twice in a year instead of twice a week! I would spend at least an hour a week trying to keep the weeds under control and I really don't think I spent total . . . of three hours weeding that area this whole season!

You have helped to educate me so that I can feed my family healthy food regardless of what the future may hold.

Thanks very much,
M. G.
Roy, Utah

Paul,

The information you have shared through the movie and L2Survive's videos have truly changed my life. I don't yet have a garden as I am living in Philadelphia, but you don't need a garden to appreciate the information.

Your relationship with God is inspirational, and the information God has shared with you uplifts everyone, including me.

If I am ever tired or a bit down from a long day or long week at work, watching you working in your garden brings me right back to what matters in life. It has certainly changed plans for myself and my daughters in the future.

Thank you, again, for not mincing words, speaking your Truth, and giving us all inspiration to follow a spiritual path.

J. B.
Malvern, Pennsylvania

Dear Paul,

Greetings from India!

Our country depends on monsoons; we have rainy season, winter season, and summer season. . . . In our district area we have only paddy rice crop. The lands are suitable for this paddy rice only, but after viewing your video, I came to implement your idea in our empty land in front of our orphanage building and surrounding. Thanking you!

Evangelist G. Y.
Machilipatnam, India

Dear Paul,

My name is [T. C.] and I live in the island of Jamaica (Caribbean Sea). I just finished watching your video and it was awesome. My husband saw it last week and was raving about it. We operate a five-acre farm.

I am really impressed with your relationship with God because, I totally get it. That's how God speaks to me also. I sanction every word you have said. God will talk to you all day once you are available.

Yours in Christ,
T. & K. C.
Jamaica

Dear Paul,

I already know this note will not cover all the gratitude I have for you . . . but it's all I have to convey my heartfelt thanks.

To accomplish the task of healing our planet and bringing people to understand their Maker, requires that there are already a few people in place that can teach how to do this in His way. You are one of those people.

The knowledge that you imparted to us, will be as a stone dropped into a pool of water; its ripples spreading out as long as there are willing, open minded people to receive it.

. . . All things are in His timetable . . . I wished I had known about this ten years ago, but there's a reason why I didn't; one of which, I didn't ask! I relied on man's way of doing things. I am relearning this valuable survival technique . . . ASK!

Fondly,
N. P.
Florida

Dear Paul,

I was recently trying to find out some things about chickens and gardening. . . . I found the film and began watching it . . . I immediately told my husband about it and we watched it together. We were both amazed, impressed, and (most of all) refreshed.

When I was in 5th grade, the teacher was telling us about acidic and alkali soil, and that some plants like one and not the other. He also spoke of growing certain things in shade and others in sun . . . [saying] grapes needed to grow in full sun. I raised my hand and said, "That's not true, we have grape vines growing up our maple tree and they love it there. Every year my brother and I climb up the tree and pick the grapes." He told me I didn't know what I was talking about.

As the years went on, I learned to comply and write the answers they wanted on the tests. Then I guess, somewhere, I must have started believing the nonsense I was writing on the tests, because I ended up believing in the lie; that it didn't matter *how* the food was grown, it was *still* just as nutritious.

After years of eating poison[ed foods], the toll on my body began to show. I began to not be able to eat sweet things like: raisins, dates, figs, and honey. As time went on, *the list* only increased. I had to continuously adjust to what I was eating to not have blood sugar reactions. The list continued to grow, until I could not eat anything sweet; no apples, bananas, oranges, peaches, pears, plums, nectarines, grapes, grapefruit, watermelon, etc.

[B]y the time I watched the *Back to Eden* film, I could not even eat things like potatoes, and carrots, as they were now on *the list*. You spoke of how "sweet" the Lord is and that He made all things to be sweet and only the Curse brought bitterness to the ground, causing it to produce food likewise.

[When you addressed the boy who was allergic to apples,] you told him that it was the poison *on the apples* that he was allergic to, and *not* the apple: "God made all foods good, and He made the body to be able to eat the foods He made."[232]

Suddenly, I was crying, as I realized the *only* reason I could not eat those sweeter foods was because I had believed the lie. I went to Genesis 1:29-31 and 2:9 and read it in Hebrew. He gave to us *all* of the plants for food and they were exceedingly good. Then, He says that all the trees (meaning their fruit) were pleasing to the eyes and "*good for food*." They were in "order," and therefore given to provide "order" for our bodies as we eat them. It wasn't that the foods were too sweet! It was because my body was deficient in something and was not working right. So, I asked the Lord what to do.

That night, the Lord gave me a dream. He told me the reason I was having so much trouble was because my body was deficient in minerals. I started taking a really good trace mineral supplement.

Then the next night, while I was sleeping, the Lord spoke to my spirit these words: "I can eat all things through Christ Jesus who strengthens me."[233] Suddenly, the lights went on and I said aloud: "I CAN eat all things through Christ Jesus who strengthens me!" "I CAN eat ALL the foods the Lord has made, because He is Good and ONLY gives good things to eat, therefore I can eat _____"(and I named all those things I couldn't eat for years without messing up my blood sugar). Then for breakfast, I ate a whole grapefruit, just because I wanted to. I had NO side effects at all. For dinner, I had some cornbread. . . . Later, I had a quarter of a pomegranate. All these things I could not previously even consider eating.

---

232 You can read Paul's account in the previous chapter.
233 A personalized application of Philippians 4:13, "I can do all things through Christ which strengtheneth me."

I had agreed with the lie that I could not eat them, but now I have chosen to agree with the words of the Lord that *I can* eat the foods He has given to us, for they are "good" and they are good for us.

Thank you so very much, you have blessed me greatly. It was because the Spirit of the Lord was speaking through you that suddenly I was awakened to see something I had not seen.

Thank you again,
C. J.
LaPine, Oregon

———————————

Three years after C. J.'s letter was published, a lady with the initials L. J. emailed me (David) to ask permission to reprint the letter in a blog she writes. Here is the entire blog, less C. J.'s letter you just read (used by permission):

In the book *Growing Food God's Way*, David Devine shares what God has shown Paul Gautschi about Himself and how He created the earth to function. God's way is a way of abundance, life and vigor in our spiritual and physical lives and even in our gardens! That word is shouted not only in this book but also through Paul's video <u>Back to Eden</u>. A chapter of the book is devoted to testimonials that people have sent in. I read them, and they were good, but this one God brought home to me in a big way, and I want to share it with you. [C. J.'s letter follows and then L. J.'s response to the letter.]

I have had hypoglycemia, food allergies and sensitivities since childhood and when I read this person's testimony, I thought, "Oh my gosh, that's me!" I also had an ever growing "list" of foods I couldn't eat including: fruits, diary, nuts, honey, potatoes and many sweet tasting vegetables. I kept thinking that I should be able to eat the foods that God created for my good. They are the fuel He created for my body to run on, so I wondered why they would be poison to me. I asked God about this and He put it on my heart to ask for healing. So, I began to pray. The Lord spoke to my heart and said that I could also, like this person, eat all things that He created for my good—through Him who strengthens me. It was a word of healing that I had to combine with faith to find the courage to eat foods that have normally made me feel ill.

In the book, I also read the story about the boy who was not allergic to apples but rather the chemicals sprayed on the apples. Something clicked, and I figured that was why I reacted to peanuts. I prayed about it and, by faith, I tried some organic peanut butter . . . and I felt fine! Praise God!

Last summer we had apples on our tree, and my three-year old grandson picked one for me to eat. Normally, I would have refused because fruit messed up my blood sugar, and I always had to combine a carb with protein. I thought of that little boy . . . and the apple . . . and what God had said to me, and I ate it without having any reaction at all!

I would like to say that as soon as I received the word of healing from God, that I immediately picked up my mat[234] and began to leap tall buildings with a single bound, but that wasn't the case. God had to work on my unbelief and build my faith.

Dairy was the next hurdle. One day I was in the grocery store and God very clearly said, "I want you to start drinking milk." I said "Really God?? You do know it's always made me have a blood sugar reaction, don't You?" Thankfully my God is a very patient and loving God. He kindly replied that I had asked for this healing, and He was giving it to me. He led me to a certain brand of milk, and by faith (with a bit of fear to be honest) I drank it. My blood sugar didn't plummet! As a matter of fact, I didn't react at all. I was amazed! Again, I'd like to say that I suddenly found myself eating all kinds of dairy with no fear or hesitation, but that wasn't the case. I slowly, but steadily, began to walk in greater faith and trust in my God.

During this time, the Lord spoke to me several times to say that healing would come according to my faith. Healing wasn't something that God was going to impose upon me. I had to make a choice to believe what He was saying and walk in it. He put His Holy Spirit within me to give me the power to walk and the power and freedom to choose, but He won't force me to choose to believe.

L. J.

---

234 Luke 5:24.

Isn't that amazing? When she said, "I slowly, but steadily, began to walk in greater faith and trust in my God," she reminded me of a saying of evangelist **Torben Sonnegard**: "Faith is like a muscle; the more you exercise it, the stronger it grows." Do you have a weak faith? Maybe it's time to start exercising it a little.

On a surprise visit to Paul and his tour on July 14, 2019, my wife and I were driving up to Paul's, and I had a spontaneous thought that said I should have brought our second rooster to give to him. I dismissed that thought because he already had a fine rooster. At the end of the tour (which is by the chicken yard), I found out that Paul's rooster had died two days earlier. Had I acted in faith (to the prompting), he could have been blessed by God with a free replacement rooster. Obviously, I didn't exercise my faith right that day. As a result, both Paul and I were robbed of the joy we would have had.

CHAPTER 18

It Takes a Village
(of Animals and Organisms)

Go to the ant, thou sluggard; consider her ways, and be wise: Which having no guide, overseer, or ruler, provideth her meat in the summer, and gathereth her food in the harvest.

– Proverbs 6:6-8

PAUL REALIZES THAT NOT ONLY is his garden a gift from God but also it exists because of the many actors He has chosen to play their parts that lead to excellent results. We will consider a few including, but not limited to four dogs (over time), three cats, about thirty chickens, and multitudes of earthworms and microscopic helpers.

THE ROLE OF THE DOG

Tova's role in Paul's garden was that of protector. A more lofty title would be Guardian of the Garden. She was livin' the dream of dogs by getting to freely roam Paul's five-acre property day and night (especially night) to keep out those pesky deer, skunks, rabbits, raccoons, neighborhood or feral cats, and even birds of prey.

Having spent two nights at the Gautschis', I would say the curtain opened at about 11 p.m., and the guardian announced her presence with some introductory barking. Throughout the wee hours of darkness, she barked off and on as if to say, "I see you!" or "Make my day!" Altogether, she was very effective, and the deer were denied scrumptious lettuce leaves, inviting pears, and blueberries bursting with flavor. The Gautschis and their guests benefitted from Tova's relentless patrolling of the perimeter. The guardian's job was never done. Broccoli burglars take no vacations.

THE ROLE OF THE CATS

All but the most pampered felines have big cat instincts: searching, finding, stalking, strategizing, and pouncing. Paul's cats are no different. In fact, he encourages these instincts among Lucy, Boaz, and Sliha (Hebrew for "excuse me"). Because there are three of them, they can cover more ground simultaneously.

These three amigos protect the garden from or rid it of birds and various forms of rodents: rats, mice, and moles. Between the herb garden, orchard, and vegetable garden, they have plenty of opportunities to find garden-harming prey. Their objective: Take no prisoners.

The Role of the Chickens

Paul regards his chickens as critical to his garden. He refers to them as his "soil-making machines." That is, they eat whatever he brings them—his weeds, his grass clippings, and garden waste—with the purpose of converting those inputs of food into excellent compost. Moreover, since they are laying hens (rooster excluded), they lay the natural, chemical-free eggs that Paul and his family enjoy. Even Tova would eat two or three fresh (raw) eggs a day, and she had a very lovely coat. To Paul, raw food is an *eggs-essential* existence. On occasion, he consumes uncooked eggs in a breakfast drink. He has added them to pet food.

Once a year, Paul covers the chicken house floor and nesting boxes with three to four inches of a mixture composed of horse manure and wood shavings. It is a combination that absorbs moisture and reduces the odor of natural chicken byproducts like urine and droppings. Also, it is a constant source of entertainment for the chickens as they love to scratch in it. By the end of the year, it will be used as nitrogen and nutrient-enriched soil enhancer. When he cleaned out the chicken house in January of 2013, the rich material he took out was scattered amongst the blueberries. In 2015, he scattered it over the front garden area. In 2019, he spread it in the herb garden, by the wasabi.

THE ROLE OF WORMS

One cannot overestimate the inherent value of having worms actively living and working in the soil of your garden. According to the Natural Resources Conservation Service (NRCS), earthworms:

> **Stimulate microbial activity.** Although earthworms derive their nutrition from microorganisms, many more microorganisms are present in their feces or casts than in the organic matter that they consume. As organic matter passes through their intestines, it is fragmented and inoculated with microorganisms. Increased microbial activity facilitates the cycling of nutrients from organic matter and their conversion into forms readily taken up by plants.
>
> **Mix and aggregate soil.** As they consume organic matter and mineral particles, earthworms excrete wastes in the form of casts, a type of soil aggregate. . . . Earthworms can move large amounts of soil from the lower strata to the surface and also carry organic matter down into deeper soil layers. A large proportion of soil passes through the guts of earthworms, and they can turn over the top six inches (15 cm) of soil in ten to twenty years.
>
> **Increase infiltration.** Earthworms enhance porosity as they move through the soil. Some species make permanent burrows deep into the soil. These burrows can persist long after the inhabitant has died,

and can be a major conduit for soil drainage, particularly under heavy rainfall. At the same time, the burrows minimize surface water erosion. The horizontal burrowing of other species in the top several inches of soil increases overall porosity and drainage.

Improve water-holding capacity. By fragmenting organic matter and increasing soil porosity and aggregation, earthworms can significantly increase the water-holding capacity of soils.

Provide channels for root growth. The channels made by deep-burrowing earthworms are lined with readily available nutrients and make it easier for roots to penetrate deep into the soil.

Bury and shred plant residue. Plant and crop residue are gradually buried by cast material deposited on the surface and as earthworms pull surface residue into their burrows.[235]

In terms of biomass and overall activity, earthworms dominate the world of soil invertebrates, including arthropods. There are three kinds of earthworms that may roam your garden:

Surface soil and litter species – Epigeic species. These species live in or near surface plant litter. They are typically small and are adapted to the highly variable moisture and temperature conditions at the soil surface. The worms found in compost piles are epigeic and are unlikely to survive in the low organic matter environment of soil.

Upper soil species – Endogeic species. Some species move and live in the upper soil strata and feed primarily on soil and associated organic matter (geophages). They do not have permanent burrows, and their temporary channels become filled with cast material as they move through the soil, progressively passing it through their intestines.

235 https://www.nrcs.usda.gov/wps/portal/nrcs/detailfull/soils/health/biology/?cid=nrc-s142p2_053863.

Deep-burrowing species – Anecic species. These earthworms, which are typified by the "night crawler," *Lumbricus terrestris*, inhabit more or less permanent burrow systems that may extend several meters into the soil. They feed mainly on surface litter that they pull into their burrows. They may leave plugs, organic matter, or cast (excreted soil and mineral particles) blocking the mouth of their burrows.[236]

Paul experienced the earthworms dismantling his hardpan without any effort on Paul's part. The hardpan is broken up by the tunneling of the earthworms. "Earthworms eat up to thirty times their body weight in soil each day," according to **Mark Hodson**, an earth sciences professor at England's University of Reading.[237]

Earthworms are the subterranean workhorses of your garden. They give so much more than they take, and we benefit from them.

---

236 https://www.nrcs.usda.gov/wps/portal/nrcs/detailfull/soils/health/biology/?cid=nrc-s142p2_053863.
237 Robyn Williams, "The Science Show," ABC Radio National, November 15, 2008, updated September 30, 2011, https://www.abc.net.au/radionational/programs/scienceshow/worms-help-remediate-soils/3156866.

The Role of Mason Bees

Paul has mason bees in a wood-holed structure on his pump house, facing east to get the morning sun. These bees are native to his region, which is very desirable. Unlike honeybees, mason bees do not produce honey or nectar for extraction. One benefit of this bee variety is that they do not sting unless stepped on or otherwise handled aggressively. In addition, mason bees are immune from the common diseases that have devastated many honeybee hives.

These bees do not have a queen. All the females actively lay eggs in their chosen place. They tour many options for where to lay their eggs and go with the one that best suits them. Each female gathers food from flowers, packs the back of the cell, lays an egg, and then builds a partition wall out of mud (that's the mason part). The front wall of the first egg becomes the back wall of the next egg and so on till the cell is filled, and she seals the outside. Female eggs are laid in back and male eggs closer to the entrance. One of the three hundred kinds of mama mason bees will line the walls of the cells with flower petals to add an extra feminine touch and smell.

Mason bees adequately pollenate Paul's plants throughout the orchard and gardens. In winter, they go dormant and essentially hibernate. Paul says they are the first bees to be found in the spring because they have to constantly seek food, unlike their honeybee cousins who store food in their hives.

FINDING NEMATODES

Nematodes are not the typical worms we see. They are microscopic, multicellular organisms (unsegmented roundworms) that live and feed in soil and on plants. According to the University of California's Museum of Paleontology, there are over fifteen thousand known species of roundworms. It claims that "there are many thousands of individual nematodes in even a single handful of garden soil."[238]

We'll look at two categories: plant parasitic (bad) and plant beneficial (good).

High on the menu of plant parasitic nematodes are tomatoes, carrots, lettuce, and peppers. They can cause root-tip damage, distorted leaves, and damaged plant tissue, among other ills.

Cornell University concludes that beneficial nematodes help control the insects shown on the following list:[239]

238 http://www.ucmp.berkeley.edu/phyla/ecdysozoa/nematoda.html
239 https://biocontrol.entomology.cornell.edu/pathogens/nematodes.php

Common Pest Name	Typical Crops Affected
Artichoke plum moth	Artichoke
Army worms	Vegetables
Banana Moth	Ornamentals
Banana root borer	Bananas
Bill bug	Turf
Black cutworm	Turf, vegetables
Black vine weevil	Berries, ornamentals
Borers	Fruit trees, ornamentals
Cat flea	Home, yard turf
Citrus root weevil	Citrus, ornamentals
Coddling moth	Pome fruit
Corn earworm	Vegetables
Corn rootworm	Vegetables
Cranberry girdler	Cranberries
Crane fly	Turf, ornamentals
Diaprepes root weevil	Citrus, ornamentals
Fungus gnats	Mushrooms, greenhouse
Grape root borer	Grapes
Iris borer	Iris
Large pine weevil	Forest plantings
Leaf miners	Vegetables, ornamentals
Mole crickets	Turf, ornamentals
Navel orangeworm	Nut and fruit trees
Plum curculia	Fruit trees
Scarab glibs	Turf, ornamentals
Shoreflies	Ornamentals
Strawberry root weevil	Berries
Small hive beetle	Bee hives

I cannot account for the number and variety of nematodes in Paul's garden, but the lack of insects is prevalent there, so it would likely be due, in part, to these microscopic insect avengers.

UPDATE ON 2020 ANIMALS

Puppy Tova 2 was about four months old and was a favorite with the twenty-eight folks touring Paul's place Sunday, June 4, 2018. It was the first tour of the 2018 growing season. She enjoyed the two bigger dogs in attendance. By the way, Paul allows for dogs on the tour if they are on a leash and the owner "cleans up after them."

The original Tova had to be put down in the winter of 2017. Her replacement was to be Tirzah, a golden retriever, but she was too undependable in staying on the property and keeping the deer away.

Thus, Paul began praying for a more suitable replacement, and Tova 2.0 came along.

Tragedy on Craig Road

In August of 2018, Paul's son went for a bike ride, and Tova 2 tagged along. It was a nice outing, so far as biking in the country goes. At some point, Tova 2 (who was running alongside the bike) veered into the road and was hit by a passing car. For Tova 2.0, the impact was fatal.

Paul called me the next morning and broke the sad news. God had used Tova 2 so effectively to protect the garden. She was an alpha female, just like her namesake. She kept all the deer away. Rather, God kept the deer away with her as His tool. I had to ask why. There was no answer, but Paul quoted from the first part of 1 Corinthians 13:12: "For now we see through a glass, darkly . . ." Paul needs an animal guardian for the orchard and the sheep. It's one thing to lose apples and quite another to lose living sheep.

He trusted that the Lord would provide another Tova-like guardian of the garden, and Paul began the search. These were stretching times. The first thing was to thank God that the bicyclist wasn't injured. (Thank You, Lord!)

Relational permaculture dictates that Paul can take his need to the Father and then sit back and watch Him provide (again).

In the Nick of Time

Lo and behold, a young (avid) gardener from Maryland named Nick Ager started contacting Paul in late 2018. Nick has an Instagram account called "growingbacktoeden."[240] At the time of this writing, in 2020, he has nearly twenty-four thousand followers. Because of this, he was sponsored by Baker Creek Heirloom Seeds to go to Sequim and spend a year with the Gautschis.

---

240 www.instagram.com/growingbacktoeden/?hl=en.

A key aspect of Nick's arrival was his small, feisty dog Willow. In a phone call, Paul said that Willow has done a fine job of keeping the unwanted animals out of the orchard. "I haven't seen this much abundance [in April 2019] since Tova," Paul testified. He went on to say that "Willow is really working. She's a mini-Aussie. She barks all night from the porch, and that is keeping the deer out. The deer had been making such a mess of the trees. It's been such a blessing." But the blessing didn't stop with deer prevention.

Prior to Nick's arrival in November of 2018, Paul slowly started to acquire his own sheep to have in his small pasture. That experiment seemed to fade as predators started killing the sheep at night. Since Willow's presence, there hasn't been another loss of sheep. At last count (January 2020), Paul had three sheep and one ram.

Nick made two chicken tractors (movable coops on wheels) to position his sixty grower chickens around the pasture and employ the techniques Joel Salatin faithfully uses at Polyface Farm. That was a good thing because there weren't enough sheep on that pasture to keep the vegetation down.

Prior to the 2019 tours, the area that Paul uses as a parking lot for his visitors was being taken over by weeds. Removing them would be a daunting task for a human to undertake. Enter Paul's chickens. With about seven of Paul's layers in the moveable cage, they snapped up that live food to make quick work of removing the unwanted vegetation from that area. Paul did none of the work because they took care of it!

Nick's dog Willow.

Eventually, the deer figured out that Willow was going to stay on the porch and not come any closer to them. They began to take liberties with Paul's apple trees without consequence. This added to their boldness, and the orchard began to suffer.

Carol has a client mama that she did seven births for. Someone gave them a Great Pyrenees puppy, and she told Carol they had one more. So Paul went to their place and found it very peaceful and orderly. They gave Paul a male puppy he calls Micah. The first night he put Micah in the barn. The next morning, Paul went out to his porch, and Micah was lying there. "He is amazing," Paul testifies. "He has never left the property since we got him in July." The orchard is looking better, and Paul knows as Micah gets older there will be fewer and fewer deer coming around.

On a wonderful visit to the animal shelter, Paul and Carol found a chocolate lab and got her as a rescue dog. They named her Tova also, so she is Tova 3.0. May she last as long as the first. However, she is not an alpha female like the previous two. That is why Micah was added. Miss 3.0 largely serves as a companion to Nick, Willow and Micah, as well as the Gautschis.

"Favor from God is a significant reality."

– Paul Gautschi

Micah the new male protector.

Tova 3.0, the rescue dog.

CHAPTER 19

Tales of First-Year Coverings

God be merciful unto us and bless us; and cause Thy face to shine upon us; that Thy way may be known upon earth, Thy saving health among all nations.
— Psalms 67:1-2

TO ENCOURAGE EVEN THE SEASONED VETERAN GARDENER in the next chapter, "Turning a Corner," this chapter is devoted to sharing the experiences of three families and a community church that (like thousands of others) heard Paul's story and enthusiastically applied the principle of God's restorative covering to their new or established gardens. Each responded to a questionnaire about what they did and the results.

RAMIN (RAY) AND NICOLE

First meet Ramin (Ray) and Nicole. They live near Rainier, Oregon, and grew a decent traditional garden. Their six kids range from ages two to eleven and baby #7 is on the way in the photo above. A neighbor gave the *Back to Eden* web address to Nicole, and she passed it on to her husband, Ray. As Nicole tells it: "I gave the card with the link written on it to Ramin. We sat down and watched it with the kids. It was exciting! We couldn't wait to get our first load of chips and get started!"

Their fifty-by-fifty-foot garden features new crops and some perennials. They also have one honeybee super (a stack of three frames). Inspired by Paul's use of chickens for his garden refuse, Ray and friends built a new chicken coop and yard adjacent to the garden.

Ray responded to the questionnaire.

> **Occupation:** Utility worker and part-time arborist (Ray) and keeper-at-home (Nicole).
> **Location:** Rainier, Oregon 97048.
> **Elevation:** 567 feet.
> **Average annual rainfall:** 67 inches.

Age of garden: Three years.

Size: 50 x 50 feet (expanded at end of 2013 season to 75x50, then 80x100 in 2014).

When the covering was applied: February 2013.

Expenses to growing food God's way transition: I already had an established garden site that we use. The paper and the cover were free. I've spent maybe $25 in fuel to move the chips into the garden. Lots of sweat equity.

Any new crops planted? No.

Seed source(s): Gurney's seed catalog.[241]

Did you amend your soil? With what? Yes. Compost, cover crops, lime, grass clippings, and some fertilizer.

241 http://www.gurneys.com/.

Fenced? What kind(s)? Yes. New Zealand open-wire field fence around the entire garden. [to keep out the deer of the garden and a small apple orchard].

Pest issues? The most problematic were slugs.

Best results (so far): The cucumbers. We've planted them for two years with no results, and now with the cover we received a bumper crop!

Worst crop this first year: Onions.

Comments from neighbors and family: People have been very curious, and I refer them to *Back to Eden*. My parents and younger brother are also using this method and seem to be pleased with the results.

What I wish I'd done: 1. Be patient and trust God. 2. I would have been more knowledgeable if I would have watched Paul's film a few times instead of once. I've since watched *Back to Eden* four times and I'm still learning things.

Zach and Tammy

Zach and Tammy's family live in Washington State, and they also had an established garden when they learned about the covering. Because of clay soils, they originally chose to use raised beds. So this year, they applied woodchips to the beds and were able to expand their garden area by applying the chips directly on top of the grass. Like Ray and Nicole's photos in mid-September, those from Zach and

Tammy represent end of season photos of gardens that have been largely harvested already. The benefit of my showing up in September is that they have experienced a full season and can share their lessons and victories with us.

Occupation: Remodeling contractor (Zach) and homemaker (Tammy).

Location: Near LaCenter, Washington 98629.

Elevation: 166 feet.

Average annual rainfall: 42 inches.

Age of Garden: Six years.

Size: Five 25 x 100-foot sections ("I used to till each one," says Tammy).

When the covering was applied: Late spring 2013.

Expenses to growing food God's way transition: There was no additional expense to do the Eden method. I was able to obtain all the chips I needed for free.

Any new crops planted? The only new crop would be the cantaloupes. I have always tried to grow them but never have had a crop until this year. I had 20+!!

Seed source(s): Territorial Seeds.[242]

Did you amend your soil? With what? I only amended about half my garden with cow manure, then ran out of time and manure. The half of the garden that did not get amended did just as well as the half of the garden that did get amended. I just put down the manure and covered it with chips.

Fenced? What kind(s)? We did not fence our garden.

Pest issues? I had issues with aphids on my Brussel sprouts and Japanese beetles on my cucumbers.

Best results (so far): I had so many great crops I can't just name one: green beans, peas, pumpkin, tomato, cantaloupe, peppers, eggplant, onions, carrots, beets, parsnips, cauliflower, broccoli, cabbage, Brussel sprouts, cucumbers, potato, squash, artichokes, lavender, asparagus, lettuce, chard, kale, collards, corn, dill, cilantro, strawberries, raspberries, blueberries, turnips, leeks, and herbs.

---

242 https://territorialseed.com/pages/vegetables.

Worst crop this first year: My worse crop was potatoes, but it was still a better crop than I had last year.

Comments from neighbors and family: My friends and neighbors came back with their friends. I had so much fun showing off my garden; thanks be to God. I have never been so proud of my garden. I am usually stressed out, in tears, and done with gardening by August. It was just too much work with very little fruit for all the time and labor I had spent out there. This year was less work with more fruit and, so much so, I gave away sacks of veggies every time someone wanted to see my garden! Oh . . . and now I love weeding!

What I wished I'd done: I wish I had done this sooner! Thanks be to God for His creation and for Paul Gautschi and his video. I am looking forward to meeting him and visiting his garden!

Vince and Diana

Vince and Diana were brand new at gardening and didn't have a clue. They actually live in the Sequim, Washington, area so this account focuses on meeting Paul and their interactions since then, how it affected their life and their brand-new garden. Here is their story:

Vince, Diana, and their two sons survived a major car accident in November of 2011. Each family member received head trauma in varying degrees. To speed recovery, Diana looked to healthy foods and desired a Vita-Mix[243] blender to improve their food inputs. She started searching the internet about raw foods and healthy diets (including raw food smoothies). One site she was reading linked to *Back to Eden*. That afternoon, she watched it and realized that it was filmed in her area.

After seeing the movie, she craved a low-maintenance, high-producing garden for her family and called a local tree service to see if they would deliver free woodchips. The man on the phone indicated that since Paul's video came out, woodchips are in high demand.

243 https: www.vitamix.com/us/en_us/.

Diana said, "I just saw that movie and want to start a garden!" He proceeded to describe to her how to find Paul's rental property in the city of Sequim and encouraged her by implying that Paul is often over there, so she drove over right away.

She went up the driveway and met a lady that lived there. Diana gathered up the courage to say, "I'm looking for Paul Gautschi." The lady said he was her brother-in-law, but that he was not there. On second look, the woman could barely see Paul hunched over; weeding. The sister-in-law coaxed Diana, "Why don't you go see him?" All of a sudden, the thought overwhelmed Diana, and she asked herself, "What in the heck am I doing?" Nevertheless, being stirred by her resolve to meet Paul and get started on the garden, she walked over to him. The dialogue went much like this:

> **Diana:** "Are you Paul?"
> **Paul:** "Yes, I am."
> **Diana:** "I just finished watching your movie thirty minutes ago, and I believe the Lord led me here to you."
> Paul smiles and laughs, as if to say, "Yep, the Lord can sure do that easy enough."
> They talked for about an hour. Finally . . .
> **Diana:** "I want to do this right now."
> **Paul:** "The Lord is saying to me, 'Be anxious for nothing.'[244] Until you get your own garden going, you can glean from mine."
> **Diana:** To herself, she thinks, "Is this for real? Is this man for real? Will he really do this for us?"

She came to him only for advice to get started, but here he's offering her family to start eating right right away, and that was a huge "God thing" for her . . . an unexpected blessing.

Understand Vince and Diana's life situation: He had just been medically discharged from the US Coast Guard, and they were all trying to regain normal functionality after the head trauma they received in the accident. Plus they weren't sure Vince would be readily employable, but they were sure his Coast Guard pension was insufficient for

244 "Be anxious for nothing, by in every thing by prayer and supplication, with thanksgiving, let your requests be made known unto God." Philippians 4:6

their family of four. As if that were not enough, Diana had a lump on the right side of her chest (more about that later).

Diana explains how she took Paul up on his generosity. "Two weeks later, we toured Paul's [garden on Craig Road] . . . and he invited us to take some lettuce and carrots home." Afterwards, since they drove by the road[245] that leads to Paul's street when they were going to doctor visits, they would stop and pick produce "about every two weeks." (Paul's recollection is that they liked his celery and arugula.) Vince and Diana planted that fall.

God impressed upon Diana that Vince should run the garden. She adds, "We wanted to do it Paul's way . . . God's way." Vince first planted garlic, then lettuce seeds, but the lettuce was not coming up. He recalls, "The birds were eating my seeds." Every now and then, they would call Paul for advice, and he was glad to give it. This time, they told of their seed loss, and he said to replant them, but he specifically told them, "Pray over your garden." "Why hadn't we thought of that?" was their response. Diana said their training and regular way of doing things tend to approach things without thinking of prayer.

Haven't you observed that, more often than not, we treat life like a recipe? If you add this, this, and this and then stir and bake, you will end up with the desired outcome, For the garden, if you lay down newspaper and cover it with woodchips, you'll have success, right? Well . . . read on.

Diana further shares: "We laid hands on the dirt of one section of our garden and asked God to bless the soil. It grew the best, and when it grew, it grew fast." That section had kale and beans. Diana perked up as she said, "When those beans were only four inches high, they began to bear fruit. We were shocked! We've got to remember to ask God to bless the land."

That again, intelligent readers, is relational permaculture being lived out.

Diana views their first-year garden as a success, even though they were on a learning curve. She says, "It's been an awesome experience" and "It's easier than I thought it would be; we hardly had any weeds at all, and the ones we got were almost a pleasure to pull because they came out so easy."

---

245 Chicken Coop Road.

But what about the lump Diana discovered almost a year prior? Her story takes us back to months before meeting Paul:

"When I first discovered a lump, it scared me. It was about the size of a fifty-cent piece, bigger than a quarter. Two mammograms later, they [the physicians] could not tell me what it was. They said it didn't look like cancer. After an ultrasound, they still could not discern what it was.

"Three months later, the growth is getting larger and painful to the touch. My doctor sent me back for another ultrasound. That doctor was not happy to see me and chided that they already told me that they couldn't help me."

It was this health challenge that also motivated her to look into a healthy diet containing raw foods and nutritious beverages.

"I felt anything that was natural would benefit my body, but organic food is so expensive. We didn't have the time or the resources to do a conventional garden, but we felt that this [gathering food from Paul's garden] was something we could do, something we could afford," Diana relates. "We began eating Paul's food." If they couldn't eat it all fresh, she would freeze it to eat later.

Over those few months, Diana noticed that her lump was getting "smaller, softer, and the pain lessened." She testifies: "The only thing we did different was eat Paul's produce and pray [to God for healing]. Now, I can't even discern the edges."

Her female primary care physician was astounded and pleased the lump was dissolving. Paul was very blessed when she told him about this. He did not even know of her condition, but God did and had directed her to him and placed her husband in one accord to grow their own garden. For many wives, that in itself would constitute a miracle!

Later in early 2014, the growth had not fully disappeared, but Diana stated, "Until the Lord heals it or removes it completely, I use it as a reminder to me, like a little monitor, measuring how my faith and diet are doing. I am thankful for the minimal presence it has in my life."

In case you're wondering, Diana continues making smoothies consisting of at least two fruits and two vegetables and not adding sweeteners. Her liquid base is either water, orange juice, or homemade kefir (from raw cow's milk).

During my June 2019 Facebook IM with Diana, I said, "Need to ask you about the lump, OK?" Her response: "Not there! That's the short answer. Bless you!" Yay, God!

YOUR BIBLE SPEAKS COMMUNITY CHURCH

This congregation meets in an older, middle-class-to-disadvantaged portion of Portland, Oregon. After seeing the documentary, Thomas, a member of Your Bible Speaks Community Church (YBSCC) approached the leaders of the church with the idea of utilizing a large grassy area behind the church to make a garden. Initially it was not well received. The leaders felt that adding a garden would notably increase their water bill, so it was rejected on a financial stewardship (got to keep costs down) basis.

Later, **Thomas** let the leaders know that this garden would not require watering, and some of the leaders watched the *Back to Eden* film. They were satisfied that the water bill would not increase and were now anxious to see the garden come to fruition. With the help of Kenyan-born **Edward** and others, Thomas organized an effort to lay out the garden size and location. They started with a 100 x 100 foot area,[246] purchased construction paper by the roll to cover the grass, and arranged for the local electric company to leave its fresh woodchips at a designated location. A friend lent them a trailer that actually dumps, and they were on their way.

---

246 10,000 square feet or 929 square meters.

Occupation: N/a.
Location: Portland, Oregon.
Elevation: 180 feet.
Average annual rainfall: 39.14 inches.
Age of garden: New.
Size: 100 x 100 feet (10,000 square feet) or nearly ¼ acre [expanded in October 2013 to 150 x 100 feet].
When the covering was applied: March 2013.
Expenses to growing food God's way transition: The original chips for covering the 100 x 100 foot area were donated, as well as the delivery and spread of chips; since then we have spent about $1,000 on seeds, equipment, and tractors.

Any new crops planted? All were new. The most impressive were the tomatoes, peppers, squash, beans, peas, radishes, chard, collards, broccoli, corn, lettuce, cucumbers, carrots, and potatoes.
Seed source(s): Mainly Territorial Seeds.
Did you amend your soil? With what? Nothing other than chips.
Fenced? What kind(s)? Chain-link on east side property line, wood fence between lot and church west side, wood fence on north property line, and open to street on the south side.

Pest issues? Squirrels got to the corn, insects were insignificant, and no slug and snail problems until fall.

Best results (so far): All grew tremendously except cabbage, planted by seed, but were not thinned.

Worst crop this first year: Potatoes: we cut the potatoes and immediately planted the pieces. Will plant whole next time.

Carrots: we had to plant at ground level and apparently where they were planted was hard pan, not letting the carrot develop a tuber.

Comments from neighbors and family:

Everyone was amazed at the production with addition of NO water through a dry and warm summer.

What we wished we'd done: The main thing we wished we had done is put down at least 8-10 inches of chips to better control the weeds. The paper worked, but it got wet in places before we put chips on it, and the chips tore the paper and some weeds came through.

YBSCC pastor Louis Turner.

The YBSCC garden is just beginning to serve as an outreach and resource to the community. Many neighbors have inquired about it and are especially awed by seeing all the growth with no watering. The church lets neighbors harvest some things to take home and eat or store. Next season, they are planning to provide sampler food baskets to give to the neighbors, door to door, as a means of being a blessing to the community.

FUNGUS AMONG US DEBACLE

After the woodchips had been applied to the church's grass area, a sporadic growth later appeared on top of the chips. This was a mystery to the garden tenders. The crusty-looking white and yellow media looked similar to byproduct of illicit methamphetamine production. A Portland police officer viewed the phenomenon and validated that the suspicious material looked like some meth lab had dumped its waste on the church's garden.

Accordingly, the Portland Fire Bureau was called in to make its assessment. It validated the officer's hunch and summarily called in their Haz-Mat team. The garden was cordoned off with police tape as technicians, in full body suits, roamed the garden, delicately taking samples of the "likely toxic" material. After many minutes of onsite testing, they approached Tom and the other anxious bystanders and sheepishly declared, "It's a protein," and with that, they were off. Show over.

On a personal note, our former dog Dixie used to enjoy lying on the freshly dumped woodchips we received twice from Asplundh.[247] She liked the warmth it provided on chilly mornings. One day, we noticed a mess on the woodchips. I initially thought it was a rained-on slice of white bread that even the dog did not want to eat. Other family members felt the dog had eaten some grass and barfed on the chips.

What the church and the Devines encountered is commonly called "dog vomit fungus." Its real name is *fuligo septica*, or dog vomit slime mold. That is, it is not a true species of fungi, though it looks like it. It is a mold according to **Professor Thomas J. Volk**[248] of the University of Wisconsin-LaCrosse. It feeds on bacteria of decaying material, like rotted tree stumps.

So, does this slime mold ruin the woodchips? Are we to be alarmed? No, but it is good to be informed. Some folks should treat it as an allergen if they are prone to mold allergies.

247 http://www.asplundh.com/?s=wood+chips.
248 http://botit.botany.wisc.edu/toms_fungi/june99.html.

SLIME MOLD 101

Slime mold goes through life stages. It often develops its "glob"[249] during the night, and we discover it the next morning. It can be white, yellow, or orange-ish; that is its fruiting stage. Next, it hardens and becomes crusty. Finally, it seems to decompose into a powdery remnant, which is its spore stage. Millions of spores will emanate from the mold as it is crushed or even merely rained on.

The good news is that this mold has a property within it that chelates high levels of toxic metals, like zinc.

If its existence totally freaks you out, then do not spray it with water (as you would real dog vomit). Rather, gingerly gather it into a plastic bag and dispose of it if you must. (Paul says he would just bury the mold under the woodchips.)

---

249 Plasmodium: a mass of protoplasm.

CHAPTER 20

Turning a Corner

When I was a child, I spake as a child, I understood as
a child, I thought as a child: but when I became a man,
I put away childish things.

– 1 Corinthians 13:11

THE ORIGINAL GROWING FOOD GOD'S WAY began in 2012. It was
written over the course of nearly two years. One morning, while
working on the manuscript, I woke up and was pondering more about
gut flora footprints.[250] and I realized that we (particularly Americans)
can assemble a fine garden but may still be prone to destructive eating practices in the off season or even all year long by force of habit.
I thought about what I had eaten the day before, Friday, February 15,
2013. (I hope the following doesn't shock you.)

As best as I could remember, I had eaten for breakfast, two pieces
of (white flour) raisin toast (with real butter); for lunch, a processed
meat (turkey) sandwich with cheddar cheese, no lettuce or mayon-
naise, on two pieces of Dave's Organic 21-grain bread, plus a bowl of
non-sugared, rice-based cereal with raw milk (from our Jersey cow);
for an afternoon snack, a Snickers bar that was given to me as a gift
by one of my kids (so I had to eat it, right?); then for dinner, two

---

250 See "Deleted Chapters" in the appendix for an explanation.

homemade, grilled hamburgers (one on a white bun) with a piece of green lettuce, raw onions, dill pickle, and ketchup one the first and the same on the second, except it had grilled onions instead of raw and I substituted a piece of organic Lacinato kale for the lettuce. (See how Paul's influence on me finally kicked in?)

GUT FLORA FOOTPRINT

Someday, I'd like to be able to score my food intake as to what I did to my gut flora footprint (GFF) that day. But for now, let's look at our habits and proclivities when it comes to looking for food, preparing food, and eating foods, as well as drinking beverages. We should change the adage "You are what you eat" to "You are what you eat AND drink" or better yet, "You are what you eat, drink, and breathe!"

Now, seven years later, no one has stepped up to develop a reliable rating for gut flora footprint. In 2017, New York Times best-selling author **Dr. Joel Furman** developed a food scoring system he coined ANDI (Aggregate Nutrient Density Index).[251] It attempts to rank the nutrient values of foods we commonly eat. The scores range from 1 to 1000. Dr. Furman is to be commended for his laser-focus on nutrient density. Yet, we need more.

To be the gold standard of useful food ratings, the system has to rate each food item, based on cooked or raw, followed by four categories: (1) store-bought, (2) organic, (3) fresh-picked (before ripened), and (4) fresh-picked (ripened). Also, I don't take any food scoring system to the bank that doesn't have negative scoring. According to the ANDI chart, cola scores a 1, and french fries score a 12. Sorry, not going there. The greatest benefit of the chart is to note the high scorers (127 and up). The five items scoring a perfect 1000 are Swiss chard, watercress, mustard greens, collard greens, and (you guessed it) kale.

In all fairness to ANDI, it focuses on biologic results, and GFF would focus on metabolic results. The good items would track well

---

251 Nutrients evaluated were fiber, calcium, iron, magnesium, phosphorus, potassium, zinc, copper, manganese, selenium, vitamin A, beta carotene, alpha carotene, lycopene, lutein, zeaxanthin, vitamin E, vitamin C, thiamin, riboflavin, niacin, pantothetic acid, vitamin B6, folate, vitamin B12, choline, vitamin K, phytosterols, glucosinolates, angiogenesis inhibitors, organosulfides, aromatase inhibitors, resistant starch, resveratrol and an Oxygen Radical Absorbance Capacity (ORAC) score. ORAC measures the antioxidant (or free radical scavenging) capacity of a food.

between both types of scores, but the low end of ANDI would have negative GFF scores (as low as −100).

Our food, our beverages, and our air make up the inputs to our bodies that cause them to maintain, grow, or denigrate. The better the inputs, the better the growth and maintenance. By illustration, the inputs to your car, truck, or motorcycle are air, liquids (fuel/anti-freeze), and lubricants (oil, grease). The better the inputs are to your vehicle, the better it will run and last.

I grew up in Arizona. There was a fair number of horses back in the early 1960s. Horse inputs are food, water, and air (just like us). Horses, like kids, enjoy sugar. Sugar cubes were given to them as a snack, but you'd never replace alfalfa or horse pellets with sugar cubes for their main source of food. In the wild, there is no source of white, refined sugar for the roaming mustangs to eat. They eat food that is local (what's growing around them), fresh (live), raw (uncooked), and in season. Though there is no meat in their diet, their strong muscles (ingesting grasses and occasional berries) receive the protein muscles rely on. They drink water from a spring, pond, lake, or stream. As you can see, there is much we can learn about proper and healthy eating from a wild horse.

Do you remember the three things the Gautschis wanted when they moved out of Los Angeles? Fresh air, clean water, and live, healthy food, the three key inputs.

Americans eat out of habit. Most of us were trained to eat three meals a day: morning, mid-day, and early evening. We also have a tendency to eat until our stomachs are physically full and/or till a craving (sugar, salt, mineral, favorite tastes, or smells) has been satisfied. Also, to not feel guilty or wasteful, we are trained to clear our plate.

NUTRITIONAL HONESTY

You have heard the term "intellectually honest"; it's where you appeal to the other person to set feelings aside and look at something objectively and sensibly. In the following, I am going to be nutritionally honest. It may not feel good, but it is honest, nonetheless. If we could listen to our body better, we would find it is telling us when it has its quota of necessary nutrients to get us through the day. We are not used to sensing that because we don't eat the right things, don't eat enough of the right things, or cook out nutrients from the right things, any and all of which leave our bodies starved for proper attention, proper inputs.

Most Americans go through each day in various states of dehydration or what I call "water deficit syndrome." Our body asks for water, but instead we drink coffee, commercial (sugar and sodium-added) juices, and soft drinks and wonder why we're not satisfied. Most foods (and beverages) that we consume get an F for what they do to our gut flora. As a result, our bodies are left in a state of dissatisfaction and disease vulnerability.

You may be old enough to remember **Mick Jagger**'s popular hit in the 1970s, "I Can't Get No Satisfaction," which describes the food and liquid intake for many of us. And that is what our body is trying to convey to us. We go from one can of pop a day to three cans of pop, from one hot dog for lunch to two, from a regular candy bar at two thirty for a snack to a king-sized bar in an elusive effort to feel full. All the while, our bodies are trying to find the proverbial needle in a haystack: to attach to some modicum of nutrition (amongst the nutrient-free sewage we consume) and send it on down multitudinous pipelines called our circulation system.

Our bloodstream tries to share that one grain of life-sustaining nutrient with our entire body, and most areas get left out. Then we wonder why we feel anemic, why we hit a brick wall by 3 p.m. (or earlier), why we don't seem to have the energy we need or used to have, and why we don't sleep well at night. We chalk it up to aging or the stress of the day; it certainly is not our fault! We did not bring this upon ourselves, did we? Indeed, nearly all of us did and do. Day after day.

There are many seminal, powerful moments recorded for us in Holy Scripture. One is where Moses is laying out all the Lord expects of the freed Hebrew slaves in Deuteronomy. Toward the end, in chapter 30, verse 19 and on into 20, Moses says:

> I call heaven and earth to record this day against you,
> that I have set before you life and death, blessing and
> cursing: therefore choose life, that both thou and thy
> seed may live: That thou mayest love the LORD thy

God, and that thou mayest obey His voice, and that thou mayest cleave unto Him: for He is thy life, and the length of thy days.

The moral of this Bible passage is when you face a choice between life and death, choose life. In this case, choosing life means choosing to eat the foods and drink the fluids that add life to your body and not detract from it.

A Tale of Two . . . Gates

Picture in your mind two chain-link gates, both ten feet tall. Each is surrounded with higher fencing, very secure. As you study the two gates, you notice that one is almost wide open; the other is closed and locked tightly. Let's add to this image the fact that you have to get through one gate or the other to stay alive. You have to make a choice. If you are a parent, you will be also choosing for your child or children as well. Though the gates are not very far apart, there are two distinctly different forms of existence on the other sides. Before you decide which gate to go through, let's add some crucial facts and realities:

Life behind the open gate will expose you and your children (every day) to increasingly high rates of juvenile diabetes, adult diabetes, obesity, heart disease, respiratory distress (asthma, allergies, etc.), thyroid complications, juvenile rheumatoid arthritis, COPD, chronic bowel diseases, acne, fibro-myalgia, sleeplessness, skin diseases, dementia, ADHD, dyslexia, leukemia, tooth decay, gum diseases, impaired vision, all forms of cancer, and a host of other ills. Life behind the closed gate promises very little likelihood of contracting the above diseases and, in many cases, may limit or reverse said diseases.

Let's call the latter the Sanity Gate, which by default makes the former the Insanity Gate. Understand the saneness of the gate is NOT determined by which is the easiest to get through. The saneness is measured only by the quality and longevity of life on the other side. Are you tracking with me? Our only way through the Sanity Gate is to have a key! Question: Is getting and using the key worth it to you? Is it worth it to me?

This is a no-brainer. We should lovingly and relentlessly search everywhere we can to find the key to get us and our loved ones through the formidable Sanity Gate if it will spare them near-certain health consequences or correct what has already shown up in their lives. Same goes for us.

Our desire to enter the Sanity Gate must be matched with our commitment to do so. *When your commitment gets overtaken by convenience or habit, it reveals your true level of commitment.*

Former NFL player-turned-preacher, **Dr. Voddie Baucham,**[252] has given messages all over the country. Each one of his messages typically has at least one moment where he says something that hits you right between the eyes. Generally, there is silence in the audience as they grapple with how personally poignant that statement is to most of them. At that point, Voddie breaks the silence and says, "Somebody better say amen or ouch!" For me, most of the time, it is "ouch." That is how I felt when I first heard the above statement about our level of commitment.

As an American society, we are so used to getting things easy and quick. The concept of requiring forethought and effort on our part for something as basic as what we eat seems ridiculous. We place low effort and low input over the proven benefits of high effort and high input. In a nutshell, we have sacrificed our health on the altar of convenience. We have elevated convenience to a god-like position in our lives, and we need to see the consequences of this pattern of behavior before it is too late.

In a word, it's *idolatry*. Satan would like you to believe only those who burn candles and pray to idols in caves are committing idolatry. Wrong! Anytime we elevate something or someone in our lives over God, we are walking on idolatrous ground, statues or not. Most often, the idol we are worshipping is ourselves (I, me, my, mine).

~~Don't~~ Sweat It!

One of the benefits of tending our own garden (or helping others do so) is that it can make us sweat. Why is that good? Because sweat is one of the ways our body rids itself of internal toxins. So, it's a win-win. You not only are working (high input) to grow and eventually eat

---

252 https://www.voddiebaucham.org/.

good, fresh, live food, but in the process, you are discharging some bad elements resident in your body too.

The scripture at the beginning of Genesis 3, known as the "Genesis curse," includes verse 19: "In the sweat of thy face shalt thou eat bread, till thou return unto the ground; for out of it wast thou taken: for dust thou art, and unto dust shalt thou return." I also want you to see another facet of how loving God is to Adam and to us. Even God's curse had within it a mechanism for Adam to relieve his body of the wrong things that were going to enter it as a result of the fall.

How sweaty do you get when accumulating food? Even in the height of summer, your grocery stores, warehouse stores, local food banks, and cooperatives are likely cooled or air conditioned. Maybe you sweat a bit if you head out to the farmer's market in July during your lunch break, but other than that, food acquisition is probably low effort and low input. Let's resolve to sweat more and hydrate ourselves better.

But isn't a garden that grows food God's way easier and less sweaty? It is! As you eat the produce grown with a covering, you should have less toxins and, therefore, less need to sweat. The sweating comes at the forefront and the resting comes over time.

The sixty-four-thousand-dollar question is "What good is there in growing food God's way if we don't eat and drink properly? (Amen. . . . And ouch?)

FOOD LIFESTYLES

The verse at the beginning of this chapter talks of "putting away childish things." Do you still eat the same breakfast cereals—sugar coated, unnaturally colored and flavored—you ate as a kid? You may remember back in the 1960s and 1970s how we were either so decadent or brain-dead that some cereals even had the word "sugar" or "frosted" in their names as an enticement?

Before we disparage our parents for taking us through the open (Insanity) gate each morning, you have to understand that they were relying on pathetic advice from what should have been reliable sources:

pediatricians, the USDA,[253] the FDA,[254] the US surgeon general, etc. The food pyramid of the 1960s is way different from the visual guide today, MyPlate.[255] Then, eating cold breakfast cereals was a means to take in the "necessary dairy items" the pyramid prescribed.

Here was the Madison Avenue (advertising) mantra: As long as you gotta eat it (cereal), it might as well be fun, sweet, and maybe go snap, crackle, and pop. Thus, the industrial food complex conglomerates were in a race to create the next kid breakfast sensation, and have customers for Life.

Now that we are grownups, can we stop habitually eating childhood breakfast foods and start eating beneficial grains, spices, raw milk, almond milk, yogurt, honey, kefir, kombucha, eggs, fruit, nuts, and a host of other sane things for breakfast?

Won't you try to go through the Sanity Gate each morning? It sets the tone for the rest of your day.

FREEDOM ISN'T FREE

A popular (but now politically incorrect) 1965 song during the latter end of the American civil rights movement was called "Freedom Isn't Free."[256] It reminds us that we have to pay a price (sacrifice) for the liberties we take for granted. A garden with a proper covering promises a lot of freedom and rest *once it is in place*, but know that you will have to pay a price to get it to that point; to restore the cover. Implicit in the biblical term "tend" are the adjectives work, labor, dress, and keep.

God installed Adam to tend the garden, to work it. The level of work for Adam was not such that caused him to sweat, so his burden was light. Indeed, with perfect inputs of food, water, oxygen, along with a perfect environmental climate, he didn't have any toxins that needed to leach out of his system via sweating. That reasonably ensures us he did not break up the land and take off the cover. Most folks would call that tilling or plowing.

253 United States Department of Agriculture. http://www.usda.gov/wps/portal/usda/.
254 Food and Drug Administration. http://www.fda.gov/.
255 Since 2011, USDA food pyramids have been replaced with a food initiative called My-Plate. See https://www.myplate.gov/.
256 Written by Paul Colwell.

Deuteronomy 22:10 says: "You shall not plow with a donkey and an ox together." So, if the Bible talks about plowing, it must condone it, right? Let's look a little closer. God does not say: "Thou shalt plow." He is saying that if you are going to plow, don't mix animal breeds. Nor does He call plowing a sin; instead, He talks about the "plowing of the wicked." Of all the verses that speak of plowing or plow, only two are in the New Testament.

Two of the total twelve verses are related as analogies to people's attitudes and actions: "Even as I have seen, they that plow iniquity, and sow wickedness, reap the same" (Job 4:8) and "A[n] high look, and a proud heart, and the plowing of the wicked, is sin" (Proverbs 21:4). Some of the Old Covenant verses follow up the term "plowing" with "breaking up the clods."[257] Thanks to Paul, we have learned to ask ourselves, "Why were there (dirt) clods?" You know the answer. Because the soil was compacted. Because the cover had been taken off. Beware of thinking that just because a method is mentioned in the Bible it receives some sort of heavenly sanction.[258] Divorce is mentioned in scripture and goes so far as instructing men on its implementation, but it is not endorsed.[259]

Having the Will to Live Right

Jesus encountered a man who was infirmed (couldn't walk) for thirty-eight years. He asked him, "Will you be made whole?" I always thought that was a strange thing to ask, but if our lifestyles are causal to a disease or diseases (infirmities), we are living with, then it begs the question to find out how serious we are about living right to live healthier and better.

When NASCAR driver Jerrod Sessler was sentenced by his doctor's prognosis of a 95 percent likelihood of dying, he was forced to seek an alternative method to allopathic medicine (surgeries, strategic poisoning, and radiation) to find a means to survive. That path led him to nutrient-dense foods and supplements, plus a huge change in his eating habits and lifestyle. To some degree, we have to ask

---

257 Isaiah 28:24 and Hosea 10:11.
258 See Deuteronomy 24:1 and then Jesus's instruction in Mathew 5:31-32.
259 Mark 10:1-9. "For the hardness of your heart, he wrote you this precept" (v.5).

ourselves: "Will I be made whole? Do I have the determination (will) to not only survive but also thrive?"

Jesus exhorts us in Matthew 18:9: "And if thine eye offend thee, pluck it out, and cast it from thee: it is better for thee to enter into life with one eye, rather than having two eyes to be cast into hell fire." Sounds more like the allopathic approach of surgery, doesn't it? Not exactly. The point is: what should we cut out of our life (sugar, white flour, GMOs, trans-fats, etc.) that will tend to death and not to life? Jesus is not saying "all eyes are bad." He points out that if we habitually use our eye to, say, lust for people or things, we would be better off without sight. It is causing us to fall. If eating cheese puffs or smoking puts us on a collision course with cancer or other diseases, then we need to cut it out of our lives while the moratorium can do some good.

Getting back to the man who couldn't walk for thirty-eight years, what did Jesus do? He told the man: "Rise, take up thy bed, and walk."[260] And immediately the man was made whole, took up his bed, and walked. He *did* want to be made whole, and even carried his bed on the Sabbath as he was instructed. In other words, he took action![261]

WHAT'S THE PURPOSE?

Growing Food God's Way is not a get-nutrient-dense-food-quick scheme. Rather, it is an enter-into-wisdom scheme, a get-connected-with-God scheme, if you will. If you approach it as a fad, it may serve you only as long as fads last, but if you embrace it as a way of life, then you are truly entering into the joy of the Master.

To progress in turning a corner, it is optimal to learn about nutrient-dense food and what it is made up of. Here is a simple, unsophisticated, definition. Nutrient-dense foods are foods chock-full of natural nutrients such that the good things are not ancillary but are designed by God to give us maximum health benefits with relatively little consumption. To put it more bluntly, they are the foods that give us the most bang for the bite. Yes, nutritional quality initially trumps quality in taste, but that is eventually resolved when our taste buds and the portion of our brain that controls dopamine[262] and serotonin

---

260 John 5:8.
261 See John 5:1-9.
262 The caudate nucleus.

course correct to real foods. A raw carrot can evoke the same pleasure responses in our nervous system as a jelly-filled doughnut. It is a matter of conditioning.

So what nutrient-dense foods does Paul grow and consume? For starters, kale, cilantro, and apples (to name a few).

Books have been written about "super foods" or ultra-high-density fruits, nuts, and vegetables. Not surprisingly, God has provided regions all around the world with food that has unique properties that are very healthful. Apples don't tend to make anyone's list of super-foods, but consider the following about apples. They:

- have the highest ratio of free phenols[263] among commonly eaten fruit. Free phenols aren't bound to other compounds, so they are freely absorbed in the bloodstream.
- are good for lung function and reduce incidences of asthma, and even help smokers reduce the risk of chronic obstructive pulmonary disease (COPD).
- contain quercetin, a flavonoid[264] that gives apples their color and inhibits the growth of cancer cells in the lungs, prostate, liver, breast, and colon.
- lower LDL (bad) cholesterol and also raise beneficial HDL (good) cholesterol.
- provide dietary fiber via the skin that saves the colon mucous membrane from exposure to toxic substances by binding to cancer-causing chemicals inside the colon.
- protect against heart disease by slowing the oxidation process involved in the build-up of arterial plaque.

The high consumption of flavonoids and fiber in apples in some groups of people is directly associated with lower risk of coronary disease mortality and thrombotic stroke.

263 A natural and aromatic organic compound known as carbolic acid.
264 The Department of Environmental and Molecular Toxicology at Oregon State University defines flavonoids as "polyphenolic compounds that are ubiquitous in nature and are categorized, according to chemical structure, into flavonols, flavones, flavanones, isoflavones, catechins, anthocyanidins and chalcones." They further assert that: "flavonoids have aroused considerable interest recently because of their potential beneficial effects on human health—they have been reported to have antiviral, anti-allergic, antiplatelet, anti-inflammatory, anti-tumor and antioxidant activities." See https://lpi.oregonstate.edu/mic/dietary-factors/phytochemicals/flavonoids.

Eating just one apple a day can decrease serum cholesterol (LDLs) by 8-11 percent, and eating two a day reduces it by up to 16 percent.

The natural fructose and fiber in apples helps keep blood sugar levels stable for type 2 diabetics.

If you can't eat your apples fresh, optimal storage of apples is at 35-40°F[265] with 80-90 percent relative humidity. Otherwise, consider slicing apples and drying them for future enjoyment.[266] Remember, tree ripening and fruit-basket ripening are not the same thing.

Paul says: "The best apple to grow is Honey Crisp.[267] Their storage quality is incredible. I have a walk-in cooler in back, and they last for the entire year. I eat apples every day, three a day, all year long. My point is that God made them that way, and now they are telling us we can't eat them? I am telling people today to plant fruit trees because the future says you are going to be so wealthy and so blessed because [apples] won't be available in the store. Fruit trees are much less work than a garden. These fruit trees are one to thirty-four years old. The new one produced the first year. What I am doing now, because some varieties get scab, I am cutting out those and planting disease-resistant ones."

TIME TO MAN UP

Turning a corner also means that men need to be men in society again. Excuse me? Paul's motivation to grow a great garden was to provide good, healthy food for his family. That provider instinct needs to be felt by all husbands, fathers, and grandfathers. We have dropped the ball. We have confused the practice of food accumulation with the duty of food generation. Somehow, we guys count it as Mission Accomplished if we bring home a paycheck that allows us to go to the Hundred-Dollar-Store (Costco or Sam's Club) and leave with enough food to fill our cupboards and refrigerator/freezers. Somehow, that satisfies a man's hunter/gatherer instincts, but should it?

Given the opportunity to do better, a loving, protective man will always do the best he can. God put Adam (man) in the garden to tend

---

265 1.67° to 4.44° Celsius.
266 Adapted from "Apple: No Ordinary Fruit," *Young At Heart News*, September 2012, p.12.
267 Not that it is his favorite tasting apple, which is Gravenstein, but they don't store. On one visit there, he gave me a Sweet Sixteen apple and it was amazing!

it. That doesn't mean he became an expert, but he was responsible for it. Another way to put it is that he wasn't chosen by merit, but he was chosen.

Paul wanted the best food for his family because it was the only family he would ever have. If he could spare them illnesses, literally prevent harm from coming to them by poor diets, then how could he accept any lesser alternative? Again, amen or ouch! What kind of loving father or mother are you? A garden-fresh salad versus a fast food, GMO-laden, taco is quite a contrast. Twenty ounces of good water is vastly superior to a thirty-two-ounce soft drink.

By the way, what do you drink? Why would your kids drink anything better than what their mom or dad does? These are tough questions only if we are on the wrong side of them. Years ago, I heard a wise proverb that says: "What parents excuse in moderation, their children will excuse in excess."[268] Ouch and amen time again! That goes for gambling, pill-dependence, smoking, drinking that one can of beer during the weekend ball game or that double-shot latte, your computer or smartphone gaming, whatever.

In the last appendix entry, "All's Well That Ends Well," Paul and Carol repented of the way they handled the first well. They purposed to do the right thing in faith, not the fearful way of the first well. When it comes to eating and drinking, you can repent of habitually poor eating habits. Pray about what you eat plus how you prepare and eat it. It's a matter of humility and passion for doing the best for yourself, your kids, and your grandkids.

Though the road of fast, convenient, and processed food is well traveled, you can make a detour. You can follow the safer paths that lead to better health and stewardship of the only body you have. The Sanity Gate awaits your passage!

---

268 Shared by Dr. William Gothard.

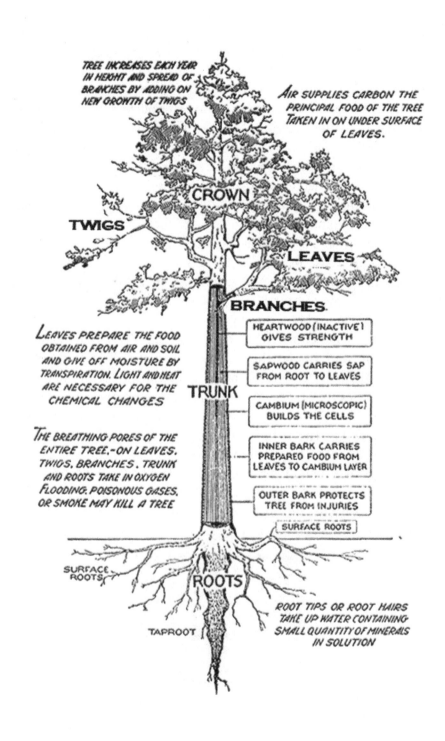

TREE INCREASES EACH YEAR IN HEIGHT AND SPREAD OF BRANCHES BY ADDING ON NEW GROWTH OF TWIGS

AIR SUPPLIES CARBON THE PRINCIPAL FOOD OF THE TREE TAKEN IN ON UNDER SURFACE OF LEAVES.

CROWN

TWIGS

LEAVES

BRANCHES

LEAVES PREPARE THE FOOD OBTAINED FROM AIR AND SOIL AND GIVE OFF MOISTURE BY TRANSPIRATION. LIGHT AND HEAT ARE NECESSARY FOR THE CHEMICAL CHANGES

THE BREATHING PORES OF THE ENTIRE TREE,—ON LEAVES. TWIGS, BRANCHES, TRUNK AND ROOTS TAKE IN OXYGEN FLOODING, POISONOUS GASES, OR SMOKE MAY KILL A TREE

TRUNK

HEARTWOOD (INACTIVE) GIVES STRENGTH

SAPWOOD CARRIES SAP FROM ROOT TO LEAVES

CAMBIUM (MICROSCOPIC) BUILDS THE CELLS

INNER BARK CARRIES PREPARED FOOD FROM LEAVES TO CAMBIUM LAYER

OUTER BARK PROTECTS TREE FROM INJURIES

SURFACE ROOTS

SURFACE ROOTS

ROOTS

TAPROOT

ROOT TIPS OR ROOT HAIRS TAKE UP WATER CONTAINING SMALL QUANTITY OF MINERALS IN SOLUTION

CHAPTER 21

DIY Like Paul

GROWING FOOD GOD'S WAY is all about doing things yourself and relying on God and not on man. Three of Paul's biggest DIY projects are pruning, grafting, and seed saving.

You can watch Paul prune on YouTube videos like https://www.knowyourfarmer?navid=KNOWYOURFARMER.

Before we look into his most active DIY project, let's make sure we're on the same page about trees.

TREES 101

First, there are two basic kinds of trees: deciduous and evergreen. The former are trees that shed their leaves or needles every year (like oak, maple, fruit and nut trees, European larch), and the latter keep their foliage (like pine, spruce, fir, and cedar trees). Even the palm trees that Paul grew up with would be considered evergreens.

Next, consider the anatomy of a tree. As you see on the opposite page, the ends of the roots on the ground are where the moisture and nutrients are taken up. So often we water a tree at its base where the trunk enters the ground, when we should be watering below the ends of the branches (the drip line) where natural rain nourishes the tree.

Grafting

Here is Paul's take on grafting: "There are many benefits to grafting. For those who don't have much space for trees, it provides more varieties of fruit in the same space. It is key to cross-pollination. I was amazed one year that I had a pear tree that was thirty feet away from another pear tree. It was not bearing fruit even though the bees were in the orchard, so it was being pollinated. When I grafted [another variety] into that pear and it bloomed, that next year it was loaded with fruit! I saw the advantages of the pollen being *within the tree*, so grafting really increases pollination. If we pay attention to what's happening to the planet with the overuse of pesticides, [we see] the bee population is declining at a scary rate. What these farmers don't realize is if you don't have bees, you won't have food. What I think is awesome about grafting is that without bees I'm going to have pollination happening just from the wind. [Grafting] is something I am doing more and more of because they keep coming up with new varieties and I have room in my orchard.

"Years ago, I asked the Holy Spirit how to do [grafting], and this is what He told me: This method of grafting is very, very simple. Onto a branch of a tree, I bring in what's called scion wood [a young twig from the other tree]. I do it branch to branch. The principle is to join the cambium layer (that's the layer below the bark) between the existing branch and the scion wood. The cambium layer is where all the life force is in the tree. You have to make sure that both cambium layers are in contact. You want to make sure the twig you're putting in and the piece you're grafting into are the same diameter [a half-inch or 1.25cm minimum], so the cambium lines up. What I do is cut the branch I want to graft flat with a saw, and with my pruner, I cut a slit in the middle of it (crack it open). This does not remove any wood from the branch I'm working on. On the piece that I'm grafting, I cut both sides at an angle (like an arrow), and I slide that into the opening (of the receiving branch). The longer the angle, the more cambium you have coming in contact. Make sure you line up both sides before you do any cutting to make sure they are the same size; like holding your two index fingers side by side, you can tell they are the same diameter. Doing that with the scion wood helps to ensure the connection is right.

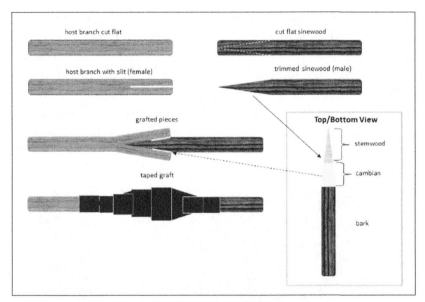

"Afterwards I apply cheap electrical tape (from Taiwan) because it stretches. As you wrap around that union with black electrical tape, it keeps those cambium layers in alignment. When you wrap it well, it is immovable. I start at the base of the union and wrap beyond the joint and back up again, probably two or three wraps. You wrap a bit tight and take advantage of the tape stretching. That's what keeps the air and disease out. When the sun hits it, it heals quicker. It is an amazing, effective way to graft. Be generous with the tape because it is cheap and you want a secure joint. As the branches bond together, the tape will eventually fall off. You know you were successful when the new branches start to bud out. It is so amazing to see, and I just say, 'Yay, God.'"

I asked Paul if there were times when the graft didn't work out right. He said, "It has happened to me when it didn't take, and I have to cut off the deadwood. Next time, I will probably go somewhere else on the tree to do another one. Occasionally it will fail.

"One thing . . . is important, and this is scary. . . . One year I grafted a tree, and the first year four apples grew. I said, 'Look at that—four full apples are growing there!' Then one day I go out there, and it's all lying on the ground because [the joint] broke off. The union was not yet steady enough to support all the weight, and I lost my good graft. So, I'm telling people that if you get apples (or pears) the first year, take them off immediately because the union has not thickened enough to hold the weight. It has to be totally enmeshed in the tree. It takes time; doesn't happen in the first year. If you get fruit, take it off at the earliest stage so bigger fruit doesn't strain the union. I was so sad because it was such a cool variety. Man, I come out and saw the thing was hinged out and dead. What a bummer! I know the temptation to leave, say, one apple to grow out, but I'm telling you from experience, that apple is not worth losing the graft." Pruning that first year means you have an eye for the next season.

Paul continues: "All the stuff you read in books about specialty pins and grafting paste are unnecessary. This is so simple and it makes it easy."

As to which branches to graft, Paul says: "Where you apply the graft is important. Put it in a place where there's plenty of room to grow. Don't put it in a place where it will grow back into the tree or be shaded by other branches. You want your grafts to be there forever, so place it in a place where it can be forever. If you put it out on an end, you'll be cutting it off next year when you're pruning. So the placement of that graft is very important. You want to place it where it can grow up, then out. The graft becomes an upright leader, and from it will spring lateral growth that will bear the fruit. When you buy a fruit tree, it's [called] a whip, and branches will spread forth from it.

This is basically the same thing. Your grafted whip will produce multiple branches later on."

When do we graft? Paul tells us the textbook way to graft is to cut the scion wood in the fall and store it in a cool place all winter. Next spring, as the sap stops being dormant and the host tree buds start to form, you do your grafting then.

Paul follows a different path: "What I'm doing now is cutting the scion wood and grafting immediately. What's the point of keeping it cool all winter when it's [already] cool outside?

"Again, so many of the things we're being told are stupid and inconvenient methods we got from the enemy to make it hard for us. What's the point of keeping the scion wood unattached? I'm doing this in the fall and I am seeing results. I don't have to wait as long to see if it will take. You get the results quicker by grafting immediately." If you do it the old way, what if you're gone, on vacation or holiday, when the sap starts flowing? Are you going to get a call to come home right away? If the graft is already in place, you can be anywhere when the sap moves and your scion wood is already there to receive it!

Paul says: "As you are out there, your brain is in gear. That's how you can ask questions like: Why keep things separate for months? It's not going to dry out in the orchard. In fact, with rain and snow, much more moisture is available than sitting in a sterile cooler.

"This one year I had an experience that made me start thinking that way. One of my tree clients had paid an insane price for a Gravenstein tree. I couldn't figure out why until I tried one. I said, 'Whoa, that is an amazing Gravenstein." I took cuttings from it and grafted it in my tree. As I was pruning my tree, I'm thinking 'I want to extend this.' So I laid some pieces on the ground, and after I was done pruning, I would come pick them up, but [this time] I never did. I spaced out and forgot about them. Next spring, I'm out there weeding (this is so hilarious), and I find those sticks on the ground. What got my attention is that the sticks on the ground were as leafed-out as the ones on the tree, and these are no longer connected to the tree! That's what got me thinking, 'Wait a minute. The only life force these are getting is from lying on the woodchips, and it's totally drawing enough off of that to create all this growth.' I'm thinking, 'Wow! That would not have happened in a cooler.' It was awesome. I love these things you consider mistakes and God uses to open you up to potential you never realized."

Where does Paul get his scion wood? It can come from another tree in his orchard or from a neighbor or nursery. There are all kinds of sources. He warns: "There are some issues that you've got to be aware of. For instance, the Gravenstein[269] I mentioned is the most vigorous-growing variety I've ever seen. Doesn't matter whether it's dwarf or semi-dwarf, it's so aggressive. The challenge is, if you graft a Gravenstein into another variety, you're going to have one branch that is extended and way developed beyond all the rest. If that's the case, you want to make sure you graft in the center and it has all the room it needs to grow out because it's going to need it. What I'm doing now is only grafting Gravenstein to Gravenstein[270] because I know how huge it gets. If you don't, your Gravenstein graft will imbalance the tree and seem way out of whack, kind of a detriment. Graft vigorous varieties to each other so they maintain the same growth patterns."

As to disease issues with grafting, Paul doesn't have any: "I've never had a problem with disease on any of my grafts because I am grafting into healthy trees." Plus, the electrical tape acts as a bandage to protect the tree.

GRAFTING GENTILES

Do not miss the spiritual implications of grafting. It is spoken of in the Bible. Remember what it takes to graft: A natural branch serves as the host, and a wild branch (scion wood) is amalgamated with the natural branch. It is a beautiful picture of provision because the wild branch (scion wood) is all by itself. It is not connected to the life source of any tree. Left to itself, it would dry out and die. But when you properly fit it in to the live host, it takes on the life of the natural branch of the living tree.

That is what YHWH (God) did for Gentiles. The Messiah is as the Tree of Life, and the Jews were divinely chosen to be became the natural branches. If you were not a Jew, you were almost certain to have no life in Him. But the Jews rebelled against the Tree, so God cut off their (natural) branches and grafted in the (wild) branches of

269 For info on this special variety, see https://www.orangepippintrees.com/trees/apple-trees/gravenstein ,
270 Paul says there are red and yellow Gravesteins.

the Gentiles. Now God, the Son, would be their life source and supply them with that which was never available to Gentiles before. But they are not to be high-minded about it. The Jews were entrusted with the oracles of God. Paul Gautschi reminds us that God gave that nation a life purpose in Genesis 22:18: "in thy seed shall all the nations of the earth be blessed; because thou hast obeyed my voice."

In Romans 11:11-24, the Apostle Paul analogizes Jews as part of an olive tree (related and devoted to God). Since God is holy and serves as the root of the tree, then the branches are holy. He speaks of the Jews falling from grace and their branches being cut off. Remember that the book of Romans was (largely) written to Gentiles. The Apostle makes this point in verse 17: "And if **some** of the branches [Jews] be broken off, and thou [Gentiles], being a wild olive tree, wer[e] grafted in among them, and with them partakest of the root and fatness of the olive tree." (Emphasis added.) He goes on to tell the Gentiles to not boast against the Jews because God has not written them off forever, but that the grafting in of Gentiles was to provoke Jews to (righteous) jealousy.

Finally, the Apostle validates God's love for Jews and issues a warning in verses 23 and 24: "And they [Jews] also, if they abide not still in unbelief, shall be grafted in: for **God is able to graft them in again**. For if you [Gentiles] were cut out of the olive tree which is wild by nature, and wert grafted (contrary to nature) into a good olive tree: how much more shall these, which be the natural branches, be grafted into their own olive tree?" (Emphasis added.)

To summarize, we (like Paul Gautschi) were likely born Gentiles that go through life abiding in a wild olive tree. Wild refers to our freewill, which allows for wild imaginations and evil living apart from God. We can't graft ourselves from the evil, wild tree to the good, natural tree. We have to be willing—actually, not just willing but passionate—to cut ourselves off from the evil tree and die to it with the assurance that Jesus will graft us into His tree and cause us to bear fruit for His kingdom.

Saving Seeds, Not Private Ryan

In April of 2020, Paul says, "I get a call from a lady in Vermont who is stressed out because all the big-box garden centers are shut down because the governor declared they were non-essential during this COVID-19 pandemic.[271] For years, I have been saying, 'There will come a time when saving seeds will be non-optional. We are approaching that really quick.'" This worldwide plague has been a wake-up call that we need to use what God gives us now to provide for the future. Paul has been saving seeds from the very beginning of his gardening experience. His mom saved seeds. He admits it involves effort and intentionality, but the benefits far outweigh the hassles.

Paul says, "I called Fedco to order some seeds over the phone. The recording says. 'We are totally overwhelmed with orders and are not taking any new orders.' It is amazing the volume of calls coming here [Paul's house] now. People are waking up and saying, '*We've got to grow [our own] food.*' My neighbor went to a local farm to buy compost and was told they were sold out. The owner said it was the first time in their history that they had run out of compost. This is definitely a wake-up call for those who are paying attention.

"I was watching a man from Victoria, BC, doing a presentation in front of about one hundred people. He was saying how it was essential to grow our own food and not rely on corporate supply chains. If prophesy in the Word says there's going to be a lack, then it's obvious we need to be prepared. He shows a picture of a house with a garden and says, 'Now you all know about the Back to Eden gardening method. It is the most amazing way.' Carol said to me, 'Paul, did you hear that? All those folks act [as if] they know what he's talking about.'

"I sort my dried seeds in the winter. I don't have that much to do then anyway, so it is good for me to attend to it. When you save your own seeds, you know the quality of the plant you got the seeds from. You don't know that when you buy seeds in a package."

Even if they claim the seeds are organic, you still can't be sure of the integrity. There is also the matter of cost that should motivate us to supply our own. How many of us have bought an envelope of seeds to find out there are only five seeds in the packet? Paul advises we pay attention to the weight of the package as our only indicator of volume. Seeds are very light, so it is not unusual to buy a quarter-ounce packet. He likes that Fedco shows the weight of their seed packages.

---

271 To be fair, the governor's Addendum 6 to Executive Order 01-20, item 6 k. adds "the production and delivery of seed" as essential. However, they closed Lowe's and The Home Depot, which forced Vermont residents to buy from smaller local garden centers.

Paul does have a warning about which plants we should save seeds from. "You need to isolate the seed plants from the rest of the garden, in a place that is out of the way. Also, you want to grow healthy plants for seed." Before Paul planted everything in the orchard, it was his out-of-the-way place. He grew kale for seed out there. He warns: "Keep it separate from your production plants." Later, he shared: "When I plant my seeds next to the stuff I buy, there's no comparison. There's a major difference on how vigorous my seed is compared to the seeds I buy because my plants are good here, so the seed is very potent. You should be improving every year. This is not a static thing with proper soil care."

Timing is critical. Paul says, "If you harvest too early, they're not fully developed. If you wait too long, the pods open up and the seeds fall on the ground, so I like to get to them right before they're fully dry. Then I bring them into my shed to finish drying." Again, pray about your timing. The reason to have some distance between your dedicated plants for seed is the reality of cross-pollination. Paul shares: "I once grew some wonderful cucumbers from seed Carol got from Israel. They were so extraordinary that I wanted to save seeds, but the plant was next to a different kind of cucumber, and it wasn't till I planted my saved seeds that I got the shock that my seeds had been compromised. It was not good; a total disappointment!"

In the winter, Paul gathers the seeds he had placed on paper towels and laid on a cookie sheet. He puts the trays in his shed and keeps them there to dry out naturally. When he has the time, he gathers the seeds and places them in a regular paper envelope. "Be sure you label it with the plant the seeds came from *and* the date you got them. One thing people need to know is not all seeds have the same shelf life. You look at the pyramids in Egypt and find corn that has been there for thousands of years that can still sprout when you plant them. With onion seeds (I don't care how healthy they are), the second year, they're dead. They only last one year, so that tells me that I need to save seeds each year if I want to grow my own onions. Each plant's seeds have their own shelf life, and you need to start knowing that." I asked if he had a list of things like that, and he said no; he is still determining seed shelf-life by trial and error. "If I plant older saved seeds one year and they don't do as good as the year before, I look at the date and can tell myself that I need to plant these seeds by year three (for example).

"A woman that I rented my place to in 1999 moved to Canada. Recently, she got on Nick's website[272] and sent him some Russian kale seeds I had given her back then. He planted them, and they grew! Those seeds are as old as he is—we're talking over twenty years! It depends on the cultivars [as to] how long the seeds last."

Paul doesn't recommend any particular environment to store your seeds in. He does not think they need to be refrigerated, but you do need to keep them dry.

"I come back to God's storage method for seeds. He lays them on top of the ground in the fall, then they spend a harsh winter with rains, snow, ice, floods, whatever, and the seeds come up in the early spring (long before the last frost date) and they come out just fine. Are you hearing what I just said? It's doing everything *the opposite* of what we do . . . and it works! [He chuckles.] Seeds are pretty resilient."

Another benefit of seed saving is seed sharing. Like trading baseball, football, or soccer cards, gardeners can share seeds among one another. Early on, Paul would mail seeds to anyone he thought could use them for free, but that became untenable. Now there is a small circle of family and friends he shares with. That is how we would get started—with a core group of seed sharers. It may take a few years to build your seeds up to that. Meanwhile, nothing stops

272 https://www.instagram.com/growingbacktoeden/?hl=en.

you from gifting some seeds to your kids or neighbors if you have more seeds than you can realistically use. Additionally, Paul says, "When people come on tours and want seeds, I say to take a part of the (cucumber or zucchini) home, eat what you want, and save the seeds. You want the biggest, mature plant. Remove the seeds and place them on a paper towel in a tray and let them dry out with ambient air. There's no reason to put them in a warmer or dehydrator; that's just extra work."

A few years ago, a local friend asked Paul for any seed potatoes he could spare. Every year she would get seed potatoes from the local feed store in Sequim, but that year she found out they were affected by GMOs. That reminds us that the vast majority of seeds out there have been corrupted in one way or another. Saving your own gains you peace of mind, and Paul is all about living the peaceful, stressless life.

To recap:

- Be intentional about saving seeds.
- Grow healthy plants for seeds away from your production plants.
- Beware of variety cross-pollination.
- Don't harvest too soon or too late.
- Store the seeds in a dry area in envelopes with variety name and date.
- Be attentive to different shelf lives of your seeds.
- Share some seeds with others and maybe get a few to try.

CHAPTER 22

The Good, the Bad, and the Ugly

And by the river upon the bank thereof, on this side and on that side, shall grow all trees for food, whose leaf shall not fade, neither shall the fruit thereof be consumed: it shall bring forth new fruit according to his months, because their waters they issued out of the sanctuary: and the fruit thereof shall be for [food], and the leaf thereof for medicine.

— Ezekiel 47:12

GMO CONTROVERSY

REGARDING GENETICALLY MODIFIED ORGANISMS (GMOs), it is not the purpose of this book to be an exposé of agricultural moguls that seek to dominate the world's food supply. Having watched informative videos and read germane material on GMOs, I would simply like to add a term that aptly describes the status quo: *agronomics*. It is not a brand-new term,[273] but below is how I define it:

---

273 Wikipedia defines it as "the application of economic methods to optimizing the decisions made by agricultural producers." http://en.wikipedia.org/wiki/Agronomics.

Agronomics is the pursuit of agriculture that is most profitable for those who can strategically position themselves in the food and seed supply chain.

This pursuit is driven by profits at the expense of, and borders contempt for, consumers and farmers. The bright-line test of whether a person or corporation (legal entity) is a practitioner of agronomics is whether the person or entity puts profits before safety and/or heavily relies on gray technology[274] (chemicals and/or extreme biologic processes) to do business and subscribe to one or more of the following laws of agronomics:

1st Law of Agronomics: The end justifies the means.
2nd Law of Agronomics: The truth is what we say it is.
3rd Law of Agronomics: Never eat or drink too much of what you sell to the public.

The main point to be made is that genetically modified organisms in seeds (and whatever else has GMOs) is not God's way of growing food. GMOs are the antithesis of growing food God's way. It is not a matter of science versus God but rather, science versus what's right, What's right is what promotes human health and nature, and does not threaten us. God loves you and wants your best. Modern science does not love you and thinks little of your best. In fact, it may decide that you would be a good subject for its next experiment (whether you want to participate or not). The process of making the American public unwitting GMO lab rats (which other countries refuse to be) emanates from what I call *trickle-down agronomics*.

Trickle-down agronomics: *Recklessly exploiting nature to accommodate unnatural and industrialized utilization (tending) of the land, resulting in nutrient deficient plants and mutant food, beverages, or food derivatives.* That is the sum of it.

Paul defines GMOs as the following: "Un-creating what God created. It's not a science thing, but a spiritual thing; an affront against God." So, I asked him what should be our *call-to-action*? He said: "We need to take responsibility to grow our own food and save our

---

274 If green technology is earth- or nature-friendly, then gray technology is patently earth-UNfriendly.

own seeds. If everyone did that, there wouldn't be a market for GMO products." That seemed like a utopian approach, but he reminded me that it has only been within the last century that people quit growing their own food. Since it has been 80+ years, both the students and the teachers in schools have always lived that way (food supply chain dependent), so we've greatly lost our historical context of food sufficiency around the world, and self-sufficiency it isn't even being presented as optional.

In **Michael Pollan**'s book, *The Omnivore's Dilemma: A Natural History of Four Meals,* [275] he states:

> Imagine if we had a food system that actually produced wholesome food. Imagine if it produced that food in a way that restored the land. Imagine if we could eat every meal knowing these few simple things: What it is we're eating. Where it came from. How it found its way to our table. And what it really cost. If that was the reality, then every meal would have the potential to be a perfect meal.

Over the years, the U.S. political system has discovered that the bane of democracy is the *low-information voter*. With that in mind, let's admit that the bane of healthy food choices (let's avoid the word "diets") is the *low-information omnivore*.[276] Low information, in this context, means not knowing or caring about where our food comes from, who handles it, how it is processed, and whether the supply chain lacks nutrition, safety, common sense, or exploits laborers.

DOES THIS DESCRIBE YOU?

Do you really not care about GMOs in your baby's infant formula?

Do you really not care about the effects of high fructose corn syrup on your teeth and in your bloodstream?

Would ignorance and apathy best describe your food and beverage choices? It very aptly describes my former way of thinking. Years ago, a co-worker (**Neil Hundtoft**) jokingly said someone once told him he was "ignorant and apathetic." His classic, witty response: "Well I don't know, and I don't care." Don't let that be your response to

275 Published by Penguin Books, 2007.
276 Or the low-information herbivore (vegetarian).

health and nutrition as it relates to your food inputs. Recall the classic computer adage—garbage in, garbage out—and know that the same goes for human bodies (and minds).

What makes you think you are immune to the effects of fake, dead food? Please don't say "exercise." That would only serve to put you more at risk because your muscle, breathing, and circulation systems create a higher demand for real food and hydration when exercising.

Without apology, I confess that I am a meat eater. Paul is not of that persuasion. He enjoys what he eats, and I enjoy what I eat—plus I enjoy what he eats. But is personal enjoyment the right litmus test for what we should or should not be eating? It's modern science again, tricking our minds. It has answered the question: "How can we get people to have a Pavlovian[277] response to our food products?" The answer: by adding powders and liquids that send our taste buds into hyperspace. Ultimately, God cares deeply about our *salvation*, but commercial food biologists only care about our *salivation*.

GUT FLORA FOOTPRINT

Modern environmental analysts have quantified activities and energy usage to derive a carbon footprint[278] of businesses and industries. It seems to be an expensive exercise in futility that will only serve to infringe our liberties and offer no measurable relief to this planet, but we can benefit by the concept if we take stock of our personal activities and food/water/air inputs. As mentioned earlier, I call it our gut flora footprint, or GFF.

The purpose of measuring one's own nutrition footprint (GFF) is to get a feel for where you're at and where you're heading. A high footprint (A, or 100%) tends to healthy, sustainable living. A low footprint (D, or <50%) tends to (you guessed it) unhealthy, unsustainable living. To put it succinctly: a shorter life with greater likelihood of debilitating diseases, addictions, and unnecessary pain. So the goal

---

277 Reference to **Ivan Petrivich Pavlov** 1849-1936. He was a Russian physicist and 1904 Nobel laureate who observed salivation responses of dogs to foods.
278 The amount of carbon dioxide and other carbon compounds emitted due to the consumption of fossil fuels by a particular person, group, etc.

is to be a bowler, not a golfer. That is, a high score is good, and a low score is bad but improvable.

CHAPTER 23

Paul's Walk with the Holy Spirit

Walk in the spirit and ye shall not fulfill the lust of the flesh.
If we live in the Spirit, let us also walk in the Spirit.
– Galatians 5:16, 25

FOR MANY PEOPLE AT PAUL'S TOURS, he speaks a different language. Sure, it's understandable English, but he continually refers to God speaking to him. It's a life that about 96 percent of us cannot relate to, even if we've been going to church all our lives. Why?

Because we don't seem to be able to track with God as simply and faithfully as Paul does. One advantage Paul has is that he realizes he is not under the curse. This has given him a new identity in Christ, not only to be saved from the curse of the law but also to be saved from the Genesis 3 curse upon the land by tending soil God's way.

So, how can we learn to track with God as Paul does? Is there a book called "Connecting with God for Dummies?" No, but this chapter was written to help us in that pursuit.

Larry Bird was an exceptional NBA basketball player for the Boston Celtics. He was a great ball-handler and could make shots effortlessly from just about anywhere. Many players wanted his skill level, but few made the efforts Larry Bird did to be one of the greats. You see, he was the first Celtic player on the practice court and the last one to leave. He would shoot and shoot and shoot and then drill and drill and drill till he obtained a level of mastery unreached by 99 percent of NBA players. I'm told NHL star **Wayne Gretsky** was the same way.

That reminds me of Paul and his connection with God. We all want it, but we haven't made the efforts Paul has to have continual communion/communication with God. Perhaps we haven't spent years and years memorizing God's word. Perhaps we haven't been faithful in a little so God could give us much.[279] Though effort can be profitable, the life he has is a free gift to all who truly surrender their hearts and lives to Christ and get the indwelling of the Holy Spirit. Yet it takes intentionality to memorize and meditate upon God's word.

Recall Paul's testimony in chapter 6, "Relational Permaculture and You"? His preconceived notions of how God talked to His children prevented Paul from recognizing that God often speaks to us through spontaneous thoughts, as well as a "still, small voice."[280] Have you noticed that some of the hardest chains to shake free of are the ones we place on ourselves?

The teaching Paul got from Mark Virkler is summarized below:

1. Enquire (ask God).
2. Patiently listen as you seek guidance from His word (oftentimes the book of Proverbs is enlightening).
3. Pay attention to your thoughts (particularly ones that you usually wouldn't go to in your mind).
4. Write down those thoughts so you don't forget them.
5. See if the thought aligns with Scripture. If it does, you know you've heard from the Lord.
6. Pray about it in faith.
7. DO WHATEVER God tells you to do as confirmed by His Word.[281]

---

279 Luke 16:10. He that s faithful in that which is least is faithful also in much: and he that is unjust in the least is unjust also in much.
280 1 Kings 19:12.
281 Many hurtful people have done bad things and say that "God told me to do it." Without exception, none of those acts line up with Scripture, which reveals that it was the enemy (disguised as an angel of light) that told them to hurt someone.

It all begins with step 1—enquiring. The first mention of a person making such an inquiry is a woman named Rebekah. In Genesis 25:22, she asks God why there was such a tumult in her womb. She didn't ask her husband; she didn't ask a priest. In the next verse God answers her directly: "Two nations are in thy womb, and two manner of people shall be separated from thy bowels; and the one people shall be stronger than the other people; and the elder shall serve the younger." Read on and you'll see the older was named Esau and the younger was Jacob. The former was the progenitor of Arab people, and the latter was the progenitor of the twelve Hebrew patriarchs. Yes, over two thousand years later, the friction and fighting remain as living proof that God's answer to Rebekah was spot on.

The key to hearing from God is opening yourself up to the Holy Spirit to be a willing receiver of the promptings of the Spirit. Like the college football tight end who's downfield without defenders, we need to say to God, "I'm open! I'm open! Pass it to me!" It takes effort to shake off the opponents that want to prevent us from receiving God's gifts: old habits, pragmatism, confusion, bad advice, fear, indoctrination, traditions, religiosity, and so on.

Paul faced the same challenges we all face. His main opponent was confusion. Yours may be different. The opponent called indoctrination comes from two opposite directions. There is an indoctrination of religion (which says that "God speaks only to a select few") and an indoctrination of academics (that says "there's no God to hear from"). Both can serve to shipwreck our ability to connect with the Spirit and heart of God.

But what if you don't have the Holy Spirit? How can you receive the Spirit of God in your spirit, soul, and body? ASK! In Luke 11:9, Jesus says, "I say unto you ask." In the following verses He talks about our earthly fathers giving good gifts to their children. Then He concludes (in verse 13): "If ye [dads] then, being evil, know how to give good gifts unto your children: how much more shall your heavenly Father give the Holy Spirit to them that ask Him?" Ask our heavenly Father to give you His Spirit. Ask in faith, then receive in faith and full assurance that He will keep His word. Confirm His gift by observing manifestations of the Spirit in your life: love, joy, peace, patience, kindness, gentleness, self-control, a deeper connection with

God (as evidenced by receiving His promptings) and even speaking in tongues (for many).

I queried Paul if there were any Scriptures that opened his spirit to hear from the Holy Spirit. He said: "Draw near to God and He will draw near to you." (James 4:8) Also, Jeremiah 33:3: "Call unto me [ask], and I will answer thee, and show thee great and mighty things, which thou knowest not." To those, let's add Matthew 7:7: "Ask, and it shall be given you; seek, and ye shall find; knock, and it shall be opened unto you."

So, how do we draw near to God? Pray, read His word, ponder the words you read, and memorize the verses the Holy Spirit prompts you to. Be in constant prayer for big things, little things, your needs and weaknesses, others' needs and weaknesses; praise and thank Him in your prayers.

There is a model of prayer in what is known as the Lord's Prayer.[282] We can pray that word for word, by rote, or we can consider it more closely and recognize the elements of that prayer. ACTS is an acronym to help us remember:

Adoration
Confession
Thanksgiving
Supplication (pray for the needs of others ahead
    of your own needs).[283]

I also asked Paul if he would share the type of prayer he said to get connected with God. Guess what? There was no single prayer. He said we should have a heart of prayer that reflects the Word of God. Scripture-centric prayer looks a lot like this:

God, I am drawing near to You, and You promised to draw near to me. I am calling upon You, I am seeking, I am knocking, I am asking to hear from You, Lord. Close my eyes and ears to my mind and the world, and open them up to You. In Jesus's name, amen.

282 Matthew 6:5-13.
283 Encouraged to pray this way by Cynthia Briganti, a California believer and millionaire.

The Bible reference we read in Luke 11:13 speaks of an impartation of the Holy Spirit. If you look up the word "impart" in a dictionary, you'll see definitions like "to give, to tell, to make known." The Bible tells those who have two coats "to impart one to someone who is without a coat." (Same goes for food.)[284] What's catchy about "impart" (in English) is that we can separate the letters to *I M Part*, as in: *I am part* of God's Kingdom, *I am part* of His will, *I am part* of His love, and *I am part* of His generous nature.

Once the Holy Spirit is imparted to us, as blood-bought saints, then we are empowered to impart this to others to make disciples. How? By prayer and/or the laying of hands, but sometimes that doesn't work. Why? Because something bad needs to leave us (like wrong spirits of pride, greed, lust, anger, or unbelief) before the holy and righteous Spirit of God will enter in and take residence and pre-eminence.

Perhaps a root of bitterness sprang up in our lives way back when, and it has only grown in our hearts (as an invasive species would). If so, then that root needs to be cut out by forgiveness. In Romans 12:21, we are told to "overcome evil with good." Just that (God-replicating) act of forgiveness could trigger the indwelling of the Holy Spirit in thousands of believers who don't truly experience Him now. Let the fragrance of your violet be on the one who crushed you.

Even Jesus didn't go full-on in His ministry until He was baptized with the Holy Spirit. That's right. Please don't be shocked. John the Baptist didn't baptize Jesus for the remission of sins (He was sinless). Rather, two heavenly events took place: (1) The Holy Spirit came upon Him (in the form of a dove) and (2) God's declaration of who Jesus is was heard from above.[285] Also, Acts 10:38 records that "God anointed Jesus of Nazareth with the Holy Ghost and with power: who went about doing good, and healing all that were oppressed of the devil; for God was with him."

Charis Bible School founder, **Andrew Wommack**, wrote to Christians about the spirit connecting with our soul:

---

284 Luke 3:11.
285 See Matthew 3:13-17.

> Surely, you've read a scripture and felt like, all of a sudden, you "saw" it. You may have read it a hundred times before, but all at once, everything within you shouts, "Yes!" That's your spirit and your soul becoming of one mind. When your soulish realm gains a truth and begins to embrace it, your spirit connects [with it] and agrees. Once the connection is made, that truth just *goes off* inside of you. It's now *revelation* and *reality* to you. Because of your inner witness, you don't necessarily need anyone else to prove it; you just know. [Italics added.][286]

That is what Paul has experienced for years, and he desires every believer to walk in this vital path: truth validated by the Spirit, experienced in our soul, and affecting the way we do things with our body. Isn't this the life you yearn to live?

This book begins and ends with the life and testimony of Paul Gautschi. But for his faith in God, he would be just another man in Washington State. We would have never encountered him. There would be no *Back to Eden* video, no book, no YouTube videos and Instagram posts about him. He would be like thousands of other men struggling against nature to grow food, stuck on his never-ending treadmill.

Is that where you are now? Imagine how far you can go with a similar, or even greater, faith in God. Not a mere assent that God exists, but an active faith that lives it out. Our goal shouldn't be to be like Paul or even the man he looked up to; Pastor Arthur Corey. Our goal is to *be like Jesus*, to love as He loved, to care for others as He cared, to walk in submission to the Father and heavenly wisdom.

Anything less than that is just . . . normal human existence that leads to destruction. Choose life!

---

286 Andrew Wommack, Spirit, Soul & Body, Tulsa, OK: Harrison House, 2010.

Appendix

M OST APPENDICES HAVE SUPPORTING DATA, sometimes photos. This appendix is different. When my family watches a video together, we often check out the menu after the video is over, scroll to "Special Features" and then scroll to "Deleted Scenes." I know this isn't a video (or even a book about a video), but I want to devote most of the appendix to what I call "Deleted Chapters."

The following chapters are good yet didn't make the starting team, largely because of their brevity. But it is my prayer that one or more will be a blessing to you. So here goes.

HOW DOES YOUR GARDEN GROW?

Build ye houses, and dwell in them; and plant gardens, and eat the fruit of them.

– Jeremiah 29:5

Paul planted these winter crops mostly in early August:

2013/2014	2019/2020
Beets	Beets
Carrots	Carrots
Cilantro	(plants in Sept.)
Kale	Kale
Onions	Onions
Parsnip	Parsnip
Potatoes	(in Sept. when he harvests)
Rutabagas	Rutabagas
Swiss chard	Swiss chard
Turnips	Turnips
Flowers	Flowers

Paul shares that in 2011, "I planted nasturtiums under three of my apple trees. The nasturtium package tells you to plant in full sun. The Bible tells you your Father is an ever-present help in time of need.[287] Are you tracking with me and doing the math? There is nothing you will encounter that God does not have an answer for.

"I was walking down my driveway one day, and I'm telling God that my wife wants me to grow nasturtiums. She loves nasturtiums. They go in salads; they are kind of tart and good. The flowers in salad really look nice. 'God, where can I plant that plant?' God says, 'Look under the apple trees.' I am so brain dead. I'm telling God, 'You have to plant in full sun.' I am telling God! This is how stupid I am. I love God, He does not argue. He says, 'Just do it.' I was planning to plant nasturtiums every year; that's what people do. But as soon as they finish blooming, they create seed that falls to the ground; now this is perennial. It's been three years [now seven in 2020], and those things keep coming up on their own. God knew where I was going. God says, 'See, if you do it My way, you will never have to do it again.' I was planning to have to do it every year. He tells me go plant them over there and you will have them for life. No work! You see, my brain just

287 Psalms 46:1 "God is our refuge and strength, a very present help in trouble."

can't go there, thinking of all this effort, but God (Jesus) said, 'It's an easy yoke, My burden . . . track with Me.'[288] It's so cool."

Too-Good Results

Because his soil is being enriched every year, Paul is finding it too productive. That is, he has to plant his winter crops later and later each year because the plants want to grow right away, acting more like late spring crops than fall or winter crops. He relates: "I used to do my winter garden in June because things grew so slowly. Then last year I did it in July, but they got so big I knew they wouldn't make it through the winter, so in desperation I planted in August.

"Now I'm looking at the size of this stuff and thinking that next year I'll plant the first week in August [again] because everything is growing so much faster and bigger than it ever has before.

"I have to keep adjusting how I do stuff because I have this compounding interest program working here where this just did not used to be. I love it! It is challenging but such an encouraging challenge. I have to plant later because things grow so fast, much faster."

His garden in late October 2012 was remarkable for all the summer produce that remained,[289] and the carrots he planted the previous August were already harvestable!

Paul plants hard yellow winter onions. He shares: "They grow all winter. Even in the summer, they will keep better in the ground rather than picked. Most people will pick them because the ground is wet and muddy and they will rot, but because the [covered] ground is really porous, full of air, they store really great. *So my garden is also my root cellar.* These are the things you come across after having done it wrong for so many years that you just literally get blown away with the benefits. Every day I come out here, there are new benefits God shows me that are so awesome."

Because Paul no longer has to slog through a muddy garden in April, he tries to plant the summer crops that first week. As he tells it,

---

288 Paraphrasing Matthew 11:30.
289 Lettuce, celery, cucumbers, onions, etc. The first overnight frost in Paul's neighborhood came November 8 that year.

"April 1 is when I do my first planting of all my greens.[290] I've tried to push it. One year, I planted bean seeds, and they stayed in the ground a whole month before they came up and did not rot. Bean seeds will rot if they stay in soil and do not come up. The bean seeds stayed in my woodchips thirty days and did not rot. The first of May, when the weather warmed, they came up. I realized you cannot push nature; you cannot make things happen earlier. There is a time and a season for everything.[291] I don't care how much you want to; you are not going to change that. God has a reason for what He has done. Why would I want to mess with it or change it?"

The springs of 2013 and 2014, Paul planted kale, celery, parsley, lettuce, spinach, arugula, broccoli, cilantro, cabbage, cucumbers, beans, corn, squash, and zucchini with his own seeds, plus those purchased from Johnny's Seed Co. and Fedco Seeds. The spring of 2019, he planted some seeds he kept from previous plants.

FEED MY SHEEP

Jesus saith unto him; Feed My sheep.

– John 21:17

Of the Gautschis' five acres[292] of land, one and a quarter acres of it is pasture. Looking from the street, it is left of the orchard. The orchard and garden are at a higher grade than the pasture; therefore, the subterranean gravity fall of Paul's compost tea drains or flows into the lower pasture land. The result of this phenomenon is that the grass gets extraordinary nutrition and grows extremely thick and healthy.

From the third week of June till the end of October 2012, a local sheep grower needed to rest the twenty acres where he raised his sheep, so he brought fifty-three sheep to graze on Paul's pasture. In the sustainable animal grazing biz, there have been conclusive studies to determine how many acres can sustain so many animals of various

---

290 In 2019, Sequim had a warm March, and Paul planted seeds then. In 2020 he planted in April again.
291 Ecclesiastes 3:1: "To every thing there is a season, and a time to every purpose under the heaven."
292 About two hectares.

kinds called animal unit months (AUMs). The bigger the animal, the greater acreage required to give them adequate forage.

Knowing this, I asked a resident sheep expert in my area about this very thing. **Margaret Macgruder** owns Oregon Shepherd, a company that converts less-than-clothing-grade wool into natural blown-in insulation for environmentally superior home construction. She raises sheep near Clatskanie, Oregon, as well. When I asked her how many sheep I could graze on a one-and-a-quarter-acre pasture, she said, "Five, maybe six."

So, the enormity of Paul's pasture began to sink in—his grass sustains ten times the usual animal-carrying capacity because of the richness of the grass! Those sheep went all summer before they were repatriated in October to their home pasture (which is about twenty times larger!). At Paul's, they ate in the morning and lay around the rest of their day in satisfaction. Much less volume (quantity) of grass was required to satiate them, and much fewer calories were burned foraging.

Paul reflects: "The commercial shepherd came by here twice a week to check on his sheep. One day, the sheep owner calls me, and says, 'I had to call you. I've been raising sheep for thirty years. When my sheep are on the home place, they roam all day, but when I come by your place, they're all lying down.' I said, 'Fred, they're satisfied here because they're eating nutrient-dense grass. On your pasture, with chemical fertilizers, they're never satisfied. This pasture is nutrient-dense, and your sheep get satisfied.'"

Fred Hatfield, the owner of the sheep, testified to me that his sheep put on weight while at Paul's pasture. It was a good experience for him, and for the sheep!

ALL WE LIKE ESAU

And Esau said unto his father, Hast thou but one bless-
ing, my father? Bless me, even me also, O my father. And
Esau lifted up his voice, and wept.

– Genesis 27:38

This man's account is revealed in Genesis 25:34. His spiritual birthright from his father Isaac was to be in close fellowship with God. That is every created human's birthright and eternal need. The US Declaration of Independence is based on the premise that true rights come from God, not from governments or kings. It testified to **King George** of England that the Creator has endowed mankind with "certain unalienable rights." This chapter is testifying to you that chief among those rights is the birthright every man and woman, boy and girl has: to live by faith *in* God and to have fellowship *with* God.

The Bible tells us that **Esau** despised his spiritual birthright, as well as the physical birthright provided to firstborn sons in that culture. He placed no value in it and chose not to live in the light of its benefits and blessings. He sold it to his kid-brother for a bowl of soup (homemade, not Campbell's).

We all tend to be Esaus. We want to live according to our preferences, even if they are bad for us (like smoking). The Hebrew prophet Isaiah wrote: "All we like sheep have gone astray; we have turned everyone to his own way; and the LORD hath laid on Him [Jesus] the iniquity of us all."

We resist the reality that we shall face a righteous Judge at our death or the Lord's Second Coming.[293] It's inconvenient to serve a Holy God, so we devise our own god who thinks like us and promotes our desires as the measure of all things. Thus, we lightly esteem our Creator (at best) and completely ignore Him (like Esau) at worst.

---

293 "So, then every one of us shall give account of himself to God." (Romans 14:12)

ALL'S WELL THAT ENDS WELL

If you confess your sins, He is faithful and just to forgive
you your sins and cleanse you from all unrighteousness.

– 1 John 1:9

During my 2012 hot August visit to Paul's gardens, one highlight was getting a drink from his well. Surely this wasn't the well that yielded only one-half gallon a minute! I asked Paul about it, and he said, "In the late '80s we dug another well because well drilling went from twenty-four dollars per linear foot to only fourteen dollars per linear foot due to little construction activity." Paul told Carol that there wouldn't be a better time to try for another well, so they called a drilling company.

He admitted to me, "The first well was motivated out of fear, and Romans 14 tells us that 'whatever is not of faith is sin.'" [294] Paul and Carol prayed and repented of the fear and said to God,: "We are going to trust You for a good well." Soon afterwards, Carol told Paul she believed the Lord informed her that the drilling would be only 130 feet and that the well would yield 20 GPM. Paul was astonished at such a statement, as she was now expecting forty times the volume of their first well! They agreed to let the well driller determine where to drill.

On drilling day, Carol was away at a midwife event, and Paul decided to not be there as well. The drillers came, did their job, and left. When Paul got back, he talked with a neighbor on his way up the drive. The neighbor said the driller was "in and out in about four hours." This was an ominous report, as that seemed too short a time to drill the minimum 150 feet to even begin looking for traces of water, which was the norm in that part of the county.

Paul quickly called the driller, who informed him that they did finish drilling the well. The well driller said, "You have something here I've never seen before—an underground river running in a five-foot space of rock surrounded by blue clay." The driller's well log indicates 133 feet of depth (130 feet plus three feet of casing the driller adds) and the flow indicated 20 GPM! Carol's testimony of God's leading was spot-on!

---

294 "And he that doubteth is damned if he eat, because he eateth not of faith: for whatsoever is not of faith is sin." (Romans 14:23)

Moreover, the Lord promises His believers that He will do "above that which ye shall think." He provided not only forty times the water but also the drilling at much less cost than was budgeted *and* the water, as tested, at 7.3 pH, which is ideal drinking water at slightly alkaline.

TAKEAWAYS

I remember the days of old; I meditate on all thy works;
I muse on the work of thy hands.

– Genesis 27:38

- It is foolish to build one's worldview on the philosophy of evolutionism, as it is not scientifically replicable, nor is that belief supported by the fossil record and other revealing artifacts. There are zero transitional species because a species can only produce its own kind (i.e., canine, fowl, fish, etc.).
- God created the universe in six literal days and rested on the seventh. It remains a pattern for us to live by.
- Jesus is the Son of God, and He came to Earth to redeem humankind from the fall of Adam and Eve to give us peace with God, provide hope for the resurrection, and destroy the works of the devil.
- Relational permaculture is bringing God into your food-growing equation by believing in Him, coming under His authority, and bathing your soil and seeds in prayer for the Lord's favor as you seek His wisdom by hearing His voice.
- Hearing God's voice can come by spontaneous thoughts that are consistent with Holy Scripture.
- Follow through with God's promptings to do things and His warnings to avoid things.
- Chipped branches and leaves are the best organic matter to heal and enrich your soil.
- Practice the 7 effective habits of relational permaculture and do them with joy.

- God loves you and has pursued a relationship with you, even when you disregarded Him in ignorance or on purpose.
- Invest your time in God's Owner's Manual. Memorize key verses that speak to you.
- The only thing more important than woodchips in your garden is love in your heart. Without love, everything else is meaningless. See 1 Corinthians 13:1-3.
- Grafting is the best way to pollinate your tree. Proper pruning is a game-changer.
- Reject the lies that you cannot grow your own food and realize that God can provide you the helpers you may need.
- Be sensitive to observe God's blessings and favor in your life and thank Him for all of it.
- Share the Good News with others and, when appropriate, share this book too.

Bibliography

You will be the same person in five years as you are today except for the books you read and the people you meet.

– Charlie (Tremendous) Jones

FOLLOWING ARE A FEW BOOKS PAUL recommends between Bible reading:

5% Chance
Jerrod Sessler
ToDoBlue Press (2009)

"A must read for using good food to treat your body." – PG

Animal, Vegetable, Miracle
Barbara Kingsolver
HarperCollins (2007)

"This lady gets it when it comes to food." – PG

Expendable
Phillip W. Keller
Prairie Press (1967?)

"A great biography and my gateway to Prairie." – PG

My Father, My Father
Sam Solelyn
Solelyn Publishing & eGenCo, LLC

"Sam articulates the orphan spirit so well." – PG

Pilgrim's Progress
John Bunyan
Various publishers

"A classic Christian allegory." – PG

Finding The Father
Herb Montgomery
Review & Herald Publications (2009)

"Herb communicates the incredible love of the Father." – PG

Re_Orient
Kevin Wheeler

"This book moves you out of the religious box." – PG

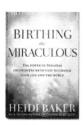

Birthing the Miraculous
Heidi Baker
Charisma House (2014)

"This is like a current version of the book of Acts." – PG

By Divine Design
Michael Pearl
No Greater Joy Ministries

"A profound explanation of salvation." – PG

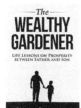

The Wealthy Gardener
John Soforic
EGH Publishing

"Perfect for homeschoolers. Lots of wisdom." – PG

A Holiday for August
Thomas P. Brankin
Self-published

"Amazing demonstration of developing gifts of the homeless." – PG

Free
Angie Ruble
Self-published

"A redemptive and healing novel." – PG

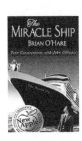

THE MIRACLE SHIP
Brian O'Hare
Crimson Cloak Publishing

"A faithful man that loved God and brought healing to the masses." – PG

You Can Farm
Joel Salatin
Polyface

"You can't go wrong with the wisdom of Joel. He encourages people." – PG

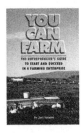

Dead Doctors Don't Lie, 2nd ed.
Dr. Joel D. Wallach & Dr. Ma Lan
Wellness Publications

"#1 exposé of allopathic medicine." – PG

Alkalize or Die, 11th ed.
Dr. Theodore A. Baroody
Holographic Health Press

"How alkalizing your body keeps you well." – PG

Hallelujah Diet
George Malkmus, Peter and Stowe Shockley
Destiny Image Publisher's
"He points us to Genesis 1:29 eating, and this has healed so many people, eating as God designed." – PG

Pots, Pans and Peace
Eleanor Corey
Self-published
"A detailed memoir of Margaret Corey,
Pastor Arthur Corey's wife. It is a blessing to read
about my pastor and his special family again." – PG

Playing in the Dirt
Dr. Benjamin Page
Self-published

"A practical book that connects all the
health issues of life in a clear, plain way." – PG

Illustrations

Index

Bold numbers indicate images. Page locators followed by "n" refer to footnotes.

Made in the USA
Coppell, TX
28 March 2022

75690122R00184